M000165103

Understanding Poverty

Understanding Poverty
A Relational Approach

Elizabeth Seale

polity

The right of Elizabeth Seale to be identified as Author of this Work has been asserted in accordance with the UK Copyright, Designs and Patents Act 1988.

First published in 2023 by Polity Press

Polity Press
65 Bridge Street
Cambridge CB2 1UR, UK

Polity Press
111 River Street
Hoboken, NJ 07030, USA

ISBN-13: 978-1-5095-5332-7
ISBN-13: 978-1-5095-5333-4 (pb)

A catalogue record for this book is available from the British Library.

Library of Congress Control Number: 2022951311

Typeset in 10.5 on 12pt Plantin by
Cheshire Typesetting Ltd, Cuddington, Cheshire
Printed and bound in Great Britain by TJ Books Limited, Padstow, Cornwall

For further information on Polity, visit our website:
politybooks.com

I dedicate this to
Mom and brother Rod,
the imprinters

Contents

Acknowledgments		*page* ix
1	**On Understanding**	**1**
	Poverty in the USA	3
	My Research Experience	5
	How We Think and Talk about Poverty	7
	A Relational Approach	8
	What a Relational Approach Contributes	13
	Relations of Vulnerability and the Desire for Dignity	17
	Aims and Overview of the Book	18
2	**Who Are the Poor?**	**20**
	Defining and Measuring Poverty	20
	Mobility	36
	Diversity	38
	Similarity to and Difference from the Nonpoor	53
	Conclusion	57
3	**Family and Parenting**	**60**
	Single Mother Households	61
	Young Moms	71
	Child Maltreatment	77
	Conclusion	85

4 Culture   **92**
  Historical Context   96
  Culture of Poverty and Policy   103
  Problems with the Culture of Poverty Arguments   107
  Contemporary Research on Culture and Poverty   114
  A Culture of Dependency or a Culture of Blame?   120
  Conclusion   124

5 Structure and Social Relations   **126**
  How Structure Creates Poverty   127
  Social Policy: Punishing the Poor   135
  The Limits of Structuralism   142
  A Relational Approach   145
  Conclusion   150

6 Opportunity and Personal Autonomy   **151**
  Going to College   151
  Finding (Better) Employment   156
  General Autonomy   168
  Conclusion   172

7 Vulnerability and Dignity   **174**
  The Relations of Poverty   175
  Changing Our Thinking about Poverty   177
  The Significance of a Relational Approach   179
  Conclusion   188

References   189
Index   222

Acknowledgments

This project was supported through the granting of a sabbatical for the Fall 2017 term by State University of New York at Oneonta. Undergraduate research assistants funded by the College Foundation of SUNY Oneonta also contributed to this project; special thanks go to Krista Green, Katie Kilichowski, Juliana Luna, and Samantha Palermo.

Thank you to the many colleagues, editors, and reviewers who read drafts of related material and provided enormously useful feedback. I also extend my thanks for and admiration to the professors who assisted in my early studies.

I am grateful for the research participants over the years who graciously gave their time and permitted the intrusion into their privacy. This book could not have been written without you; thank you so much.

Thank you to the community members in Michigan who opened their homes and hearts to me during a crisis in my youth. I have never forgotten.

And I thank my life partner, Michael Koch, for reading many, many drafts, and whose unwavering support has been nothing short of absolute.

1

On Understanding

"I'm not poor, I'm broke. Poor means you can't pay your bills. I pay my bills but then I have no money left."

"I'm happy to be alive. God lets me live. I'm not saying I'm not stressed. I used to cry myself to sleep every night. I'm not used to asking for help. I've been on my own since I was 18 years old."

"You say you are poor every day. Get out of it. It's a mentality."

(Quotes from fieldnotes and interviews with participants in antipoverty programs)

Poverty is thought to be a cause of many social problems. It is considered both a cause and effect of violence. It is believed to undermine public education and is associated with a variety of negative health outcomes as well as plain, old-fashioned despair. In the United States, a wealthy and powerful nation, poverty marks the lives of millions. Child poverty rates are particularly high. Such high poverty rates shape how people develop psychologically, emotionally, and socially. Poverty is the curse that keeps on cursing.

Given this, how do we understand the experiences of people in poverty, this already stigmatized state? Are individuals in poverty best perceived as their own worst enemies? As victims? As heroes? What are the best ways to help people in poverty? And how do we understand poverty without further stigmatizing "the poor"? This book is an effort to guide our answers to these questions using what I refer to as the relational approach, and with the United States as the focus.

How we think about people in poverty matters for the sorts of relations formed in society, from national social policies to everyday encounters between primary school teachers and low-income families. How the public and key gatekeepers think about people in poverty helps form the structure and culture that all people must navigate as they try to make a life for themselves. There is a potential paradox here: Can we recognize that, while poverty itself is damaging, the people who have been, and continue to struggle, in poverty are not necessarily damaged? Yes, because the damage is not just to the individual, nor is it primarily a feature of individuals. The damage is to social relations. Whether that damage becomes a semi-permanent feature of an individual is always an open question. While we can recognize that some individuals are severely hurt by poverty, it does not follow that all individuals in poverty are affected in the same way. The trick is to shift the focus from the individual as the problem to seeing the individual in the context of social relations.

We pay real costs – moral, social, and economic – for allowing poverty to encroach on so many lives. The amount and severity of suffering are enormous. Yet this suffering is easily prevented socially when concerns about preventing fraud and idleness among the *least* powerful are not dominant. People in poverty put up with treatment that many of us could not imagine putting up with ourselves. In the United States, we address poverty through such fragmented halfway measures, with so many stipulations and bureaucratic requirements, that it typically becomes more effort to rely on the safety net than it would to have a(nother) job. I have repeatedly seen this for myself in agencies that serve the low-income community or people in crisis. The need to justify helping someone out and to demonstrate that clients are not taking undue advantage becomes a major stumbling block for anyone who wants to assist, and certainly for clients themselves looking for a safety net before they become stripped of any dignified recourse. We sometimes never do find out what happens to those who fall outside the safety nets. But why do so many people fall in the first place?

Reader, I say "we" throughout this book *not* because I assume you have no knowledge about poverty or that you only entertain bad thoughts about people in poverty. In fact, there is a very high likelihood that you have experienced poverty yourself and/or have close interactions with people in poverty. Social scientists believe that there are important implications for understanding people depending on how close the observer is to the situation of the observed. Too far away, and there is a tendency to see the characteristics of the observed as natural and unvarying. Too close, and there is a tendency to see characteristics as ingrained and unchangeable, and to miss the larger picture. It is thus important to be attentive to such tendencies and attempt to correct for them. In addition, I purposefully address not only the "deserving poor," as they are sometimes referred to, but also the "undeserving poor" – the ones *we* – myself included – tend to categorize, even if only for a second, as less deserving of our full consideration. I want to go even further and explore our notions of what poverty is, what it involves, and who it involves. By necessity, this is very much a "we" endeavor. I hope you are willing to take this journey with me.

In our attempts to understand poverty, we are confronted by difficult questions about human value and worth; issues of race, class, and gender; and whether inequality is beneficial in stratifying people by ability and will. We have to take into account how people benefit from poverty, particularly the wealthy. Studying the most disadvantaged people in society tells us much about the human experience. For one thing, we learn about the role of human agency under severe constraints. Human agency is the capacity to take action in the world out of one's own free will, as opposed to having those actions determined by circumstances and other people. It is important to recognize that people – even those in poverty – are not helpless. Often, they do not need our help so much as the same respect and basic rights that the nonpoor have. And in many ways, despite surface appearances and markedly different circumstances, we are not so different across social classes. It can be difficult sometimes to see our similarities when we are socially distant. But if we were actually placed in similar circumstances, how would we act?

Poverty in the USA

Poverty is the lack of the basic requirements to live a decent life in a given society – that is, the inability to acquire that which one needs to live a decent life in society. Although what is considered "decent" is partially subjective, we can identify certain needs as fundamental: reliable shelter, food, and healthcare. Some definitions of poverty go further than this, but let us begin with the official poverty measure, which is aimed at identifying those who cannot afford the necessities. In the next chapter, I identify some of the many ways researchers and policy experts define and measure poverty, but for now, here are some basic figures. The US government measures poverty by multiplying by three the estimated minimum cost of food for a given family size. That is the threshold for poverty by family size, and any household with a total income below that threshold is considered in poverty. In 2020, the annual income threshold for a family of three was $20,244. For 2019, around 34 million Americans were identified by the Census as living in poverty (US Census Bureau 2020c). This was 10.5% of the population, the lowest percentage since such data were provided, beginning in 1959. Poverty increased as the COVID-19 pandemic impacted the economy in 2020, rising to 11.4% of the population (Shrider et al. 2021).

Poverty rates in the USA are higher than those in nearly all other affluent countries. One measure of poverty used by the World Bank calculates the percentage of people who live on $1.90 or less per day (using 2011 US dollar equivalents). The World Bank (2022) found that the poverty rate by this measure is higher in the USA (at 1% for 2019) than it is for 69 other countries out of 171 total countries for which they had these data. An alternative used by the World Bank measures the percentage of people whose income is half the median income for that country, or lower. By this relative poverty indicator, the World Bank ranked the United States in 55th place out of 159 countries (17.8% in poverty) (World Population Review 2022). Thus, at extreme poverty levels ($1.90 per day) and relative poverty levels (half median income), the USA fares significantly worse than many other nations. Of course, many countries have much higher rates of extreme poverty than the USA – as high as 78.8% for the $1.90 per day level. However, given our very high levels of productivity and income, the USA tolerates an excessive amount of poverty compared to many other countries.

It is important to recognize, however, that these one-point-in-time measurements of poverty do not take into account how many people live through poverty throughout their lives. Rank et al. (2021) estimate that around 58% of Americans experience poverty for at least a year of their lives. The majority of Americans are at risk of experiencing poverty at some point in their lives. A quarter of Americans are at a particularly high risk, often bouncing in and out of poverty over the years.

Younger ages are associated with greater risk for poverty. Typically, about one-fifth of American children are living in poverty at any given time. One in ten (nearly 9 million) US children grow up in poverty for more than half of their childhood (Ratcliffe and Kalish 2017). A majority of these children are African American (56%), followed by Whites (36%) (Ratcliffe and Kalish 2017). However, 40% of African American children grow up in persistent poverty, compared to only 5.5% of Whites. Although there are a lot of White people in poverty in the United States, one is still at greater risk if one is Black.

Poverty is not a monolithic experience or state; rather, it is wide-ranging and diverse. Geographically, the assistance available to people varies drastically, both between and within states. The amount of concentrated poverty or the level of chronic poverty varies geographically as well, generally being worse in the US south. Poverty is not just an urban phenomenon, and, although rural areas have the highest rates of the poor, suburban areas are catching up quickly. Some of the poor are disabled; most are not. Some of the poor struggle with addiction or substance abuse; most do not. Some of the poor are homeless. But most are not, though they may live perpetually with the risk of losing a roof over their heads. There is also a difference between people who are: (a) low-income but not poor; (b) in poverty at a given point in time; and (c) chronically poor, often moving in and out of poverty, and never secure. The lines between these populations are not always clear, and often concerns apply across groups. Because people move in and out of poverty, there is no defined, clear group of people we can identify as "the poor."

Furthermore, poverty does not affect everyone equally and is itself reinforced by and made up of other forms of social stratification, including gender, race, citizenship status, ethnicity, and disability. It is now customary – indeed, it is almost automatic – to say that academics must consider race and gender as a researcher embarks on any analysis. But there are very compelling reasons to do so here, as we will see. Anyone who is disadvantaged in one regard, be it due to race or citizenship status or having a disability, is at greater risk for poverty, especially to the extent that a status affects their prospects for education, employment, and control over their lives. In some cases, one's position in the stratification system may work to one's advantage – having cultural identity and familial support related to one's ethnicity, for instance – but the total advantages and disadvantages emerge in ways we can understand by studying the precise social relations entailed. These complexities will be further unpacked in later chapters.

My Research Experience

I have studied poverty since I became a research assistant for Dr. Barbara Risman in 2005 on her project examining the effects of welfare reforms on local nonprofits. Then, after considerable agonizing over a dissertation topic as a North Carolina State University Ph.D. candidate, I decided that ultimately what I cared most about understanding was poverty. I designed a comparative case study of two counties in North Carolina, one rural and one urban, that drew me into 6 different nonprofit agencies and over 100 interviews with a variety of community members, including people in poverty and officials or agents of nonprofits, community colleges, churches, local governments, and cooperative extension. I worked at nonprofit agencies, including shelters, food banks, and emergency assistance. I worked alongside client-workers in the warehouse devoted to providing for people in need and attended the classes assigned to the client-workers. At another organization, I attended weekly open community meetings among people who were engaged in the fight against injustice of all kinds. I shared cigarettes to ingratiate myself with the client-workers (to later "bum" from my graduate student peers – note the underlying meaning). In turn, I accepted generous offers of food, advice, and the time and trust of others. I struggled to help people at many nonprofits, falling physically ill from the stress on a couple of occasions. Day after day, I worked to conquer shyness, always be respectful to everyone, and put my nose to the grindstone of nonprofit work because I was so privileged in the first place to pursue this research and earn a Ph.D. I am thus aware of the struggle that many bear, and that I have only experienced for relatively short periods of time over the past couple of decades.

I did not have a chummy relationship with all of the people in poverty I encountered during this time. Some heckled the non-profit workers – like one particularly memorable occasion when a woman mooned the entire staff and the director. Some were under-standably hostile to my efforts to pry into their lives (though such efforts were often a necessary requirement for assistance). Many were disappointed at how little I could assist them in their time of extreme crisis. Since my dissertation research, I have occasionally volunteered at agencies serving people in poverty. In such cases, I was not conducting research, but simply helping my community. Across all of these experiences, I was despondent at how little I could actually help people. In 2015, in New York state, I began a research project on family planning among people in poverty and encountered individuals who seemed completely inept at basic life tasks, such as making and keeping appointments or remembering medication. These various experiences drove me to ask challenging questions about how to think about people in poverty, how to help those few individuals who do not seem to want to help themselves, and what all of this means sociologically. For instance, how do I reconcile the perspectives of people working with the poor day after day with those of poverty scholars who rejected culture of poverty understandings in favor of structural explanations? As you will see, I found a way to answer these questions.

How We Think and Talk about Poverty

How people think we should address poverty is very much related to ideas about why people are in poverty and how different forms of assistance might affect their behavior. One explanation for why people remain in poverty is known as the culture of poverty theory, which is very influential in American culture and politics. The culture of poverty theory in its popular form is the idea that the poor navigate the world in ways that are inferior to those of the middle class and that serve to maintain their lower position in society. As discussed in a later chapter, culture of poverty ideas are not completely wrong, but the general notion that there is a single set of values and behaviors that characterize the poor – or, indeed, any social class – is demonstrably nonsensical. Culture of poverty explanations, despite their fall from favor among poverty scholars, remain stubbornly present in the wider consciousness, in policy circles, and even in some of the ways that we continue to study the poor. It is in part due to such culture of poverty assumptions that the United States has gutted social services, and when the USA does invest in antipoverty efforts, these efforts often focus on the wrong problems or become tied up in bureaucratic requirements aimed at controlling supposedly pathological behaviors.

People in poverty are often characterized as dependent, lazy, fraudulent, criminal, violent, untrustworthy, unintelligent, dirty, loud, addicted, unmotivated, passive, bigoted, and ignorant. They are sometimes compared to animals or parasites. This occurs in the media, in schools, in social services, in politics, and in the labor market. On the other hand, sometimes people in poverty or poverty itself are romanticized, viewed as character-building, or as some sort of state of innocence. Helping people in poverty makes those of us "better-off" feel virtuous and kind. And few people think of themselves as poor, even when they are by federal standards. As the quote above says, poverty is "a mentality" – and it is the *wrong* mindset. Attempts at personal change typically fail to lift an individual out of poverty, however, unless accompanied by a change in their relations to others (Seale 2017; Obernesser and Seale n.d.). Moreover, it is an odd thing to claim that poverty is a mindset when very few people in poverty consider themselves different from the middle class.

A Relational Approach

A relational approach focuses on the social relations in which individuals are embedded and the multiple ways in which their conditions and actions are products of more than just individual circumstance or development. Conditions and actions are products of *social relations*, the unavoidable ways in which we are connected to one another. This means that individual-level actions can be understood through attention to structural and cultural conditions as well as interactional dynamics. From a relational perspective, the dimensions that make up intersectional inequalities and power dynamics are important because they indicate social relations that profoundly affect experiences and opportunity. For instance, it is not the fact that someone is disabled that matters so much to the relationist as the social relations that occur as a result of an ableist society that renders disability a problem in the first place. For example, the inability to travel via public transportation can be located as an inability in the public transportation set-up to accommodate certain bodies, as opposed to in the individual or body itself. The focus should therefore be on ableism, racism, sexism, heterosexism, nationalism, and ageism, as opposed to the individual attribute (a similar argument is made by intersectionality theorists such as Aguayo-Romero [2021]). In my review of what we know about poverty, some of the key interactional dynamics that end up most relevant for large portions of people in poverty are relations of dignity and vulnerability. Using the relational approach, I will provide a set of guidelines for thinking through issues of poverty.

Poverty itself is a social relation. Poverty exists only as a matter of relation to other people and institutions that have the ability to acquire goods, wealth, and/or status. Although poverty can be defined as a lack of fundamental necessities, such a lack when disconnected from a larger social economy is not poverty – it is a struggle for survival. The lone person in the wilderness who struggles to shelter and feed themselves is not best considered "poor"; they are best considered a hermit or a survivor. Race, gender, and dis/ability can also be thought about in terms of social relations, that is, how they acquire meaning and consequence through relations between people. Social inequality as we use the term is a durable type of relation that involves groups of people and relational factors that vary on the basis of categorical distinctions. One can think of inequality as a key characteristic of any relation between two or more entities. Thus, when I mention inequality as a factor, I am by default referring to social relations. However, we must go deeper. It is not enough to say inequality exists. We need to examine how unequal relations develop, persist, change, and manifest at both the interpersonal level and the level of how society is organized.

Social relations involve the positions people have relative to one another, including: (1) how we relate to one another and thus form identity; (2) interactions at the micro (face-to-face or equivalent) level, such as relationships; and (3) the macro-level relations (which encompass structure) whereby the action of one person, group, or institution affects another or is dependent on another. Any sense of the self occurs in relation to another: "I" am a teacher only in relation to others who are students. Or "I" am a considerate person in relation to those who are less considerate. "I" enact these identities in interactions with others; they must be confirmed and are shaped by my interactions with others. The ability to become a teacher and engage in that relationship are influenced by one's position in society. These abilities are also shaped by the pathways that permit a person to become a teacher, and the consequences of becoming a teacher in the society. Social relations as practiced by everyone recreate both the organization of people and resources ("structure") and the meanings of those arrangements and reactions to them ("culture"). Indeed, structure and culture are the effects of prior social relations that then provide the preconditions for other social relations.

If we ask why any particular person is in poverty, looking at the individual characteristics of that person alone cannot really answer this. What can? Consider each of the following bullet points:

- how their labor is valued and rewarded by their employer and the labor market
- the opportunity they have had to build valued skills
- whom they know, and the access to resources and opportunities that provides
- the duties and obligations they have to other people (such as dependents)
- the ways in which they create meaning in their life (such as valuing having children over having a career)
- the ability they have to do a job in the formal labor market, relative to others (such as reliable transportation).

Each of these points refers to the relation that person has relative to other people and organizations. It is that relation that matters, not the personal characteristics per se. The whole becomes greater than the sum of its parts.

Let's consider this further with a simplifying hypothetical. Consider a world where two human beings are completely alone and separate. There is no society. Then, they encounter each other and decide to live in cooperation. They effectively form a society. As these two people – let's call them Kiz and Phan – live together and find ways to cooperate, they form social relations. This involves a lot of different subprocesses and outcomes. In the process of living together, for instance, they form expectations of each other and themselves. They form inside jokes. They form routines. There is a division of labor. They develop new identities. Kiz is a really good fire-starter. Phan is the better fisher. That becomes part of their identity, their social role, and forms their worldview. They in effect develop all of these things – identities, expectations, routines, stories, vocabularies, justifications, and a history – that form a greater whole than if you took the sum of each of their personal characteristics and abilities in isolation. How Phan treats Kiz affects how Kiz thinks of themselves, and vice versa. For sociologists observing this small, new society, they might notice that personal characteristics can influence how they treat each other, but it is how they treat each other that really matters, not the personal characteristics. If Kiz had found someone else to cooperate with, they might not have become the fire-starter. They would not interact the same way with this other person as they do with Phan. The jokes and stories would be totally different. You cannot take *who Kiz is* and *who Phan is* and develop the whole of their social world living together. It becomes something apart from them as individuals – its own *thing*. Their social relations are what adds up to *society*. It's their social relations that best inform and explain the society that results.

Relational sociology has deep origins in classical sociology, as well as social philosophy, including Marxism, feminism, Pierre Bourdieu's theory of social reproduction, symbolic interactionism, and social network analysis. Symbolic interactionists have focused their efforts specifically on how social reality is inherently perceptual and communicative. They taught us, for instance, that even "the self" is constructed through interaction (Crossley 2015). As George Herbert Mead pointed out, the mind, the self, and society develop out of interaction. The self is performed interactionally and identity is relational. Erving Goffman gave us important tools to identify the processes of interactions by emphasizing how social action is performative and ordered on the basis of shared meanings (Collins 2010). The actions taken by people in any given field – education, say, or the welfare eligibility office – depend on the attributes of the other and the shared understandings of how the interaction is supposed to work. Goffman (1959) points out that the scene provides important cues to order the interaction as well. Similarly, for Bourdieu, physical space organizes social interactions and can reinforce division, union, or other social dynamics (Fogle 2011). To what extent does a classroom look and run like a prison? To what extent is the welfare office set up to enact discipline and humility? These processes have the effect of communicating to people where they are in relation to the other (i.e., the professor, the case worker, etc.) and what they should and should not do. Impression management can become about retaining dignity, often working against the purported objectives of the school and the welfare office. Hence, the high school student may be embarrassed about the real reason she did not do her homework, and so acts as if she chose not to do it. The single mother of two may strive to distinguish herself from other welfare dependents, and so the eligibility workers begin to doubt this client is really in need.

The relational approach as I define it is not a theory but a set of guidelines that can be applied in conjunction with a particular theory. It fundamentally guides the questions we ask about the social world. As Tomaskovic-Devey and Avent-Holt (2019:226) indicate, the relational turn is not so much a new theory as a systematic turn back toward sociology's strengths: "We think that much, perhaps most, social theory is already relational in its causal assumptions but that relational dynamics are hidden by explanations of action that exaggerate the autonomy of individuals or the homogeneity of social structures." The task, then, is to uncover these relational dynamics. In the relational framework I have developed for the purposes of understanding poverty, we ask this set of questions about any action or problem of interest: (1) What obligations and expectations affect the behavior or outcome of interest? (2) How are these obligations and expectations shaped by structural and cultural arrangements? (3) Who are the relevant players in affecting the outcome? (4) How do they use power, and from what structural or cultural arrangements do they gain this power?

Obligations and expectations are critical for human behavior and involve consideration of multiple relations. Parent–child relations are also influenced by the relations a parent has with other people, such as other children, romantic partners, and their own parents. Relations between an employee and employer are affected by relations between the employer and other workers or potential laborers, and between the employee and their obligations as parents. And obligations and expectations are very much influenced by race, gender, and dis/ability, which takes us to the next issue.

It is also important to consider the contextual and macro-level factors that shape relations at the interactional or micro level. For instance, not having dependable childcare can interfere with a parent's relations to both their employer and their child. Racial segregation of schools reinforces the message of disadvantage that racial minority students who do not show exceptional ability (and even those who do) are not expected to succeed. Standard expectations for workers devalue the contributions and abilities of those persons with limited mobility, different sensory abilities, or cognitive disabilities. This line of interrogation is more difficult in that such factors are often less visible or obvious to the investigator. Certainly, it tends to be ignored by those involved in the interaction at issue. For the employer, it only matters that the employee is not fulfilling expectations or obligations as an employee. If the employee wanted a better job, they should have gone to college, or not have had a child before achieving financial stability. Such a perspective fails to recognize such outcomes are not merely individual choices, but are subject to multiple social relations. In turn, the employer has their own social obligations and expectations with which to deal. It is not a matter of who is at fault, but understanding what social relations, including macro-structural and cultural factors, lead to what sorts of outcomes. To widen that perspective to consideration of macro-level factors, a general understanding of how society works is essential. Practice helps. But, more practically and precisely, identifying the relevant institutions is a useful first step.

I use the term "player" as a way to think about who is invested in the macro-level set of conditions, as well as individuals and institutions closer to the individual. Considering the relevant institutions is a useful step here as well. But sometimes players are not immediately identifiable through institutions. It becomes essential to consider the explanations that people have for the actions they take. Sometimes an unexpected connection comes from in-depth observations of people's lives. For instance, Burton (2009) found that, for some women having trouble getting off welfare, the problem was not their relations with employers so much as their relations with abusive partners or ex-partners. But we need to go one step further to ask why these (ex-)partners should have such power over these women? This takes us to the next question.

Finally, we can consider what power players use and from what structural or cultural arrangements they gain their power. Many sociologists argue that the cultural allowances for domestic violence that come out of patriarchal beliefs, as well as a flawed criminal justice system, make domestic violence the problem that it is. This is part of the web that we are all stuck in: we are connected, constrained, and enabled by the different strands of social relations that make up society. That does not mean we do not exercise any individual choice or agency. But the consequences of our choices, the opportunity we have to exercise agency, and the power we have to realize our hopes are compelling products of social relations.

What a Relational Approach Contributes

E. P. Thompson, in *The Making of the English Working Class*, writes that:

> By class I understand an historical phenomenon, unifying a number of disparate and seemingly unconnected events, both in the raw material of experience and in consciousness. I emphasise that it is an *historical* phenomenon. I do not see class as a "structure", nor even as a "category", but as something which in fact happens (and can be shown to have happened) in human relationships. More than this, the notion of class entails the notion of historical relationship. Like any other relationship, it is a fluency which evades analysis if we attempt to stop it dead at any given moment and anatomise its structure. The finest meshed sociological net cannot give us a pure specimen of class, any more than it can give us one of deference or of love. The relationship must always be embodied in real people and in a real context. Moreover, we cannot have two distinct classes, each with an independent being, and then bring them *into* relationship with each other. We cannot have love without lovers, nor deference without squires and labourers. And class happens when some men, as a result of common experiences (inherited or shared), feel and articulate the identity of their interests as between themselves, and as against other men whose interests are different from (and usually opposed to) theirs. The class experience is largely determined by the productive relations into which men are born – or enter involuntarily. (1966:9)

And so we cannot have poverty without wealth, or homelessness without the housed. There is no "pure" specimen of poverty. We can examine the social relations that make up the experiences of people in poverty in specific cases to identify relevant sets of conditions. My review of the research points to how many problems of the poor are relational in nature – that is, they are not problems in or with the individual, but problems that arise out of the imbalanced social relations that characterize the lives of the poor. Such social relations can be brutal at times. They are in other cases quite subtle, and hardly visible to the outsider. Erdmans and Black (2015) reveal the ways in which young women in low-income families in their study experienced abusive relations that sapped their ability to *own* their life, leading to lax self-protection, and, eventually, early pregnancy. A more subtle example can be drawn from Garcia's (2010) work on addiction and the overlapping institutions of the criminal justice system (including drug courts) and the detox clinic that provide scripts and roles for the "patient-prisoners." Over time, the addict comes to adopt the claims and roles provided by these institutions, which ends up reinforcing a sense of personal failure and hopelessness. The recent coronavirus pandemic also provides a clear example of how the personal problem of contracting an illness is more a product of social and relational factors – e.g., the ability to isolate ourselves or the local interpretation of mask-wearing – than of individual choices alone. In addition to meeting the standards for interrogating class as set forth by E. P. Thompson, the relational approach as I use it has the benefit of fulfilling several ideal aims in addressing poverty. Specifically, this approach entails a combined but nuanced approach to culture and structure; a need to recognize intersectional inequalities, particularly race, gender, and disability; and allowance for individual agency.

Discussing sets of conditions might help us better envision development and change rather than reinforce rigid, monolithic images of social forces. I use the concept of *sets of conditions* to refer to structural and cultural products of human relations that provide the context for social relations at the interactional level. Neither structure nor culture is given primacy over the other, but neither is the possibility ruled out that one may have some primacy in a given situation. This approach addresses the problems entailed by merely structural or merely cultural understandings of poverty. Structure refers to the durable and material outcomes of social action, such as law, institutions, technological capacities, and the physical characteristics of places. Structure represents those difficult-to-change conditions that people confront and live by. Structure shapes opportunity, resources, and exposure to harm or help. Culture, on the other hand, refers to the symbolic resources that are formed through social interaction and relations. Structure does rely on culture, as culture is also influenced by structure; the two are intertwined. When we change our minds

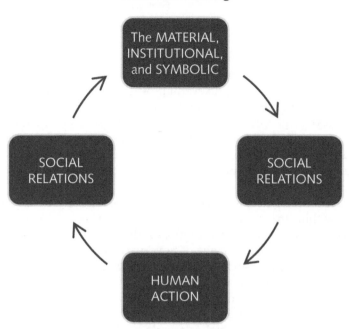

A representation of the relationship between structure and culture and individuals

about the meaning of some structural feature, that feature can come under attack. We follow constitutional law because so many people believe in it, and it thus legitimizes certain actions. In turn, past decisions made about what is lawful and subsequent rules influence ideas about nationalism and lawfulness. But the circle can be interrupted – for instance, changing interpretations of the US Constitution combined with institutional change feasibly endanger traditional ideals and processes of law in the United States.

Sets of expectations and transactions are conditioned by structure, culture, and direct individual action. In turn, individual action is shaped by social relations and individual-level factors. We do not typically experience structure, culture, and the material as social realities directly. Rather, we experience these phenomena through interactions, through how we come to think of and present ourselves in relation to others, and positions we hold relative to others. So why do we need structure and culture as overarching concepts at all? Because even those immediate social relations are shaped by temporally durable effects of other human action occurring through social relations.

A relational approach also highlights the intersectional nature of poverty. Poverty is not just a structural feature or an individual characteristic, but a matter of positioning relative to others. If we address the production of and the experience of poverty as operating through a series of relations, we find several processes that operate according to different logics. By examining the actual social relations that form the context of people's lives, we find that these social relations are shaped strongly by ideas and institutionalizations of race, gender, age, disability, citizenship, and other social constructs. The production and experience of poverty are shaped by these other positions and relations.

Intersectionality is, in part, about the positioning of individual actors within these larger relations of domination. A relational approach is well suited to recognizing that racism is implicated in the production and experience of poverty. Multiple power processes operate in any given social relationship. Yet these power processes are subject to change as well as variation in their salience. A Latina woman in poverty without citizenship or legal documentation, an African American male in poverty, and a White single mother each could have a different social relation to a law enforcement officer. The outcome of any interaction or action with relevance, such as a decision to call or not call the police about a domestic violence incident, is affected by the particular social relation. If interaction ensues, the race, ethnicity, or gender of the officer is also likely to impact the relation to the extent that these constructs bear on expectations and resources. So too will the race and gender of the higher authorities to which this officer is accountable, though they are more distant. In turn, a given interaction between any of the two parties has the potential to alter or perpetuate common expectations and resource differentials. The point is that the decision to call the police is not just formed by one individual in isolation. It is formed within and by social relations, and the specific impact of these social relations varies according to the different positions of actors relative to larger social relations of domination and inequality.

Finally, a relational approach rejects the notion of the individual and society as independent realities. The individual and society act upon each other in fluid and constant development, and we need to recognize how the individual is both agentic and constrained. Power is not something that people have or do not have – power only exists in and through relations. As other researchers such as Edin and Shaefer (2015) have pointed out, eliminating poverty requires integrating the poor into society. Many nonpoor are more susceptible than they think to being cut off from society, and falling into poverty. An uncontrollable crisis, the subsequent loss of employment and thereby income, and the spiral begins. Until we eradicate the conditions for poverty, we are all insecure.

Relations of Vulnerability and the Desire for Dignity

Though the problems encountered by people in poverty are, as we will see, highly diverse, there are larger patterns. The social relations that contribute to the actions of people in poverty are often characterized by their vulnerability and the desire for dignity. Relations of vulnerability refer to sets of transactions and expectations between two or more individuals or groups in which at least one actor has significantly lower bargaining power to draw upon, and thus is in a vulnerable position. For instance, the relations between landlords and tenants as described in Matthew Desmond's (2016) research are an example of a relation of vulnerability for the tenants. Tenants who are behind in paying rent refrain from asking for basic housing maintenance because of the ability of the landlord to evict them. Indeed, I know from my own experience in nonprofit relief agencies that when a person in poverty is evicted, they often lack the knowledge or legal support to challenge it. Evictees often have their belongings thrown out, and if they do not find housing or storage for their belongings, they lose most of them. Moreover, there is little people in poverty can do if they are denied housing – legally or illegally – on the basis of bad credit (legal), large families (not typically legal except in the case of fire codes), criminal record (legal), race (illegal), employment status (legal), or lack of an initial payment that is three times the cost of one month's rent (legal). While landlords may find poor tenants bothersome and risky, ultimately landlords have the backing of the law, based in part on the sanctity of private property, and they have better access to the rules of the game. People in poverty may take advantage however they can, but that is often a creative recourse in the face of few options. The origin of the advantage – as "taking advantage" implies – lies with the owners and rule-makers in society.

In such relations of vulnerability, spanning the sectors of employment, childcare, social services, creditors, housing, and personal relationships, people in poverty must struggle to attain dignity. These two realities are at odds with one another. And sometimes this means that the person in poverty chooses dignity regardless of the costs. The desire for dignity is a human need. Although survival will often take precedence, the desire for dignity will nonetheless emerge in consequential moments, especially in a nation such as the USA that values individualism and status above all. Together, relations of vulnerability and the desire for dignity help us perceive the predicament of poverty. But to gain a complete picture of poverty, we must also examine how these relations and desires are shaped in the context of the phenomena we call structure and culture.

For those who struggle with chronic and deep poverty especially – what Edin and Shaefer refer to as the $2-a-day poor – their circumstances may be "worlds apart from the experiences of most Americans" (Edin and Shaefer 2015:173). Surviving deep poverty may entail doing that which one finds morally objectionable, thus isolating one even further from mainstream society or a sense of normality. Deep poverty may very well entail "deep physical and emotional wounds" (Edin and Shaefer 2015:173). I think that many of the behaviors and worldviews of people in chronic poverty can be understood as products of the existential tension between the struggle to live – to keep body and soul together – and the search for meaning – a reason to live. While this tension exists for much of humankind, it is exacerbated among the poor. Nonetheless, in addition to recognizing diversity among people in poverty, I see a need to identify the circumstances of people in poverty that tend to lead to particular behavioral outcomes and ways of living. These relationships, interactions, and sets of conditions are all characterized by the vulnerability of people in poverty, and what one must do to maintain dignity under relations of vulnerability is not always conducive to future security, as we will see.

Aims and Overview of this Book

There are three major aims of this book. The first aim is to demonstrate how the culture and behavior of the poor are not the cause of poverty. I explain what sociologists know about the culture and structure of poverty, and how popular portrayals misrepresent poverty. Chapter 2 – "Who Are the Poor?" – tackles issues of misrepresentation and addresses the basic question of how poverty manifests in the United States. Chapter 3, "Family and Parenting," addresses issues of family that are associated with poverty – namely, single motherhood, teen pregnancy, and child abuse. Now that the reader is acquainted with some key empirical research on poverty, I take us back through a broad view of how social scientists have tried to understand poverty through culture and structure. Chapter 4, "Culture," focuses on the study of culture and poverty, including the historical context of such study and alternative ways to understand culture. The prior two chapters provide a good counterpoint to some of the claims of the culture of poverty approach. The other main approach to understanding poverty – structure – is the next subject. Chapter 5, "Structure and Social Relations," takes on the role that the durable and material results of social relations play in creating and perpetuating poverty. In Chapter 6, "Opportunity and Personal Autonomy," I consider how individuals act within this structure, specifically examining college attendance, employment, and immigration. Altogether, I find that, while individual agency is not irrelevant, we must consider agency in the context of oft-imbalanced social relations. When addressing a social problem, rather than identify behavior that needs to be changed, we should identify relations that need to be changed. If it is a *social* problem, then, by definition, the root of the issue must reside in social relations.

My second aim is the pivotal one: to demonstrate a different approach to poverty. I argue that, to understand the behavior and lives of people in poverty, one must consider the relational context, especially the relations of vulnerability and the human need for dignity. In Chapter 2, race, gender, and dis/ability feature as important dimensions for understanding both the experience of people in poverty and the persistence of poverty. To demonstrate these ideas further, I identify two important dimensions in the lives of people in poverty and summarize what we know about these issues: family, and opportunity – in Chapters 3 and 6, respectively.

Third, I make the case that it is important to recognize that persistent poverty has harsh effects, and that we can and should eliminate much of the poverty that exists in the United States. Furthermore, the people *are worth* this effort. Edin and Shaefer (2015) note that there is much in the lives of the deep poor "to cherish," "protect," and "nurture." I argue that this should be one of our central aims as a society, with major implications for our general future. As part of this, Chapter 5, "Structure and Social Relations," discusses how poverty policy tends to punish and criminalize poverty and the poor. Throughout all of the chapters, however, it becomes clear that a reassessment of poverty is due. We need a different approach.

2

Who Are the Poor?

Defining and Measuring Poverty

Defining poverty is necessary in order to adequately measure it and thus ascertain how much of what sort of poverty we have and determine appropriate responses accordingly. Definitions and corresponding measurements of poverty include two approaches: the absolute and the relative. The aim of absolute definitions of poverty is to identify a threshold at which it is impossible to adequately care for oneself and one's family, given living expenses. An absolute definition and corresponding measurement of poverty is often necessary in order to efficiently identify who needs assistance. Many programs and researchers thus rely on official national measurements of poverty such as the US Official Poverty Measure (OPM). The relative definitions of poverty help us remember that poverty is a relational condition – it is about what people have in relation to other people, and how that affects their ability to live a worthwhile life. It thus turns our focus away from just meeting basic needs and toward empowerment. Since there are many different ways of defining and identifying poverty with important implications for how poverty is viewed and addressed, I have included a separate box outlining and summarizing some of the different types of poverty that may be referenced in this book or that are influential in terms of policy and practice.

Of course, meeting basic needs is among the basic requirements for empowering people. But, as Haugen and Boutros (2014) indicated in *The Locust Effect: Why the End of Poverty Requires the End of Violence*, addressing institutions that provide basic levels of security and rule of law is a necessary component of antipoverty efforts; otherwise, efforts to provide all manner of goods and services will be futile. After all, poverty is not just about not meeting basic needs; it is about not being able to meet basic needs in the context of a society in which others are able to. If everybody is "poor," nobody is poor. Even when someone identifies a whole community that is poor, that designation is coming from the perspective of someone who is not "poor." Poverty becomes a possibility when someone has much less than others in their society, and survival is a struggle for those with less even with the technical capability to provide enough for all. Status distinctions in such a society serve to deny some people of the opportunities and privileges of others because they are less valued. Poverty is not just about not having much in terms of material resources. It is about not having the opportunity that others have to acquire material resources. This is why the disabled are especially vulnerable to poverty if the disability interferes with getting a job in the labor market. It is why having an address can make such a difference. It is why not knowing the right people, not speaking the common language, or having a major stigma all contribute to the likelihood of someone ending up or remaining poor.

The degree to which we need to go beyond an absolute definition and embrace a more relative notion of poverty depends on the purpose of the measurement. I know of three reasons to measure poverty: (1) to identify eligibility for and need of social programs; (2) to identify the extent of suffering, vulnerability, and risk present at a certain time and place; and (3) to understand a social economy. Absolute measures tend to be more useful for purpose (1), whereas relative measures are better for purposes (2) and (3). These three purposes are sometimes confusedly referenced as the same – for instance, it might be assumed that if the number of persons eligible for a given program has decreased, then poverty overall has decreased. This might not be the case at all; rather, people could have access to food, but still lack access to basic healthcare. Or households may not meet a certain income threshold for poverty, but that does not mean they can afford to send their child to college (or indeed to primary school). While these three aims are closely related, they involve different considerations.

Relative definitions emphasize the importance of status, social comparison, and general social expectations in order to capture the experience of poverty and identify deprivation that may be psychological as much as physical. For instance, the notion of social exclusion advocated by UK researcher Townsend (1979:31) defined poverty as when people "lack the resources to obtain the types of

Definitions and Measures of Poverty:
Origin, Use, and Additional Information

Chronic

In my usage, this category refers to poverty that recurs often enough throughout the life course for an individual's health or well-being to be significantly impacted. The lack of social mobility is a central feature of chronic poverty. It is sometimes conceptualized strictly as including "those whose mean income (or consumption) over time is below the poverty line" and/or "where the chronically poor are those households (individuals) who are below the poverty line half of the time or more" (Israeli and Weber 2014).

In some uses, chronic poverty also implicates intergenerational transmission of poverty (Green and Hulme 2005). Chronic poverty may be conceptualized as absolute or relative.

- Clark and Hulme (2010) argue that the experience of poverty depends a great deal on how long it lasts, which is in turn directly related to social and political processes.
- One general advantage is that chronic poverty can be measured at the individual level rather than at the household level, thus recognizing inequality within households as well as change in household composition, though relevant data at the individual level can be difficult to access.
- The use of the term "chronic" may be critiqued for pathologizing poverty. Yet, Green and Hulme (2005:868) advocate for the concept of chronic poverty as a means of "highlighting the outcomes of the entrenched social relations," that is, "the social and political processes that make people poor and keep them in poverty."

Deep

Also known as extreme or absolute poverty. The United Nations (1995:section 19) defines absolute poverty as "a condition characterized by severe deprivation of basic human needs, including food, safe drinking water, sanitation facilities, health, shelter, education and information. It depends not only on income but also on access to social services."

Jensen and Ely (2017) use income below half the poverty threshold as the indicator for deep poverty. It can be conceptualized as absolute or relative. When defined in relation to others, it is a relative measure, but when used as a measure of material hardship, it is better categorized as absolute. Commonly conceptualized as an amount a person must live on per day – such as the $1.90-a-day poverty set by the World Bank in 2018 as the threshold for extreme poverty – such measures propose to make the depth of the poverty less abstract.

• Though similar to chronic poverty, deep poverty focuses less on the length of time someone is in poverty and more on its severity.

★ ★ ★

Absolute Definitions

The aim of absolute definitions of poverty is to identify a threshold at which it is impossible to adequately care for oneself and one's family, given living expenses. An absolute definition and corresponding measurement of poverty are often necessary to identify who and how many require assistance. As Fisher (1992) notes, if a purely absolute definition of poverty is derived without any reference to consumption or income patterns of the population as a whole, then many of the examples I provide are not purely absolute. However, it is difficult to develop an absolute definition of poverty that can be applied across place and time without taking one time point and standard as the norm. The closest we come to such measures are assessments of how often people go without food, shelter, warmth, and other forms of material deprivation that might be considered universal, but which thereby cannot account for the possibility of social mobility. As a compromise, I determine absolute measures as making some determination of a minimum standard of living without explicit regard to how that affects or involves one's position in society.

The Official Poverty Measure (US)

The OPM is also known as the federal threshold for poverty. It is an example of a pre-tax and transfer measure. Such measures do not reflect actual hardship so much as a need for assistance in the first place.

In the United States, this measure was created by the Office for Management and Budgeting. It was developed by an official in the Social Security Administration, Molly Orshansky (1965), initially to compare different levels of opportunity and risk among families in different demographic groups (Fisher 1992). It calculates the estimated expense of food for a given family size, multiplied by three. The OPM uses gross income before taxes and does not take into account noncash government assistance, such as Supplemental Nutritional Assistance Program (SNAP) benefits that a family might be receiving. The threshold it uses is calculated using the national Consumer Price Index for All Urban Consumers to estimate the minimum cost of food for a family, taking into account the number, gender, and age of household members. This outcome is then multiplied by three. Any household with income below this amount is considered to be officially poor in a given year.

- This measure thus takes into account household composition and the cost of food, but does not necessarily reflect the actual cost of living, especially as it varies by place. Even access to adequate nutrition at the Consumer Price Index prices varies by place for households.
- The multiply-by-three calculation was based on a 1955 survey (the Agriculture Department's Household Food Consumption Survey), finding that households with three or more persons across income brackets spent about one-third of their after-tax income on food (Fisher 1992). It was not determined what proportion of income the poor spend on food.
- While adjustments have been made to the OPM, particularly in terms of how food costs are calculated, the basic approach has remained since 1969 despite recommendations to update the measure from multiple subcommittees, agencies, and researchers (Fisher 1992).

Supplemental Poverty Measure (SPM) (US)

Established in 2011 by the Census Bureau and Bureau of Labor Statistics, the SPM is not intended to replace the official threshold, especially for purposes of eligibility determination, but it measures hardship better across place and time.

Government officials' and researchers' desire to account for non-official sources of income, such as contributions from friends and family, SNAP benefits, housing vouchers, etc., as well as changes in household composition, led to the development of the Survey of Income and Program Participation (SIPP) in 1984 (Fisher 1992; US Census Bureau 2022).

- The SPM counts more in terms of both income *and* expenses, so it may be higher *or* lower than the OPM in its measurement of percent of the population in poverty.
- The SPM also reflects the impact of more generous social programming, such as during the first few months of the COVID pandemic.
- The SPM may be less useful for identifying rural poverty relative to urban poverty, as pointed out by Jensen and Ely (2017), because it does not reflect all cost-of-living differences, such as transportation, that pertain to rural residence (only housing). All other measures included in their study, such as the OPM, deep poverty, and subjective poverty, indicated higher rates of poverty in rural areas than urban areas.

Asset Poverty

Asset poverty "refers to the percentage of households that lack sufficient net worth to subsist at the poverty level for three months in the absence of income" (Rist 2022:11). Assets are in many ways more important than income because they represent a more durable form of security. Having assets to draw upon is critical for weathering a crisis. This approach identifies families who are vulnerable to poverty as well as those experiencing poverty at that particular time.

The first asset-based approach to measuring poverty was Weisbrod and Hansen's (1968) effort to explicitly account for wealth as well as income (Caner and Wolff 2004). Asset poverty was initially used to determine the inadequacy of one's wealth to meet basic needs, but is sometimes expanded to address "assets" besides wealth, including intangible resources such as support networks (Green and Hulme 2005).

- This approach to poverty is credited with inspiring the 1998 Individual Development Account (IDA) Demonstration Act, by which the government proposed to match dollar-by-dollar the amount that eligible families saved to designated accounts.
- McKernan et al. (2014) found that assets were especially critical for low- and middle-income households' ability to recover from crisis.

- The most common asset of importance is home ownership, but savings are also very important for the ability of a family to deal with crisis, including spells of unemployment or medical bills due to accident or illness.
- Some research suggests that chronic intergenerational poverty is closely linked to "asset poverty" (Carter and Barrett 2006).
- Assets are distributed more unequally across the United States than is income.

Consumption-Based Poverty

Another version of the absolute definition is a consumption-based approach that examines what people consume, in order to establish standard of living. This is useful for taking into account the resources that people can access.

Though arguably relative in that consumption depends first on what is widely available in a society, which is in turn historically relative, I categorize it as absolute because the emphasis is not on what people have relative to others, but simply on what they have. One issue is deciding what consumption to measure. Meyer and Sullivan's (2017) model appears to include – though they are not clear – expenditures, home ownership, and vehicle ownership.

- One advantage of the consumption-based approach is that, by going straight to what people are purchasing, it gets around the whole problem of income and expense counting, including pre- versus post-taxes and transfers.
- Those who advocate for a multidimensional approach to measuring poverty argue that the consumption-based approach excludes many important considerations, such as the quality of housing, health risks, risk of victimization, and assets (White 2017).

Fuel Poverty

Fuel poverty refers to who goes without adequate heat in the winter. "A household is fuel poor when it lives in an energy inefficient dwelling and is unable to heat its home at an appropriate standard level of warmth due to insufficient financial resources" (Fizaine and Kahouli 2019).

Fuel poverty measures are used to identify either the presence of extreme hardship in certain geographic regions, or the need for assistance with fuel costs. It is most commonly used in northern Europe. A variety of measures are used for fuel poverty, however, ranging from the proportion of income spent on fuel costs to self-declarations of inability to heat one's home adequately (Fizaine and Kahouli 2019).

- This measure developed after activists in the UK protested about the rise in winter mortality due to soaring energy costs (Fizaine and Kahouli 2019).

Food Insecurity

Food insecurity refers to who is, or is at risk of, not getting adequate nutrition. This is a useful measure when the goal is to assess material deprivation. Having a low income does not necessarily mean that a family lacks access to the basic necessities, as they may rely on extended social networks or other resources.

The US Department of Agriculture (USDA) Economic Research Service office has used a Food Security Scale since 1995 based on survey questions about food consumption and hunger. According to the USDA, "food-insecure households (those with low and very low food security) had difficulty at some time during the year providing enough food for all their members because of a lack of resources" (Coleman-Jensen et al. 2022). This same report indicates that 10.2 percent of Americans were food insecure in 2021.

- Food insecurity measures are most appropriate for identifying material deprivation due to poverty.
- This is also a measure of hardship that is more comparable across time and place.
- Food insecurity has been found associated with several adverse outcomes, including mental health problems (McLaughlin et al. 2012).

★ ★ ★

Relative Definitions

Relative poverty measures take into account the specific standards of living for that time and place. Relative definitions and measures are often used to identify the extent of suffering, vulnerability, and risk present at a certain time and place, and/or to understand the implications of a social economy. The most well-known initial proposal for a relative poverty measure goes back at least to the recommendation of a poverty line equating to 50% of the median income by Townsend (1962) in the UK and Fuchs (1969) in the USA (Fisher 1992). The United Kingdom and the European Union consider 60% of median income as their official government poverty line. The advantage of this approach is that it is relative to people in the middle of the income distribution, and thus reflects (though not perfectly) inflation, cost of living, and general social expectations and standards. Foster (1998:336) points out that relative poverty measures like these do not mean poverty is "always with us," nor are they measures of inequality (they might be considered one dimension of inequality). Relative measures capture risk – who will be unable to recover from a crisis or large expense such as illness, injury, or unemployment – better than do absolute measures.

Social Exclusion

Townsend (1979:31) defined the poor as people who "lack the resources to obtain the types of diet, participate in the activities and have the living conditions and amenities which are customary or at least widely encouraged or approved in the societies to which they belong."

Inspired by Townsend, the Poverty and Social Exclusion approach combines surveys of the public on services, goods, and standards that are considered necessary with surveys looking at related deprivations across income (Gordon 2017). Statistical procedures are then used to identify an income threshold that is based on access to a decent standard of living.

- One critique of this approach is given by Green and Hulme (2005), who note that the problem is not so much that the poor are excluded from institutions, but that social institutions operate to generate poverty.

Capability Poverty

Developed by Amartya Sen (1999), capability poverty is the lack of freedom to lead the kind of life a person has reason to value. Sen developed this approach as an alternative to the focus of development in poor countries on economic indicators like income, to the detriment of basic human rights and political empowerment.

The United Nations has adopted aspects of the capability approach in its *Human Development Reports*, the Human Development Index, and the Human Poverty Index (HPI), which includes indicators of nutrition, child mortality, years of schooling, sanitation, access to electricity, clean drinking water, and assets (United Nations 2022). Sen himself, however, cautions against confusing the HPI and similar indices with actual human capabilities (Clark and Hulme 2010).

- Sen (1981) noted that democracies never have famines; thus, the political system of a nation is tied to the ability of its people – especially its most disadvantaged – to thrive.
- Martha Nussbaum, the feminist political philosopher, has expanded upon Sen's work to identify 10 different types of capabilities to which all human beings should have access, including things like access to nature, bodily integrity, and the use of one's imagination and creativity.

The Self-Sufficiency Standard (SSS)

The Center for Women's Welfare (CWW) uses, as an alternative to the OPM, the SSS, defined as "a budget-based, living wage measure that defines the real cost of living for working families at a minimally adequate level" (Center for Women's Welfare 2022).

This measure is based on what a working family needs to budget to get by without resorting to public assistance, and is calculated separately by state. It takes into account costs of childcare, housing, the low-cost food plan (see USDA 2022a), clothing/hygiene, transportation, healthcare, taxes and credits, and sufficient emergency savings to cover half of a family's costs for 6 months of job loss.

- Housed in the University of Washington's School of Social Work, the CWW provides SSS measures and reports for all states in the USA.

diet, participate in the activities and have the living conditions and amenities which are customary or at least widely encouraged or approved in the societies to which they belong." The social exclusion approach suggests that there are three inter-related forces reproducing poverty: disconnection from mainstream society, mainly through lack of employment leading to isolation; educational and social barriers preventing entrance into higher-paid technical and "high-touch" occupations; and the institutional hostility of welfare systems, penal systems, and "related bureaucracies that make the poor the victims and dependents of public charity rather than participants in generating resources for themselves or their families" (Goldsmith and Blakely 1992:10).

The capabilities approach is another example of a relative definition of poverty. When it comes to addressing poverty, Amartya Sen (1999) argued that the widespread capability to *choose a life one has reason to value* should be the guiding premise – not just economic access. Sen is most concerned with addressing development efforts of institutions such as the World Bank, and nongovernmental organizations working in the least affluent nations of the world. He argues that common indicators of development like income should be viewed as simply means to improving life conditions. Rather than focusing on income, we should view income as the means to an end – the end being the freedom of a human being to lead the kind of life they have reason to value. There are ways in which you can have income but not freedom, and ways that you can lack income but still have more freedom than someone with more money than you. The capabilities approach directs us to focus on what deprives us of *capability*, in conjunction with the deprivations that are intrinsically important to people. It also asks us to consider that the relation between income and capability varies between different communities, and even for different individuals. For instance, Sen (1999) pointed out that, if we compare the capability to live to a mature age without succumbing to premature mortality, certain populations suddenly appear more disadvantaged than previously considered. African American men are worse off in this regard than poor men in China and India, even though their incomes are much lower. When we consider mortality rates as an indicator, African American women are also much worse off than White American women, even when controlling for income. This has implications for Sen for how we address poverty alleviation, which I return to in Chapter 7.

Federal estimates of poverty using an official measure began in the 1960s, with the Official Poverty Measure (OPM). The OPM compares gross pre-tax income of family units to a threshold. This threshold is calculated using the estimated minimum cost of food for a family, taking into account the number, gender, and age of household members. This outcome is then multiplied by three. Any household with income below this amount is officially considered to be poor in a given year. This measure thus takes into account household composition and the cost of food, but does not necessarily reflect the actual cost of living, especially as it varies by place. The OPM does not take into account taxes or noncash government assistance, such as Supplemental Nutritional Assistance Program (SNAP) benefits that a family might be receiving, so it does not reflect actual hardship so much as a need for assistance in the first place. The OPM does not gauge more general social status, in terms of one's access to the means for living a decent life, including healthcare and education. Rank (2004) pointed out that the official threshold for poverty has edged further away from the median income over time. Thus, while food hardship may not be as much a problem if the OPM declines, the ability of people, per the capabilities approach, to improve their living standards may actually increase. The originator of the OPM herself indicated that the calculations would provide "a conservative underestimate" of poverty, but was at least a reasonable approach to identifying "how much, on an average, is too little" (Orshansky 1965:3; Fisher 1992).

For this reason, and others, administrators and researchers have commonly used measures less conservative than the OPM by multiplying the threshold for that year by 1.25 or 1.3, or sometimes even by 2, so that we can look at numbers of households at 130% of the poverty threshold, for instance. Government officials' and researchers' desire to account for non-official sources of income, such as contributions from friends and family, SNAP benefits, housing vouchers, etc., led to the development of the Survey of Income and Program Participation (SIPP) (Fisher 1992).

In 2011, the Census Bureau began using a new measure of poverty that takes into account government and noncash assistance, which it calls the Supplemental Poverty Measure (SPM) (Fox and Burns 2021). As "supplemental," it is not intended to replace the official threshold, particularly for purposes of eligibility determination, but provides an improved way of measuring hardship across place and time. The SPM may be higher or lower than the OPM in its measurement of percent of the population in poverty because it counts more in terms of both income and expenses. The SPM also reflects the impact of more generous social programming, such as during the first few months of the COVID pandemic. In fact, in 2020, for the first time, the SPM was lower than the OPM, and showed the sharpest annual decline (Fox and Burns 2021). This is primarily attributed to the stimulus payments and extensions of assistance programs, including unemployment compensation and SNAP. In Fox and Burns's (2021) analysis, the 2020 poverty rate would have increased from 2019 to 2020 if not for the economic stimulus payments. Instead, the SPM poverty rate declined from 11.8% in 2019 to 9.1% in 2020. The decline in poverty occurred regardless of race, Hispanic origin, region, or age, disability status, or work experience. The OPM rate, however, was 11.4%, an increase from 10.5% in 2019 (Shrider et al. 2021). Social Security continues to have the largest impact of all poverty alleviation programs in the USA on moving people from poverty to non-poverty status. But the 2020 expansions in programs helped children in particular, since most of the antipoverty programs outside of Social Security – such as the school lunch program, Women with Infants and Children, SNAP, Medicaid, and tax benefits – focus on children. Fox and Burns (2021) estimate that about 3.2 million children were prevented from falling into poverty by the stimulus payments alone. Thus, as an indicator of where people are at with the income–expense equation once government and nongovernment forms of assistance are calculated, the SPM is far more comprehensive than the OPM. It makes sense to use measures including government aid and noncash assistance for identifying levels of suffering and hardship, especially for comparative purposes, while focusing on cash income for the purpose of program eligibility.

Other population-based measures of poverty used in policy reports include fuel poverty and food insecurity. Assessing fuel poverty is an effort to identify who goes without adequate heat in the winter. This is usually not a stand-alone measure, but used to identify the presence of extreme hardship in certain geographic regions. Food insecurity is an effort to identify who is, or is at risk of, not getting adequate nutrition. Even these definitions do not take into account risk – who will be unable to recover from a disaster or large expense such as a medical bill, sudden unemployment, or disability.

We can also measure poverty based on what people consume. The consumption-based measure of poverty has advantages over the income-based measures, in that it reflects what people can actually access (Meyer and Sullivan 2017). However, along with income-based measures, it is critiqued for understating the amount of deprivation and social exclusion. The other issue is deciding what consumption to measure. Meyer and Sullivan's (2017) model appears to include – though they are not clear – expenditures, home ownership, and vehicle ownership. However, as the *New York Times* columnist Nicholas Kristof (2016) has noted, having air conditioning in the USA does not mean you can go to college. Having a television does not mean you do not go hungry.

Other measures of poverty aim to incorporate a more sophisticated reflection of hardship, vulnerability, and/or risk. The social exclusion approach inspired by Townsend and developed by a United Kingdom-based conglomeration of universities and organizations compares what the public deems necessary for a decent life with deprivations of those necessaries across income levels (Gordon 2017). Statistical procedures thereby identify an income threshold required to access a decent standard of living. The Center for Women's Welfare uses a similar but simpler approach, called the Self-Sufficiency Standard (SSS). The SSS is based on what a working family needs to get by without resorting to public assistance, taking into account costs of childcare, housing, clothing/hygiene, transportation, and healthcare; the low-cost food plan; taxes and credits; and emergency savings. Yet another approach to measuring poverty and/or economic sufficiency is the asset-based approach. Assets are in many ways more important than income because they represent a more durable form of security. This approach identifies families who are vulnerable to poverty as well as those experiencing poverty at that particular time. McKernan et al. (2014) found that assets were especially critical for low- and middle-income households' ability to recover from crisis. Some research suggests that chronic intergenerational poverty is closely linked to "asset poverty" (Carter and Barrett 2006). Salamon and MacTavish (2017) find that mobile homes are marketed to low-income and working-class individuals and families as an affordable route to home ownership, but their value as an asset is highly questionable. The asset-based approach has two main implications: (1) it separates out from the general group of poor those who have a temporary loss of income but who will weather this loss and exit poverty within a year or so; and (2) it brings to our attention those households who are not among the poor, but who are nonetheless vulnerable, and perhaps worse off in long-term security than those who might count among the income-poor at a given time (Brandolini et al. 2010).

And what about assessing the overall state of our social economy? Are we reducing poverty over time? Not surprisingly, it depends on how you measure poverty. In 2018, the Council of Economic Advisers declared that the War on Poverty has been a success, proposing new work requirements for program beneficiaries. The primary problem with the report by the Council is that it underestimates the number of people receiving benefits who already are working (Peterson 2020). Their recommendations for requiring the poor to work do not make sense, given that many are already working in a volatile labor market (Peterson 2020). But let us consider the argument that the USA has triumphed over poverty, which is based on a consumption-based measurement. While it measures certain kinds of material hardships, the consumption-based approach used by the Council of Economic Advisers does not reflect the psychological impacts of one's social position. It also flies in the face of other evidence, as provided by Edin and Shaefer (2015) and Hacker (2006), that indicates poverty has deepened in terms of possibilities for social mobility.

The year 2020 brought a pandemic and an economic recession, which consisted of a major increase in unemployment (Shrider et al. 2021). In response, the federal government passed several acts to alleviate loss of income and stimulate the economy by providing cash benefits to taxpayers through the Coronavirus Aid, Relief, and Economic Security Act and the Coronavirus Response and Relief Supplemental Appropriations Act. Median household income declined significantly in 2020. The highest declines in income were for those without a high school education and the foreign-born. These measures do not take into account the stimulus and tax benefits of 2020. The percentage decrease in income is less for Black-headed households, but this racial group also has the lowest median income ($45,870 compared to $74,912 for White non-Hispanics). The official poverty rate as defined federally increased in 2020 from 2019, but 2019 recorded the lowest rate of poverty in the United States, at 10.5%, since comparable data started to be collected in 1959. The child tax credit expansion enacted by President Biden in 2021 is considered responsible for cutting child poverty nearly in half, from 9.7% according to the SPM (which, remember, includes tax credits) in 2020 to 5.2% in 2021 (Burns et al. 2022). This shows that federal policy can do much to counter poverty, but also that progress can be easily undermined by political opposition. The extended child tax credit, a feature of the 2021 American Rescue Plan legislation, expired in 2022 due to political opposition, despite evidence that child poverty was markedly reduced by the credit (Curran 2022).

On the whole, therefore, the poverty rate has declined according to most absolute measures, up until the recession of 2020. Far from suggesting the poor should be put to work, this suggests that people are working more than ever. Confusingly, while the poverty rate has declined over the past few decades, researchers remain as concerned as ever about deep poverty and general economic insecurity. How can deep poverty and economic insecurity have worsened while poverty overall has decreased? Edin and Shaefer (2015) identified a category of poverty that changes the picture of poverty from the mid-1990s to the mid-2010s. When we examine the proportion of people living in deep poverty – measured by Edin and Shaefer as $2 a day per person (similar to a World Bank metric) – we find that such deep poverty was nearly nonexistent in the 1990s prior to welfare reform, whereas about 4% of families in the USA in 2011 were living on this amount or less. To put this into perspective, the federal threshold for poverty amounts to $16.50 per person per day.

I suggest we think of poverty as comprising three different types, recognizing the fluidity between them and the fact that these types are very historically and contextually specific: (1) the deep and chronically poor; (2) the insecure, including those above but at risk for poverty; and (3) the temporarily poor, such as those who have some assets, tangible or intangible, that allow them to weather the bad period. Groups 2 and 3 are not always easy to identify using most absolute measures, save for when the assets-based approach is used. In addition, the numbers of individuals who fall under group 2 may increase substantially without being reflected in the OPM, SPM, or consumption-based measures. And as Edin and Shaefer's (2015) study suggests, the individuals falling into group 1, the deep poor, may also swell disturbingly as a proportion of the population without drastically impacting the poverty rate as measured by absolute indicators.

These different types also reflect the relativity and relational aspects of poverty, in that our relations with others are what matter for our ability to live a life we value (Khader 2011). Deep poverty reflects extensive social exclusion from the institutions so many of us take for granted. The insecure (group 2) are also vulnerable in their relations to employers, institutional gatekeepers, and even intimate others potentially, to the degree that, while not totally excluded, they are at risk of falling into hardship. And finally, the temporarily poor continue to hold some advantage in relations with others and with institutions, although they are also, clearly, not free from some level of vulnerability.

There is no one correct measurement of poverty for all uses and all times. The percentage of median income approach, for instance, is good for reflecting the likely numbers of people in the different groups, but it may not always reflect actual hardship. On the other hand, income and consumption may not reflect the position of an individual or household with regard to the larger society, in the sense that they can seek without undue restraint a life they have reason to value (Khader 2011). As Green and Hulme (2005) indicate, definitions of poverty that view increases in income or consumption as the solution are unlikely to reveal the underlying causes of poverty, which are the social relations that close off opportunity for some to the benefit of others. In contrast, a definition of poverty that recognizes it is not just the lack of something or a characteristic of the individual, but is grounded in the relations between people, is preferable for the big-picture view. One might even argue for dispensing with the notion of poverty as a focus, and instead reference "structures of violence" to target the real problem (Farmer 2003). In short, defining poverty is an ongoing project of large political import.

Mobility

People in poverty are heterogeneous – they differ year to year and as a cross-section. This is important to keep in mind even as we aim to make some generalizations about poverty. Many people experience poverty, and most people in poverty will only be there for two to three years. Even among the deep poor, there is considerable diversity in terms of characteristics, problems, and behavior. Very few poor people actually fulfill the stereotype of the idle ghetto-dweller dependent on welfare propagated by media (Tienda and Stier 1991; Kneebone and Berube 2014). In fact, Jargowsky and Bane (1991) found, during the height of the urban ghetto scare, that 9 percent of all poor persons, nationally, lived in what they defined as ghettos. However, there are selection effects in determining who ends up mired in poverty. Poverty is more of a risk for certain groups of vulnerable people, such as those living with a disability or mental health issues. First, I examine mobility and the movement in and out of poverty. Then, I look at the diversity of people in poverty, including critical intersections with race, gender, citizenship status, and place. In effect, the diversity of people in poverty is such that we must recognize that there is no one face of poverty; there is no sense in stereotyping. Making assumptions about who people in poverty are is futile – except that, like any other group of people, they deserve basic respect.

America is supposed to be the land of opportunity. Compared to some times and places, it certainly is. One of the ways people have justified poverty is by pointing to the open mobility in American society, presuming that, if you work hard or develop a skill of a valuable kind, you can move up the ladder. But how easy is it to move from one class or status grouping to another? How much intergenerational mobility actually occurs? And, how much mobility occurs with reference to poverty specifically – in other words, how much do people enter and exit poverty?

Consistent with the story of America as the land of opportunity, people's subjective perceptions of mobility – including their own chances of mobility – are higher than what data actually show to be the case (Davidai and Gilovich 2018). Those with lower incomes are more prone to overestimate the levels of mobility (Milanovic 2016). Perhaps this is necessary motivation to strive. At any rate, it suggests hopelessness is not the primary roadblock.

Evidence from multiple studies strongly suggests that the more unequal a society is, the lower the amount of social mobility that occurs, especially for those in the lowest ranks. This makes intuitive sense, as there would be more competition for the fewer good places in a society with greater inequality. Wilkinson and Pickett (2009) found a relationship between high social inequality and low social mobility by studying eight countries – Canada, Denmark, Finland, Sweden, Norway, Germany, the UK, and the USA. The USA had both the highest economic inequality and the lowest economic mobility, with very low mobility on the lowest rungs of the socioeconomic ladder, and with mobility increasing slightly as one moves up the ladder. According to additional research, however, on the top rung of the ladder, mobility again decreases, suggesting that people at the very top ensure they remain there (Isaacs 2008).

A study by the Pew Trust found that 70% of children born in the bottom income quintile (the lowest 20%) never reach the middle quintile, and 43% remain in that bottom quintile (Pew Charitable Trust 2013). Race, education, employment status, and assets seemed to be the most important differences between those who moved out of the bottom quintile and those who remained. While 68% of White individuals were able to leave the bottom quintile, only 45% of Black individuals were (Pew Charitable Trust 2013:3). And while 35% of White individuals made it to the middle quintile, 25% of Black individuals moved from the bottom to the middle quintile. College graduates and dual-earner families tended to be more successful in reaching higher quintiles when starting from the bottom. When these factors are considered, the race gap shrinks significantly, suggesting that having a college education and being in a dual-earner household made a difference for everyone, but are more easily attained by some than by others. The discussions in later chapters of single-parent households and attending college are thus all the more critical.

Another major explanation for this phenomenon of limited mobility is proposed by network theorists: social ties. Mark Granovetter (1974) asserted that personal contacts are clearly the most common way of finding a job. Personal contacts are also the best way of finding a job, as using them is associated with better jobs and higher retention. One of the more important implications of social networks is that one's network is less controllable by the individual than many other forms of direct advantage (education, skills, and so on). If someone lacks the necessary contacts, there is not much they can do about it. This is a structural factor in job distribution, something discussed further in later chapters. Notably, however, our relations to others again factor as important determinants.

Rebecca Blank (1997) found a lot of movement in and out of poverty using a random sample of Americans surveyed over 13 years. She found that about half of those who were ever poor during these 13 years were only poor for between 1 and 3 years. About 5% were poor for more than 10 of these 13 years. Among Black families in the study, however, 17% were poor for more than 10 years. The two major factors for entering poverty were a change in family composition, such as loss of a partner, and a change in economic situation, such as the loss of a job. There was one major factor for ending poverty, which was an increase in earnings.

Perhaps it is less surprising by this point to learn that researchers estimate that nearly two-thirds of Americans are at high risk of experiencing poverty in their lifetimes for at least 1 year (Rank 2011). More specifically, analysis of longitudinal data showed that 60% of American adults fell below the bottom income quintile threshold for at least 1 year of their life, but typically for only 2 or 3 years (Rank et al. 2015). And, using the OPM, over a third of Americans between the ages of 20 and 40, and 60% between the ages of 20 and 75, experienced poverty according to longitudinal data collected between 1968 and 1992 (Rank and Hirschl 1999). As I discuss later in the chapter, this is not likely to improve much for this or future generations, as economic insecurity and inequality have both increased.

Diversity

Intersectionality is a recognition that inequality as people experience it and as it develops is not reducible to one category of difference, such as just class, just race, or just gender. Poverty is not just about class. It is also about race, gender, and ableism. This accounts for how poverty is reproduced in terms of who is susceptible, and in terms of how it is experienced. "Membership in the intersectional category results in specific experiences and forms of oppression distinct from those faced by individual categories" (Bernstein 2020:321). One category – race versus class, for instance – is not more fundamental than the other; the best understanding results from approaching the intersections of categories as their own categories (Bernstein 2020). Black poverty is different from White poverty. That does not mean there are no similarities or interests held in common across race, but that there will also be differences in both the roots of the poverty and the experience of the poverty. Power relations operate in many different ways, and these ways both differ among and crosscut gender, race, and class, such that the precise power relations an individual experiences are a product of this intersection of their multiple social positions (Collins 2015). A woman in poverty is subject to different forms of exploitation – though they often overlap – from a man in poverty. Her body is viewed and used differently than is a man's, and in ways that are also related to racism and ableism.

For our purposes, this means we must admit to immense diversity across the experiences and relations of poverty. This is an important recognition on its own. It does complicate the understanding of poverty, but only because poverty is complex. Poverty occurs through the construction and reproduction of categories that align with understandings and attributions of social worth. How Whites and people of color relate to one another, how men and women relate to one another, how cisgender and nonbinary individuals relate to one another, how upper classes and lower classes relate to one another, continue to develop and to influence the nature of poverty. Consider how a non-cis woman may be treated differently in the context of a homeless shelter than would a cis-woman. It is not merely that she would be treated in additional problematic ways because of being non-cis. She would be viewed in ways related to the simultaneity of being transgender and being homeless. Most likely, her body might be viewed as *uniquely* less worthy of respect than the body of a cis-woman in poverty or an affluent transwoman (see Crenshaw 1989; McCall 2005).

Race and Ethnicity

The likelihood of becoming poor is higher for Black Americans, Hispanic Americans, those in households headed by women, and those with lower levels of education. Poverty entry rates are about twice as high for Black Americans as for White Americans – about 11 percent versus 5 percent (Ribar and Hamrick 2003). Race is perhaps the most visible and controversial factor in who is at risk of poverty in the United States. Indeed, no other form of inequality in the history of the United States has been more brutal *and* more lucrative than racial inequality, particularly in the form of slavery and genocide. The legacy of this inequality remains evident in terms of both material deprivation and the privileges many Americans enjoy. Sociologists have documented many reasons for the differences in rates of poverty by race, including the impact of discrimination, segregation, and historical legacies in land ownership and wealth.

Although individuals and communities have made adaptations to the effects of racism, these adaptations have not created a culture of poverty. Many common assumptions made about the Black and Hispanic poor are simply incorrect. In this section, I review how race affects how we understand people in poverty. Several problematic tendencies can be identified, including: (1) viewing the Black family as the primary representation of the poor; (2) transferring racial stereotypes to all of the poor, regardless of color; and (3) viewing people of color in poverty as the undeserving poor, often because of assumptions about culture. The legacy of Moynihan ([1965] 1967) and Banfield (1970), among others (see Chapter 4), who viewed the Black family as representative of a cultural crisis, has lived on in research that is less explicitly about the culture of the poor but continues to pathologize low-income communities of color. More recently, pundits point to the White poor as evidence that race is less important than class, and to explain the rise of President Trump (see MacGillis and ProPublica 2016). To counter such simplistic interpretations, a relational approach is essential.

Wealth is a major form of inequality that renders Black Americans more vulnerable on average than White Americans. White Americans have more assets at every income level when compared to Black Americans. As mentioned, wealth and assets are critical for weathering any kind of unexpected or unavoidable period of trouble, such as illness, losing a job, or other financial crisis. According to 2019 Census SIPP data, households headed by a White, non-Hispanic person had a median net wealth of $187,300 (US Census Bureau

2020b). Households headed by a Black person had a median net worth of $14,100; by a Hispanic person (any race), $31,700. Addo and Darity (2021) found in their examination of race and occupational sector in the aftermath of the Great Recession that race actually has greater predictive power for the wealth holdings of households than occupation. Indeed, among White households, the working class actually experienced the greatest relative increase in wealth during the economic recovery of the 2010s, though this may be due partly to taking a greater economic hit in the first place compared to more affluent white households (Addo and Darity 2021). Their sample includes heads of households aged 25 to 64 who were not retired, disabled, or out of the labor force. Thus, the analysis pertains to people who are employed or looking for work, and does not include the most disadvantaged households. Nonetheless, the analysis is useful for demonstrating that, despite greater employment and occupational achievement, not only working-class Black but many middle-class Black households remain economically vulnerable compared to White working and middle classes.

A major wealth gap exists for several reasons, including the historical legacy of low wages, affecting what could be passed on intergenerationally, and past discrimination in housing and in credit markets (Conley 1999; Mather and Jarosz 2014). Promises of land in the antebellum period were not honored; instead they turned into sharecropping arrangements and other debt traps. Then, during the twentieth-century farm expansion, White Americans received low-interest loans to form farms in the mid and western USA, while Black Americans were drawn by the Great Migration to industrial sectors in the north. One result of the Great Migration was the creation of segregated urban neighborhoods, facilitated intentionally by the housing and financial industries and reinforced by Whites who left neighborhoods that became more populated by Black Americans. The occupations disproportionately filled by Black individuals were more likely to be denied Social Security, or salaries were not high enough to qualify. The loan program for home buying after World War II channeled loans to suburbs and away from central cities with higher proportions of minorities. More recently, evidence continues to accrue of the negative impact of discrimination in housing and credit markets, including redlining policies that denied loans or increased interest rates for investing in high-minority areas. The Great Recession that began in 2007 also had a disproportionate impact on the home ownership equity of racial minorities and the non-wealthy, leading to a high number of foreclosures (Addo et al.

2021). Nowadays, not only are African Americans less likely to own their home, but a home has, on average, less value in a non-White neighborhood than a similar one in a White neighborhood. Research has also shown that Black Americans, especially Black women, experience higher loan rejection rates and higher interest rates (Cheng et al. 2014).

McDermott, in *Working-Class White* (2006), demonstrated how Whiteness is situational, and argued that being White does not always confer relational privilege for some working-class Whites. While this argument is limited to specific types of interactions, it is worth considering its implications. McDermott used participant observation as a method to gather data. She worked as a convenience store / gas station clerk in two urban areas with considerable interaction between Whites and Blacks during the 1990s. Specifically, McDermott found that working-class Whites in a majority-Black area in Atlanta experienced their race and class combination as a double shame, since Whiteness in general is supposed to confer success. On the other hand, the working-class Whites McDermott (2006) studied in the Boston area experienced their Whiteness as a privilege, and distanced themselves from non-Whites. Both sets of working-class Whites sometimes indicated that they experienced the prejudice that often coexists with a sense of political correctness and civility, even friendliness, toward Blacks. This is an interesting study precisely because it shows the differences in how Whites in the working class can experience and perceive race. The local context shapes the ways in which Whiteness is viewed and experienced among the working class. In racially mixed low-income areas, Whiteness can be a liability *if the person is seeking a low-skill job*. McDermott (2006) wrote that many people in the Georgia area – Black and White – assumed that White individuals living in such an area must be damaged somehow. On the other hand, in a tight labor market with a history of working-class consciousness, such as Boston, Whiteness can continue to serve as a "mark of superiority," with the attitude that Blacks are less deserving because they haven't worked as hard as the White residents and their immigrant forebears have. McDermott noted that Whiteness still by and large functions as a marker of privilege and continues to "pay big dividends," but it is partly this reality that makes "failed" Whites so bitter. Because Americans perceive status so much in terms of race, we fail to identify class disadvantages and shared interests.

But the common assumption that poor Whites are more likely to be bitterly racist is at least sometimes wrong, and often not well supported empirically. The greater social proximity of White

Americans in poverty to Black Americans has been associated with the temptation to identify oneself as better than someone (McGhee 2021). But the social proximity has also at times encouraged greater identification and cooperation. Isenberg (2016) explores a history of poor Whites in *White Trash: The 400-Year Untold History of Class in America*. Upper-class Puritans and southern planters in early America were by some accounts highly concerned by the prospect of interracial cooperation and subsequent class warfare, and did what they could to sow discord and maintain separation between White indentured servants and Native Americans, and between poor Whites and African slaves. The lingering specter of Bacon's Rebellion of 1676 in Virginia – a cooperation of slaves, indentured servants, and other frustrated Whites – indicated a strong possibility of such alliance. In 1969, Fred Hampton of the Black Panther Party formed The Rainbow Coalition, an alliance of poor and working-class people from across the race spectrum, including The Young Patriots, a Confederate flag-wearing contingent of young White men (McPherson 2019). The members of this alliance were able to work together because they identified a common enemy: the political and economic elites of Chicago. Unfortunately, these efforts were cut short when Hampton was shot by the Chicago police during an FBI-led raid on his home in 1969 at the age of 21. More recently, the Occupy Wall Street movement promoted class solidarity across race (Syrek 2012; Quinn 2016). Overall, however, we lack research specifically on racial ideology among people in poverty, and the ways in which context affects interracial interactions and perceptions of race for White Americans in poverty, particularly those in deep or chronic poverty, as opposed to the larger and heterogeneous category of working-class White individuals.

Some historians have argued that racism itself has in fact directly and powerfully undermined the very public goods in the USA that would improve life for the poor (Quadagno 1995; McGhee 2021), such as education, public recreation, healthcare, and urban social spending. Indeed, there is powerful support for this perspective, but we do not know for sure the degree to which other factors, including concerns about the poor, might have eroded support for public goods. Resistance to public spending is not always motivated by racism. What is evident is that racism has been a large factor. McGhee (2021) suggested that the hollowing out of public goods has ironically embittered Whites, who are convinced the government is helping others, but not them. Whites also enjoy the psychological wages of Whiteness: knowing that one is better than somebody else.

McGhee's point was that, at the larger social level, this comes at some cost to Whites as well. It is not just racial oppression that is the problem – it is racial division. McGhee argued that it is not class that matters the most, because overcoming racism will be crucial to the advancement of the working, the impoverished, and the struggling classes. While this might seem to downplay the costs of racism borne by people of color throughout the history and present of the United States, it is a perspective worth full consideration. Historical and contemporary political analysis repeatedly demonstrates that racism is used as a tool by elites to consolidate power. Of Whites who suffer in addition to people of color, it is mainly Whites in poverty who suffer from racist-motivated public hollowing. Nonetheless, White people are often invested in their own innocence and in justification of the status quo, and their fears of people of color too often drive political action, with powerful repercussions.

To address poverty in general, we must confront race and racial inequality. The burdens borne by the most vulnerable pose a collective threat since we are socially intertwined whether we like it or not, the COVID-19 pandemic being a very apt example (McGhee 2021). Black, Latinx, and Indigenous people were the first ones to die in many US cities, such as Chicago, where 70 out of 100 of the first deaths were of Black Americans (Eldeib et al. 2020). Trauma, mental illness, physical illness, inability to work – these issues have consequences that feed back into society at large. Indeed, as McGhee warned, disinvestment in public health caught up to all of us during the pandemic.

Intersections with Gender and Sexuality

Like race and class, gender and sexual identities translate into social positioning and affect our relations to others in many complicated and compelling ways. Women in poverty are at a major disadvantage because they tend to be situated in more vulnerable relations to family members, the labor market, and other institutions. The difference in likelihood of becoming poor between those in female-headed households with children and married-couple households with children is one of the largest demographic differences. Single-mother households become poor at a rate of 15.7% a year, compared with just 2.8% for married-parent households (Ribar and Hamrick 2003). Being a single parent is a major disadvantage in the labor market, as is closely examined in the next chapter. But even aside from the single-parent issue, women face disadvantages in the labor market.

On average, women earn about 83 cents on the dollar compared to men (AAUW 2021; US Department of Labor 2022). In addition to the wage gap, there is also a wealth gap between men and women. Women only own 36% as much wealth as men. Such gaps are, as we know, compounded by race. Latinas were paid 57% and Black women 64% of what non-Hispanic White men were paid in 2020 (AAUW 2021). Yet women of higher-class status may be much better off in a number of ways than many men and other women.

Men and women end up in different types of jobs and different sectors of the labor market. The US Bureau of Labor Statistics (2009) shows a fairly equal representation of women and men in management and professional roles, but moving up the corporate ladder tells a different story. Women are overrepresented in certain types of work, including informal work, nonpaid labor, the secondary sector, and part-time work (Mather and Jarosz 2014). Evidence suggests that, broadly speaking, positions are value-ranked according to whether men or women hold them, and, afterwards, segregation is justified with the rhetoric of sex difference (Padavic and Reskin 2002). Women also shoulder the burden of care work and emotional labor. Emotional labor includes work done for wages that is meant to achieve a desired emotional effect in others, such as being an airline attendant or salesperson (Hochschild 2012). Such work can be stressful, demeaning, and exhausting. It is often considered to be a "soft"-skills type of work, which is paid less than other kinds of work despite the challenges of these positions. Women in poverty may have to do more emotional labor in the workplace than if they were men in poverty or women of a higher-class background.

LGBTQIA+ is an umbrella designation for several different gender and sexual identities that differ from the traditional heterosexual binary of man and woman, standing for lesbian, gay, bisexual, transgender, queer (or questioning), intersex, asexual, and other nonconforming gender and sexual identities. LGBTQIA+ status confers vulnerability in relations with others, and people with this status are highly vulnerable to poverty due to processes in schools, families, the labor force, healthcare, and experiences with violence and trauma. For instance, LGBTQIA+ youth may find themselves on the street after revealing their LGBTQIA+ status, or having it revealed, to family (Álvarez et al. 2022). They are more likely to be placed in foster care (Álvarez et al. 2022). Violence against people with these identities remains common, resulting in a criminal justice record if one fights back, and certainly resulting in trauma that can be debilitating (Robinson 2020). Indeed, LGBTQIA+ youth are disproportionately represented in juvenile detention centers (Robinson 2020). Discrimination in the workplace remains a widespread problem (Sears et al. 2021). It is well documented that healthcare and health education for LGBTQIA+ persons are inferior to that for cisgender heterosexual individuals (Burton et al. 2021; Human Rights Campaign 2021). And legal status and recognition of one's relations to others – whether an intimate relationship with someone of the same sex, parenthood, forms of nonsexual intimacy, or a nonbinary identity – remains elusive in many parts of society (Cahill and Tobias 2007; Polikoff 2016). This all translates to additional vulnerability relative to others for LGBTQIA+ persons in poverty, and additional vulnerability to falling into poverty. LGBTQIA+ persons are disproportionately represented among the homeless and are targeted to become sex workers in the informal labor market (Wesling 2008; Human Rights Campaign 2021). Researchers have found that LGBTQIA+ youth experience punishment and bullying in some schools, which creates a school-to-prison pipeline effect (Snapp et al. 2015). Even if recognition of LGBTQIA+ youth improves in the coming years, it is important to remember that the effects of generations of abuse and discrimination will continue to play out in people's lives for decades.

The intersections with poverty are thus profound for gender and sexuality, and both forms of inequality must engage with the other to redress such inequality. LGBTQIA+ persons often face discrimination in programs that serve people in or at risk for poverty (Rosenwohl-Mack et al. 2022). LGBTQIA+ persons of color or with a disability have an even higher likelihood of experiencing discrimination, as these intersections compound their vulnerability (Williams and Anderson 2020). Vulnerability to poverty takes many forms, including those related to gender and sexual nonconformity.

Immigration

Immigrants to the United States are another category of people who are vulnerable to poverty and may experience poverty in specific ways. Discrimination appears to be a factor for people of Latinx descent, as well as the large variety of Middle Eastern immigrants, who are often assumed to be Muslim. How secure immigrants feel in general in their lives differs by local context, including the prevalence of anti-immigrant sentiment and policy for that area (Cleaveland 2013). In a national longitudinal study, Hall and Farkas (2008) found that Latino (male) immigrants receive lower returns on education than Latino natives or Asian, Black, or White immigrants. For native men of all races, as well as Asian and Black non-Hispanic immigrants, education provides significant wage returns even for low-wage workers and, overall, immigrant workers in the USA do increase earnings over time (Hall and Farkas 2008). However, the authors also found that immigrants of all races earn 24% less than the US-born in the study (restricted to men with a high school diploma or less at time of first interview) and are less likely to obtain managerial positions. Economically, immigrants tend to be more vulnerable, but they can also be vulnerable to crime and exploitation, particularly if their status in the country is unassured (Cleaveland 2013). Lack of skill in the English language is an additional barrier to accessing even the most basic resources. Use of public benefits can endanger an immigrant's status in the country. Overall, relations of vulnerability are magnified for immigrants in poverty but can be moderated, to some degree, by a strong system of support and community.

However, as Monnat and Chandler (2017) argue, more recent immigrants to the United States are more likely than past waves to migrate to rural areas for work, where they are at a singular disadvantage. Although most rural areas with significant migration from foreign-born people have benefited from the population and economic growth, poverty rates for immigrant residents are higher in nonmetropolitan areas than they are for US-born citizens (Monnat and Chandler 2017). Nondocumented immigrants and legal immigrants who have not yet resided in the USA for five years are not eligible for most federal social programs, and those who are eligible are often hesitant to use them for fear of jeopardizing their citizenship status (Lichter et al. 2015). Furthermore, especially among those who fear deportation, immigrant laborers have fewer recourses and legal protections from work-related abuses.

Place

Place plays an important role in the experience of poverty. Education, crime, social networks, jobs, internet access, human services, and transportation are all geographically structured. Contrary to the stereotype of the urban ghetto youth, the largest portion of the metropolitan poor are in the suburbs (Kneebone and Berube 2014). And while the rural poor are a minority among the poor, they form a larger proportion of rural residents than the poor form of metropolitan residents. Urban, suburban, and rural poverty each comes with its own set of implications for social relations, both structural and cultural (Duncan 1999; Butz 2016). I discuss here some of the ways in which social relations of poverty manifest across place, including a brief interlude on "the forgotten poor" – racial minorities in rural places – who have the highest rates of poverty and unemployment across race and place demographics (Mauldin and Mimura 2001; Slack et al. 2020).

Rural areas in the USA have long held a disproportionate share of the poor. Using US Census Current Population Survey data for 2019, 13.3.% of rural residents are in OPM poverty, compared to 10% of metropolitan residents (US Census Bureau 2020d). The Economic Research Service of the USDA (US Department of Agriculture 2022c) reports that, in 2019, 21.1% of children in the nonmetropolitan United States were poor, compared to 16.1% of children in metropolitan areas. When they look at where child poverty is concentrated, they find that 138 counties in the United States have child poverty rates of 40% or higher (averages for 2014–19). Of these, 127 are nonmetropolitan counties, many in the South where child poverty rates are high especially among Black Americans, though some counties with extreme child poverty rates of 50% or higher (there are 38 such counties) are in South Dakota, where Native Americans are the majority of the population in poverty (USDA 2022c).

For some time now, people have adjusted to the lack of secure jobs in rural places by combining different kinds of work and sometimes migrating to cities (Nelson 2006). The rural poor is more likely to be White, elderly, or in two-parent households with at least one working adult, when compared to the urban poor. But those who are the most vulnerable in cities, including racial minorities and single-parent households, are even more likely to be poor if they live in rural areas. Rural poverty is particularly prevalent in the south, where land ownership patterns contribute to a system of dependency, lack of access to education, and a rigidly stratified social system (Tickamyer and Duncan 1990; Nelson 2006). In other regions of the USA, rural poverty is often linked to extractive industries such as mining or to unstable seasonal employment. Tourism and seasonal work play a big role in many rural economies – especially as jobs related to agriculture and energy or raw materials decrease with technological advancement, boom and bust cycles, and industrial consolidation. It is important to note, however, that rural poverty is not just a result of a lack of jobs or growth, but is the result of an inequality in the distribution of income, jobs, and resources within communities and regions (Tickamyer and Duncan 1990; Fulkerson and Thomas 2014). Harvey (2017) notes that places with high rates of minority poverty in particular follow a certain pattern, including weak, undiversified labor markets; a dependence on government funding, especially in terms of jobs among the middle class in education, health, and nonprofits; political institutions that are unresponsive to non-elites, and corrupt; and a highly divided civil society lacking an orientation toward democracy and the common good.

Escaping poverty is difficult in many places, but appears especially tough in rural America. Wages are lower in rural places than in metropolitan places, resulting in higher rates of poverty among rural workers relative to urban workers with comparable skills and education (Lichter et al. 1994; Slack 2010; Thiede et al. 2018). Thiede et al. (2018:185) found that "Rural employment growth since 2008 has also lagged behind urban growth, and employment has yet to return to pre-recession levels." This is all the more disturbing if what Nelson (2006) found remains the case: that access to formal work actually enabled other survival strategies. Apparently, there is a certain level of investment needed in the informal economy, just as there is in the formal labor market. Self-provisioning activities such as gardening or hunting, informal economy labor, and reciprocity with neighbors and friends are enabled by attachment to the formal economy (Nelson 2006). Eason et al. (2017) further note that substance abuse in rural areas has increased so much recently that related rates of prison admissions have surpassed those in urban areas. In many rural areas, the lack of rehabilitation options may exacerbate the drug problem.

There are several reasons why rural economies have declined and poverty has become entrenched. Stoll (2017) noted that Appalachia became known as a "backward," isolated place when the land and its resources became desired by outsiders. The characterization of Appalachia as backward helped justify the dispossession of people who did indeed make their living off the land, but were by no means impoverished until they lost access to the land. As Appalachians lost access to land, they were recruited as low-paid workers. Stoll (2017) pointed out that living off the land – that is, being a peasant – is not necessarily the same as being poor. He argues people became worse off when exploited as low-wage workers without other options. More broadly, the concentration of prime agricultural land in fewer hands, the decline of the industrial economy, the centralization of community functions and concentration of programs and services in more densely populated areas, lower education rates in rural areas, and new land-use patterns related to suburbanization are all likely culprits (Nelson 2006). Suburbanization leads to a rise in rural land and housing costs. Meanwhile, many have become trapped in low-income work, and vulnerable to mechanization. Nelson (2006) also found in her research that the rural poor are socially excluded from mainstream institutions and organizations. They are not integrated into the wider community, even though the wider community now services this area.

Critically, racial minorities and other people vulnerable to poverty are even more likely to be poor if they live in a rural area, especially a rural area in the southern USA (Mauldin and Mimura 2001; Harvey 2017). Monnat and Chandler (2017) note that immigrants in rural areas are at higher risk due to limited employment opportunities and greater isolation, because of small co-ethnic populations and residential segregation. The odds of being poor increase for people with disabilities, households headed by women, those who are foreign-born, and those without a high school education if living in a rural area. Rural residence, it seems, exacerbates these vulnerabilities. As a result, some of the most disadvantaged Americans are racial minorities living in isolated, rural areas, including Black Americans in the Delta, Latinx Americans in the Rio Grande Valley, and Native Americans in South Dakota. Mortality and morbidity rates and persistent, intergenerational poverty are higher for these populations, while access is lower for basics like water and privileges such as college attendance rates.

But what about the deleterious concentration of poverty in urban areas? Urban conditions have deteriorated as well. Poverty rates for urban workers increased between 2000 and 2013, while rural working poverty remained at high levels (Thiede et al. 2018). William Julius Wilson (1987) famously identified the cause of concentrated inner-city poverty as the disappearance of work in inner cities, which, in addition to the effect on income, creates an environment conducive to crime and disorganization. Massey and Denton (1993) identified the cause as racial segregation, which led to spatially concentrated disadvantage, thus creating a spiral of decline. The result in both accounts is the creation of an "underclass," inner-city residents of impoverished racial minority neighborhoods. Wilson (1987) explores the notion that, in a social setting of high unemployment, expectations and obligations change in such a way as to further disadvantage people. This is partly because of the disappearance of the Black middle class, leaving these neighborhoods without stable leadership, middle-class norms, and middle-class political leverage. Youth are not encouraged to strive and see no point in trying to succeed academically, creating an underclass. As I discuss further in Chapter 4, this notion of the underclass has serious shortcomings. However, even the critiques of Wilson (Jencks and Peterson 1991; Gans 2010) do not entirely do away with the impacts of concentrated poverty. Segregating racial minorities in impoverished neighborhoods clearly has some negative effects, including restricting access to opportunity, diminishing quality of education, undermining the building of assets, and exacerbating the social network differential. While certain members of the rural poor may be highly susceptible to violence, there are likely health and other outcomes whose processes are specific to living in a high-crime neighborhood (Anakwenze and Zuberi 2013). The effect for residential behavior remains contested and likely contextual. Regardless, concerns about inner-city poverty have abated somewhat in the past few decades with growing awareness of rural and suburban poverty.

The suburbs are considered part of metropolitan areas but separate from the city proper. The suburbs have unique attributes, different from both rural areas and cities with their business districts and apartment buildings. Kneebone and Berube (2014) have charted the decades-long increase in poverty in American suburbia. More than half of the metropolitan poor are in the suburbs. Between 2000 and 2010, the number of people living below the federal poverty line in the suburbs grew by 53%, compared with 23% in cities (Kneebone and Berube 2014). In 2010, roughly 16.4 million poor people lived in the suburbs, compared with 13.4 million in cities and 7.3 million in rural areas. Poverty rates across suburban areas average about 20% or higher. A number of reasons account for this, including the displacement of people in poverty from the inner city via gentrification; the increased costs of housing in inner cities, especially during the housing bubble; the lure of safe, cheaper homes, and better schools; the movement of jobs; and the fact that loan options favor new development over housing repair. A number of problems result from this increase in suburban poverty, including fewer available transit options and social service organizations; the dispersion across space makes it more difficult to locate and serve the poor; and selling a home if one needs to move can be difficult in certain suburbs where supply outpaces demand (Kneebone and Berube 2014).

Both poor urban and poor rural areas tend to lack decent employment options and beneficial investment by local government and business interests (Tickamyer and Duncan 1990). They also tend to have inadequate and less-resourced public education. Suburban and rural areas, however, tend to lack certain kinds of infrastructure and social service resources that people in poverty depend on, such as public transportation and homeless shelters.

Estimated numbers of homeless people greatly exceed the number of available emergency shelter and transitional housing spaces (Henry et al. 2018). About 9% of the nation's homeless are estimated to live in rural places, and numbers are growing at a faster rate than urban homelessness (National Coalition for the Homeless 2009; Institute for Children, Poverty, and Homelessness 2022). But there are few or no homeless shelters in rural areas (Meehan 2019; National Alliance to End Homelessness 2022). The US Department of Housing and Urban Development (HUD) (2022) estimated that about 25% of the sheltered homeless in 2021 were in suburban areas, and that these shelters had the highest occupancy rates.

In sum, the poor are all among us, in mixed-income areas, in poor areas, in dangerous places, in prison, in small towns, in suburbs, and maybe even next door. Often, they are not highly visible – the person behind you in the grocery check-out line, the student sitting next to you in class, the person taking your order at a restaurant, could all be someone in poverty. That does not mean place doesn't matter. Where someone lives matters in all sorts of ways for their experiences, for potential sources of meaning in their life, for opportunity, for the people they know, and more. Place shapes our social relations and can exacerbate or lessen our vulnerability.

A Variety of Vulnerabilities and Strengths

Poverty status touches many different people – some for a short time, while for others never leaving. Anything that increases vulnerability relative to major social institutions such as the labor market is associated with a greater likelihood of poverty, including being of color; being a woman, transperson, or non-gender-conforming; certain types of family composition; uncertain or absent citizenship status; and/or having a disability. Thus, examination of any random sample of people in poverty will yield a variety of specific vulnerabilities, strengths, and experiences. It is important, therefore, not to overgeneralize, even when we examine a particular group. This does not mean people do not have anything in common across place or issue that can be used for collective action or political identity. But we must be careful not to stereotype or make assumptions about the people coming to the food bank. Their differences and diversity offer a path to understanding: people in poverty are a diverse group of people like any other, to be treated with respect.

Similarity to and Difference from the Nonpoor

In many ways, Americans in poverty are not all that different from their counterparts in the middle class. Poverty is neither unusual nor atypical in the United States; just over half of the population experiences poverty over the course of a lifetime (Rank 2004). An insecure economy and inadequate safety nets at the federal, state, and local levels render poverty a real risk for many. This risk is not uniformly present in all affluent nations; those with greater social investments and safety nets, such as Denmark, have greatly reduced poverty and related suffering. However, structural changes in employment and education in the USA have reduced the ability of the next generation of middle-class individuals to avoid poverty, and even older generations of middle-class households are not invulnerable.

The Conditions of Chronic Poverty

People in the United States experiencing chronic poverty do face different *sets of* risks and living conditions than other groups, including the sporadically poor. Material hardship is significantly more common for people in poverty, as is being a victim of violence, having a child with a serious disability or illness, moving residences, and being behind on paying for rent or utilities. All of these issues are true for those who are poor at any given point in time, but especially for single female-headed households and welfare program participants. Health outcomes of the poor differ significantly from those of the nonpoor, whether measured as infant mortality (especially for African Americans and Native Americans on reservations), the likelihood of contracting a chronic condition such as asthma or diabetes at a young age, or overall life expectancy. People with disabilities are often excluded from public life (Pendo 2016), and they face employment disadvantages that intersect with gender (Pettinicchio and Maroto 2017). Accordingly, when gender and disability are examined together, women with disabilities are the most disadvantaged in the labor market, whereas the largest difference in employment within gender can be found between men with disability and men without disability (Pettinicchio and Maroto 2017). Of non-institutionalized persons in the United States aged 21 to 64, 26% of those with a disability lived below the poverty line in 2018, whereas only 10% of persons without a disability did (Erickson et al. 2020). The proportion of the disabled who live in poverty is worse in the USA than in other affluent nations, even as many continue to rely on public assistance (United Nations 2019). The COVID-19 pandemic illustrates class and racial divides all too well. Social distancing among many of the homeless, the incarcerated, and certain categories of essential workers has been difficult or nonexistent (e.g., Ho 2020). When people are faced with multiple problems without the tools to cope, their lives are qualitatively different from those who do have the tools to cope. Hence, the sets of conditions people in poverty face – especially those in chronic poverty – are often quite different from what one experiences as a middle-class citizen. Such conditions as mentioned above constitute a higher level of constant insecurity and higher chances of encountering misery, trauma, and early death. People in poverty live through and within multiple relations of vulnerability.

Some research examines what officially being in poverty actually translates to in terms of living conditions. Shaefer and Gutierrez (2013) use data from 1996, 2001, and 2004 to compare people above 150% of the official poverty level and those at or below 150% poverty. They find that 6.3% of the nonpoor report experiencing food insecurity, whereas 36.5% of those at and below 150% poverty did. Using 2014 data, Coleman-Jensen and Steffen (2017) similarly found that 33.9% of those under 180% of the poverty threshold experienced food insecurity, compared to 7.3% of those at or above 180%. Other major differences between the poor and nonpoor include the likelihood of home ownership, the likelihood of eviction, the likelihood of living in crowded housing, and housing quality (Cunningham 2016). Health and well-being outcomes are significantly worse for those in deep, chronic poverty. Those at or below 150% poverty were twice as likely to report not going to the doctor when needed because of the cost (Shaefer and Gutierrez 2013). People in poverty are about twice as likely to be a victim of a crime; their odds were greater than 1 in 4 compared to 1 in 7 for nonpoor individuals in 2020 and 2021 (Thompson and Tapp 2022). Adolescents from very-low-income backgrounds are more likely to be bullied (Due et al. 2009). Infant deaths and pre-term births are also more likely for the poor, as prenatal care is less common (Feijen-de Jong et al. 2012; Partridge et al. 2012). Parents in poverty are more likely to have a child with a disability or long-term impairment (Mitra et al. 2013).

Education is significantly worse in process and outcome for students from chronically poor backgrounds. Students from low-income families are more likely to drop out of high school; a quarter drop out, compared to 11% of their peers from more advantaged backgrounds

(Feldman et al. 2017). Students with disabilities are especially likely to drop out, compared to their non-disabled peers (Civic Enterprises & Everyone Graduates Center 2016), and children from low-income families are more likely to be diagnosed with a learning disability. Both students who are low-income and those who have a disability are more likely to have to repeat a grade or experience disciplinary action such as expulsion (Schifter et al. 2019). However, Schifter et al. (2019) question whether the higher representation of students from low-income backgrounds in special education is due to objective measures of ability rather than subjective impressions. Placement is especially higher for the more subjective categories of disability, such as emotional or intellectual disability. When it comes to higher education, students from low-income families are more likely to enroll in a community college than those from wealthier families, and the college completion rate for students starting at community colleges is 18%, compared to a 90% completion rate for students starting at selective institutions (Mather and Jarosz 2014).

Overlap and Similarities with the Middle Class

And yet, in some ways, the middle class – that is, households that make less than $150,000 in annual income – are not that far removed from some of the problems and insecurities often assumed to be lower-class issues. For instance, although drug overdose is more likely among lower socioeconomic statuses, drug dependence is rampant among all social classes (Harrell et al. 2013; Cicero et al. 2014; Maclean 2021). Sexual assault, crime, hunger, and poor housing conditions have recently elicited greater attention on non-elite college campuses (Goldrick-Rab et al. 2017; Huff 2022). The quality of public education for all but solidly affluent communities is arguably in decline (Bailey 2016; Rooks 2017). Health care continues to be unaffordable for young people in particular, including college graduates from solidly middle-class families (Levey 2022). While the relations of vulnerability tend to be more consistent and persistent for people in poverty, many problems are not in themselves unique to poverty.

When we talk about the temporarily poor, or the non-poor but insecure, we are talking about lower-middle- and many middle-middle-income households that lack assets. Increasingly, more people fall into this category, which some refer to as "the Fragile Middle-Class" (Sullivan et al. 2000). This is when a person has no real wealth or assets on which to fall back, and instead relies on earnings that could disappear at any time (due to health or disability crisis, change in the economy, or many other possibilities) (Sullivan et al. 2000). This category is synonymous with the type of poverty I refer to as the insecure, though it may more properly be referred to as a type of potential poverty. People in this category may come to share some of the vulnerable social relations of people in poverty, but may also remain different in some ways from people in deep, chronic poverty. People of insecure middle-class status are often in similar situations in relation to the state. But they tend to be in better positions in relation to institutional gatekeepers such as school officials and health providers (Lareau 2003).

Relations to the labor market depend on the answer to several questions. For the fragile middle class, the answers can vary in either direction to impact their economic standing. Are they expendable in their employment? Do they lack the skills that are rewarded in the labor market? Do they lack access to knowledge about the labor market? The fact that upward mobility for middle-income quintile has declined while downward mobility has increased, suggests the answers to these questions may increasingly be, yes (Acs and Nichols 2010).

More and more, middle-income families and individuals are disadvantaged in social relations as income and wealth inequality increase. Researchers identified growing unease among middle-income families even before the Great Recession (Acs and Nichols 2010). Their status is not only less secure, but they encounter more of the pressures and concerns that plague people in poverty, including pressures on familial and intimate relations (Pugh 2015). Hacker (2006) sees this growing insecurity as the direct consequence of a change in the obligations that the government is willing to meet. The burden of risk is placed increasingly on individuals, who must both hustle to prepare for risk (i.e., insurance) and take the blow when a crisis ensues. Meanwhile, scholars such as Arne Kalleberg (2011) document the increased precariousness of the labor market, particularly for those on the bad end of the polarization, which includes younger generations and those without a college degree (Howell and Kalleberg 2019).

Pugh's (2015) tumbleweed metaphor refers to the plight of the contemporary worker, adrift in a landscape of unconcerned employers who have no long-term obligation to their employees. Not all of us find ourselves in this landscape, and Pugh's comparisons here are revealing. Those who face insecurity in the labor market must also make choices about the level of insecurity they are willing to tolerate in their family life. Some choose independence as a self-protective mechanism, similar to the approach many low-income parents take and which I explore in the next chapter. What is particularly compelling about Pugh's study is how much the security people find at work affects their ability to cope with the challenges of their domestic relations, and how much their domestic obligations influence their relation to the labor market. To what extent must Americans constantly and completely accommodate the labor market (Pugh 2015)? Thus, it may be that the challenges that pertain to family and parenting in poverty discussed in the next chapter also apply to the insecure middle class.

In terms of despair and vulnerability to manipulation, some people of insecure middle-class status may also be desperately seeking meaning in a life full of indignities. If they lack a sense of belonging and love, they may also be vulnerable in their social relations with others. If a given interaction is a threat to their core dignity, this may lead to self-defeating action and outcomes of desperation. Consider the opioid crisis. While largely due to a lack of regulation of the pharmaceutical and healthcare industries, clearly too many people have experienced debilitating pain, and too many also latched on to the use of opiates to treat their emotional pain (Case and Deaton 2020; Maclean et al. 2021). The COVID-19 pandemic has exacerbated both the mental health and economic crises, leading to an increase in "deaths of despair" – mortality due to alcohol, drugs, or suicide (Case and Deaton 2020; Petterson et al. 2020).

Despite these problems, people from middle-income backgrounds retain some advantages over those from chronic poverty. They tend to have more education, skills, and work experience on which to rely. They tend to have better social networks on which to rely. Their relations to others in terms of emotional vulnerability may be better on average. Yet insecurity is pernicious. As with many things, it is perhaps a matter of degree. We are all vulnerable. Some are just much more so than others.

Conclusion

Poverty is multidimensional and our measurements should take that into account. Maintaining a balance between recognizing our similarities and our differences can help us develop less pathologizing, compassionate, and more accurate perceptions of poverty. Generally, this chapter's long list of figures suggests that we need an intersectional approach that takes into account how poverty varies for people in different social positions. People in poverty face many of the same structural and cultural conditions we all face, but they do so through multiple social relations in which they are disadvantaged. They also face many of the same individual-level problems that exist throughout the country – substance abuse, disability, single motherhood – but these problems themselves are not responsible for their poverty. It is at the intersection of these conditions and problems that we find poverty is perpetuated – the relations through which people are denied rights, options, opportunities, or basic securities.

As a very basic guide to thinking through some of the different experiences of poverty, it helps to consider three different types of poverty statuses that appear to be relevant for early 21st century America: (1) the deep and chronically poor; (2) the insecure, including those above poverty but who are at risk for poverty; and (3) the temporarily poor, such as those who have some assets, tangible or intangible, that allow them to weather the bad period. The perception of insecurity has spread throughout much of society: 45% of adults were dissatisfied with "Americans' opportunities to get ahead by working hard," in 2014, according to Gallup, compared to 22% in 2001 (Mather and Jarosz 2014:3; Riffkin 2014). Mather and Jarosz (2014) argue that the USA is heading toward an increasingly bimodal distribution of income, with a smaller middle class and more people at either the top or bottom. High inequality in the United States means more people fall into the three categories of poverty status.

A caution as we close out this chapter and before moving forward: as researchers or service providers, we can never truly *know* the experience of people with whom we study or work. Even if we've experienced poverty ourselves, we do not know the experiences of others. We can try to understand, but we are always constrained by our own social location and positioning. As Gunzenhauser (2006:635) writes in reference to Lather and Smithies' (1997) ethnography of women living with HIV/AIDS, the authors:

> give the women voice to express these indignities, and occasionally the slights are contradictory – one woman's experience of indignity is another's experience of understanding. The multiple interpretations by the women jar the (presumed innocent) reader, who may be looking for a fail-safe guide on how to respect the dignity of women living with HIV/AIDS. The significant finding is particular and contextual: Dignity is situated, unpredictable, divorced from intention, and embedded in relation.

The same applies to our efforts to understand people in poverty. How I interpret problems that people in poverty face, based on research findings, may not always match the experiences of people. That is why we must go beyond the quantitative data to delve deeper into the issues, while also remembering that no one person's experience is representative. Just as I implore consideration of the social relations of which someone is a part, I have discovered myself that the best way to understand someone in poverty is to actually form a relationship with them and relate to them as one human being to another. In the meantime, we see through the glass darkly, but let's at least take a look.

3

Family and Parenting

The parenting practices and family structure of people in poverty are often scrutinized and found faulty. No one is a perfect parent, regardless of social class. However, for people in poverty, relations of vulnerability and the desire for dignity characterize in specific ways their struggles to form meaningful relationships and take care of their children. Families in poverty are not necessarily worse at caring for children than nonpoor families, but they do operate at a disadvantage. Again, there is much variation in the quality of relations between family members across families in poverty, and no single issue – be it child maltreatment or unstable household composition – applies to all, or even a sizable majority of, people in poverty. We can, however, identify sets of conditions and social relations under which parents in poverty struggle, or outright fail, to take care of their children. Unequal gendered relations are particularly relevant, as we will see. Most of the relevant research is on mothers. This will be reflected in the chapter content, but effort will also be made to discuss fathers as well, including so-called "deadbeat dads" and fathers as primary and secondary caregivers. In this chapter, I examine the social science on three common concerns regarding families in poverty: single mother households, early childbearing (i.e., adolescent mothers), and child maltreatment. I then analyze the research in terms of the relational framework.

Several trends become evident in examining the social relations that shape family structure and child well-being. First, relations with the state prove critical for reinforcing single parents' problems, and these relations are profoundly gendered. Second, relations with other adults in the household, which are also gendered, strongly impact family structure and child well-being. Third, support systems, or networks of relations with kin, neighbors, and friends, are critical resources that directly impact both parent and child well-being. Fourth, how one generally relates to family and to the world shapes decision-making around childbearing and childrearing. Finally, relations to the labor market directly impact ability to parent. Thus, a variety of institutions – including education, the labor market, and the law – play important roles in the well-being of families. Gender relations also intersect with many of the social relations that matter for parenting. Culturally available meanings of motherhood and fatherhood collide with structural constraints to shape the ways in which so many children in poverty grow up. Overall, parenting is a relational product.

Single Mother Households

Larger Social Trends

Single motherhood grew more common across social classes in late twentieth-century America. Middle-class women as well as working-class and impoverished women were more likely to head their own households by the twenty-first century, as a result of changes in both cultural norms and the economy. The increase in out-of-wedlock childbirth was not a phenomenon specific to the lower classes, as the stigma associated with it lessened in the second half of the twentieth century. Nonetheless, in recent decades, a divergence by class developed in single motherhood such that marriage has become more of a privilege afforded to the middle and upper classes. Throughout all of these changes, much debate has ensued as to whether single female-headed households are an undesirable family structure for raising children. Part of the difficulty is the fact that single mothering often occurs with a bundle of other factors that may independently affect child well-being, including race, household income, and stability in household composition. Furthermore, many other factors mitigate the effect of single mothers raising children, including the presence of other adults, sources of social and institutional support, and social policies of welfare and work–family balance. It is revealing how mothers in poverty are considered bad mothers if they do not work, despite concerns about child supervision, whereas mothers in professional occupations are criticized – however obliquely – for working rather than taking care of their children (White 1999; Bowen et al. 2019).

Further complicating the topic, a steady increase in cohabitation has occurred, including both unstable cohabitation and cohabitation as a long-term alternative to marriage. Many children are born outside marriage, but that does not mean they are in a single-parent household (Haskins and Sawhill 2016). In 2020, 25.5% of all children under the age of 18 were estimated to live with one parent, but 15% of households with children had only one parent present (US Census Bureau 2020c). The difference is made up by households with multiple children (who count individually in the 25.5% but not in the 15% figure) and cohabiting households. Cohabitating families that contained joint biological children represented 4.6% of the households with children, and 2.7% of households with children were cohabiting families whose children were not shared biologically. The younger the children, the more likely it was that a partner was present. Of households with a child under the age of 6, only 11.9% had no partner present. Non-cohabiting single-parent households were more common among Black-identified families, at 37.1%; and among those without a bachelor's degree, at 19.9%; but were only slightly more common for parents not in the formal labor force, at 16.5%.

Since William Julius Wilson (1996) documented the many negative consequences of high rates of unemployment for inner-city racial minority neighborhoods, sociologists have been attentive to the conditions under which single motherhood and poverty tend to reinforce each other. Crime, welfare dependence, family dissolution, and social disorganization are a few of the side effects of concentrated unemployment that Wilson (1996) mentions. He locates the problem in terms of a global economy jobs shrinkage, as wages for low-skilled and high-skilled workers polarize. Yet this does not mean that single mother households are inherently problematic, or that marriage is the solution.

The state also imposes single parenthood through incarceration. Parental incarceration has been shown to have deleterious effects on children (Phillips and O'Brien 2012; Bradshaw et al. 2021). Rising incarceration rates in the twentieth century and into the twenty-first, especially among racial minorities, have exposed vastly more children to family separation due to parental incarceration. Among children included in the Fragile Families Study, one-tenth had experienced maternal incarceration, and one-third paternal incarceration, by age 9 (Sykes and Pettit 2014). While parental incarceration is linked to a number of other family problems that may contribute both to child outcomes and to the parental incarceration itself – drug use, for instance, or violence – often the incarceration of a parent only worsens the family situation.

Relations with Intimate Partners

One of the benefits of two-parent households is the possibility for twice the income. Of course, this does not always work out in practice, and another adult can add to the economic burden as much as they can help. But the opportunity to pool resources for expenses such as rent can make a big difference in the economic stability of a household. Researchers have also tried to work out whether there are additional benefits to the two-parent household structure. Overall, there do appear to be some benefits to children's well-being. However, the difficulty is separating the effect of family structure per se from all the other factors that influence whether a household is a one-parent or two-parent household to begin with, such as parent's stability, parent's health, child's health, or economic position. For many single parents, there may be very good reasons not to marry or cohabit. The benefit to the child, while looking encouraging in the statistics, does not actually pan out in certain contexts. For instance, the other parent or potential step-parent could be abusive. And cohabitators who do not stay for long tend to cause more problems than they solve (Stiffman et al. 2002; Schnitzer and Ewigmen 2005; Levine 2013; Pugh 2015).

Marriage, cohabitation, and co-parenting are difficult enough without the added complication of low income. Some researchers have found specific forms of distrust between low-income men and women in heterosexual relations (Levine 2013). The incompatibility of men's and women's roles in impoverished communities and the strong obligations toward kin could undermine long-term relationships. In situations of limited job opportunities, men may self-present as economic exploiters of women (Stack 1974). Women, meanwhile, in such situations, have become hyper-concerned about a man making a fool out of them (Stack 1974). Opposite-gender marriage is less likely when the man is unemployed. Marriage also entails some breaking away from the kin structure of loosely intertwined and fluid households. Marriage and the accompanying home, family, and job represent social mobility for many, but often require some removal from the daily obligations in the kin network (Stack 1974:113–14). In *Making Ends Meet: How Single Mothers Survive Welfare and Low-Wage Work*, Edin and Lein (1997) also found that boyfriends could be an important source of assistance, but were not without their costs. Edin and Lein (1997:158) write that:

Mothers who relied on boyfriends for income sometimes had to choose between danger and destitution. While not all boyfriends were involved in illegal activity, many mothers reported that they or their children had been physically or sexually abused by their domestic partners at some point in the past. When mothers discovered that a boyfriend was abusing their children, most immediately evicted him. A few told us, however, that they had ignored the evidence because they were so desperate for their boyfriend's money. Most did eventually evict the abuser, but the damage had already been done.

Stack (1974) found that the social and economic lives of people in her study of a low-income African American community were highly intertwined. Not paying one's dues when called upon could have dire consequences for both parties – the debtor loses future support, and the collector may not be able to feed a child that day. The more desperate one was, the more likely one was to pay back. Such exchanges included child-minding, and also constituted a sign of trust. In fact, people began to trust Stack more after she let them mind her son. This system – what Stack called the "collective power within kin-based exchange networks" (1974:33) – helped people survive, but it also kept them from escaping poverty. That is the huge risk entailed by social mobility. People could not move up the SES ladder without giving up the kin support system, which rendered them vulnerable. Pressures on intimate relationships between men and women were considerable, and fatherhood was precarious. However, if the father took an interest in the child, then that child could call upon the father's personal kin network as their own. The more involved and helpful a father and his kin were, the more likely they were to have rights to the child. However, it was hard for many Black men to obtain secure income. This hindered the relationship with both the mother and the child.

Kin links, however, were more stable and consequential (Stack 1974). Children were part of what may be exchanged in any kin-based or close network. Taking a child was often a form of helping out. Although Aid to Families with Dependent Children (AFDC) statistics suggested that one-fifth of child-residents of The Flats live with someone other than their mother, Stack thought that fostering was actually more common. This was an example of how interpreting statistical data out of context leads to confusion. And such confusion has led to the misinterpretation of Black family life. For instance, it's often assumed that "black children derive all their jural kin through females," and that Black families are matrifocal (Stack 1974:71).

However, most fathers of AFDC children help their children out and provide kinship affiliation. But that is not reflected in the statistics, which instead are based on household composition from the point of view of the mother or primary guardian. In some cases, fathers are more involved than they may seem.

Decades later, Edin and Kefalas ([2005] 2011) produced similar results on the basis of in-depth interviews and participant observation with 162 mothers in a low-income neighborhood around Philadelphia. They asked not only why poor, unmarried women have children, but why their relationships with the father disintegrate. These participants were a mix of White, Black, and Puerto Rican women. Edin and Kefalas found that women in their study who have children while unmarried are typically romantically involved with the father not only at the time of the conception, but often again at birth. And 4 in 10 lived with the father at the time of the birth. Thus, it was not being unattached that was the problem so much as relationship instability. These relationships often failed within several years of the child's birth. Relational instability, they find, is a major feature of the lives of these low-income women. Not only are nonmarital unions more vulnerable to dissolution, but these families survive in precarious environments – neighborhoods with high unemployment, high crime, substandard schooling, and reduced social services. Though 8 out of 10 poor, unmarried mothers who gave birth were in a romantic relationship with the father at the time, two-thirds would have split up by the time the child turned 3. Nonetheless, many of these women still clung to the hope of a lifetime partner. The dynamics are thus complex.

Consider the fallout from finding out one is pregnant, as described by Edin and Kefalas ([2005] 2011). In their study, some relationships went downhill when the woman gave the news of pregnancy. The costs relative to the rewards were greater for the father than for the mother. Pregnancy brought transformation to the young woman's life, including in the way she was treated; it was not so dramatic for most men. The soon-to-be-father's failures might be repeatedly brought up as the soon-to-be-mother planned their future. In other cases, the men suddenly became controlling and possessive. Edin and Kefalas note that domestic violence was common among these families. Many of these women did not have great records themselves, dating or legal, and certainly do not have the dating pool that middle-class women have. Meanwhile, kin are disappointed by the news of early pregnancy. They realize this is not the ideal way to do things. But they typically end up being supportive. The loss of opportunity did not seem great, as, typically, opportunities for the young woman were not ample to begin with. The new mothers often became focused on being the best mother they could be, viewing it as their new life's work (Edin and Kefalas [2005] 2011:68).

The domestic situation may have changed again with the birth (Edin and Kefalas [2005] 2011). Some fathers became interested in their child and, thus, in the mother again – at least temporarily. The relationships often fell apart. Edin and Kefalas identify four main reasons why the relationships between the mothers in poverty and the fathers of their children tended to fail: (1) criminal behavior and/ or incarceration; (2) intimate violence; (3) chronic infidelity; and (4) alcohol or drug dependency. "The transition to parenthood means that the demands on young men dramatically increase just as the rewards of the relationship are radically reduced" (Edin and Kefalas [2005] 2011:100). For the fathers, the possibility of having to make child support payments, even when one cannot afford them and even when they are shut out of their child's life, was real. Edin and Kefalas ([2005] 2011:69) describe it as an 18-year financial commitment that they will be hunted down for trying to evade (as Pennsylvania and New Jersey have tough child support laws).

These women appear to be accustomed to romantic turn-abouts. Edin and Kefalas ([2005] 2011:112) go as far as suggesting that "Low-income women are waging a war of the sexes in the domestic sphere, and they believe their own earnings and assets are what buys them power . . . [and] provide[s] insurance against a marriage gone bad." For instance, Deena and Patrick in Edin and Kefalas's study appear to be doing well as a couple, yet Deena is hesitant about taking the marital step. Remembering past experiences of happiness turning sour, Deena desires financial security and independence before marriage. She says, "I want my kids to be stable before I do anything to alter their lives. . . .. I wanna have an established environment for my kids so that my kids are happy, my kids are healthy, they're safe, they have their own house, their own toys, their own couch, their own television" (107). Giving inspiration for the title for the book, Deena refuses to make "promises that I'm not gonna be able to keep" (107). Though strongly opposed to divorce, many see marriage as risky and divorce as a major hazard. Vows are held to be sacred and literal. Thus, the moral high road entails taking years to consider marriage. In one quote, a young woman participant ridicules the idea of marrying just for love, saying people have to be prepared to live up to their vows (133–4). A fear that marriage will turn the husband traditional is expressed, and some of the women indicate that you can't tell what sort of husband a man is going to be by living with him for a few months. Mistrust may be the result of harsh childhoods or the difficulties of pregnancy and birth, but for Edin and Kefalas "seems to permeate the very air in these neighborhoods" ([2005] 2011:126). In a study of low-income women with children in Chicago in the 1990s and 2000s, Levine's (2013) interviewees also turned out to be highly distrustful of men. This distrust developed in response to involvements with men who proved untrustworthy, sometimes in relation to drug use, abuse, or sapping the women's emotional and financial resources. Indeed, the decrease in decent-wage employment situations for less-educated men reinforces this problem. Overall, it simply does not make sense for many low-income women to delay motherhood until the unlikely event of a marriage, especially when singlehood or cohabitation are acceptable.

After *Promises I Can Keep* (Edin and Kefalas [2005] 2011), Edin and Nelson (2013) conducted a similar study with low-income men in the Greater Philadelphia area, resulting in *Doing the Best I Can: Fatherhood in the Inner City*. They ask: Is it true that low-income inner-city men don't care about their children? What does fatherhood mean to these men? Consistent with the 2005 study, the relationship with the child's mother usually does not last. But the men often want to continue playing a role in the child's life. This is difficult. They have to radically redefine the role of the father. They don't want to be just a paycheck – they want to spend quality time with the kids. But the hard jobs tend to be left to the mothers, and the fathers often fail in various ways. When a new child comes along, they focus their attention on doing right with this one. Fathers are more easily drawn back into the party scene or dangerous lifestyles. Part of the problem may be that their relationships with the mothers are not secure in themselves, but are mainly fortified by the presence of the children. Relationships formed by the news of pregnancy often do not last because the couple find out that they are not compatible or have little in common down the road. The couples also often have different expectations regarding obligations of mothers and fathers. The mother often expects the father to grow up and be responsible before he really feels that pressure internally, and without him realizing that she was going to have these expectations. Furthermore, as low-income men with troubled childhoods, many of them are fragile in their masculine self-confidence. "The sudden change in a woman's expectations may, in fact, be read as a betrayal, conclusive evidence that she is lacking in commitment, ready to throw him over as soon as he fails to meet her mounting demands" (Edin and Nelson 2013:92).

On one hand, the meaning of fatherhood has changed, and can be a source of self-esteem, identity, and sense of purpose. Negative family experiences in the men's past can translate to an "ache to play a positive social role" (Edin and Nelson 2013:194). Yet fatherhood, when the parents are not married, remains institutionally weak (Edin and Nelson 2013). Getting one's name on the birth certificate, for fathers, may only mean the state will enforce child support. The mother often has leverage in terms of control over the child (Edin and Nelson 2013). Since access to the child is often the primary motivator, when fathers don't see the child, they are far less likely to provide financial support of any kind. When fathers do give financial support, they often prefer the as-needed approach. And this is often tempered by the if-available clause (Edin and Nelson 2013). Their view of what providing means is fairly broad. Edin and Nelson suggest they take advantage of the notion of female independence by expecting women to take care of themselves financially. Edin and Nelson argue that, despite their machismo, these men often see women as stronger than them. Black fathers, Edin and Nelson suggest, have made greater accommodations to non-custodial fatherhood than have White fathers; they have a more articulated version of fatherhood and are more involved with their children, especially when it comes to their early years. This may be because the unwed father role has long been a part of African American family life.

Relation to the Labor Market

In Edin and Lein's (1997) study of single mothers, mothers who were in the workforce and not receiving welfare were only able to work because of some enabling circumstances – having school-aged children; receiving regular child support; paying very little for rent, childcare, or transportation; or full family health coverage. Nine of ten working mothers mentioned one of these circumstances, two-thirds had two or more of them, and almost half reported three or more of these special circumstances (Edin and Lein 1997:121–2). Single mothers who work can be disadvantaged in three ways: (1) they may be no closer to balancing their budgets because they would have to spend more to work; (2) they would have less time to generate supplemental income; and (3) their children have less parental supervision. No mother in the sample met all her expenses with her earnings – all had supplemental income, often in the form of a generous parent or boyfriend, substantial overtime, a second job, or a lot of agency assistance (Edin and Lein 1997:106–8). Interestingly, in their comparison of single mothers who were "wage-reliant" as opposed to "welfare-reliant," across all measures of material hardship (no food, hungry, no doctor, utilities cut off, housing problems, no winter clothes, no phone), welfare-reliant mothers fared better than wage-reliant mothers. Wage-reliant mothers experienced more hardships.

In a nationally representative study of labor market situations of Americans, Albelda and Carr (2014) found that the share of low-wage and low-income situations, in which workers not only make a low wage, but total household income remains low as well, has increased over time across all household configurations. Yet single women with children are among the least likely groups to be eligible for an employer-provided pension or employer-sponsored healthcare. Having children in the household, however, does make it more likely that they receive some government-sponsored assistance, including SNAP or Medicaid. In rural areas especially, women often face a labor market disadvantage compared to men. Gender segregation remains high in fields not requiring a college degree (Hegewisch and Hartmann 2014). Job training for women receiving Temporary Aid to Needy Families (TANF) assistance is typically for some of the lowest-paying, most precarious jobs, such as those of Certified Nursing Assistants (Seale 2013; Goldblum and Shaddox 2021). Gender discrimination also remains a reality, as Goldblum and Shaddox (2021:169) remark in their review of situations of the working poor: whether the women were in construction or healthcare, they faced discrimination, "because they were doing women's work, or because they were women doing men's work."

Mothers in the low-wage workforce often prioritize their children over their employment, which means their interests are at odds with those of their employers (Dodson 2007). The low-wage labor market is already precarious, but is more so for single mothers who prioritize the needs of their children over the needs of their employer or the whims of their manager (Callan and Dolan 2013; Jacobs and Padavic 2015). In the US labor market, the lower the income, the less flexibility in work hours and scheduling exists (Dodson 2007; Jacobs and Padavic 2015). Women report inadequate hours, unpredictable scheduling, little or no protection from harassment, coercion to work "off-the-clock" or without full pay, and punishment and control tactics for rebellion or missing work, regardless of the reason (Jacobs and Padavic 2015). Research also reveals that, for rural single mothers, finding full-time work can be incredibly difficult (Callan and Dolan 2013), and the gender wage gap is worse in rural places

(Thiede et al. 2018). The combined stress of parenting and work can contribute to untreated mental health problems.

Rural single mothers may face a different set of options than the single women living in metropolitan areas and on whom so much of the research has focused. The relation of rural mothers to the labor market is even less secure and more disadvantaged relative to men's places in the labor market. In such situations, marriage or cohabitation may make more sense. This is not necessarily a better situation. Researchers have found that mothers in rural areas have a harder time escaping abusive situations and finding independence from relations with men (Callan and Dolan 2013; Bhandari et al. 2011). However, research also suggests that, in some cases, rural families in poverty may find long-term intimate relationships a more important focus compared to urban families in poverty, despite also experiencing abusive relationships in their past (Obernesser and Seale n.d.).

Thus, there are not only costs to domestic partnerships and marriage for mothers, but there are costs to being "self-reliant" through the labor force. Either way they turn, low-income mothers are reliant on someone, be it an employer, a man, a family member, or the state. All have costs. Understandably, some mothers choose singledom over coupledom, relying on some combination of the labor market, kin, support networks, nonprofit agencies, and government benefits such as the Earned Income Tax Credit. When it comes to the burdens and rewards of having children, however, it seems many low-income women are more than willing to pay that cost.

Fathers' Relations to the Labor Market

Low-income fathers are important to consider in the bigger picture of American poverty. Not only do poor employment prospects for less-educated men figure into the likelihood of low-income mothers remaining single, but their ability to provide for their children is not irrelevant simply because they do not reside with their children. Fathers often continue to play an important role in their children's lives and prospects (Stack 1974; Waller 2010; Edin and Nelson 2013). Some research has found that fathers in low-income communities view child support as something that should be voluntarily provided, and they find fault with the legal system's punitive and unfair approach (Waller 2010). They felt the informal approach was better for the child, in that it established a connection with that child, as opposed to a bureaucratically mediated line of support. Mothers often agreed with this, seeing the formal child support system as a last resort. Turning a father in for child support and welfare is often not a good idea (Levine 2013). If the man can even be found, he may not have the financial footing to contribute. Mothers risk losing the goodwill of the father and his kin and may even endanger the relationship between father and child. Further, only the first $50 per month is passed on to the mother, and the rest serves to pay the state back for the cash assistance (Levine 2013). Sometimes, the fathers became more involved with their children precisely because they had trouble finding work (Waller 2010). Thus, an arrangement in which even the non-resident father provides childcare while the mother works may become more common among low-income families.

Summary

Women's dependence comes at great cost, whether it is dependence on a man or an institution. Yet some dependence is typically inevitable – the issue is whom or what one is dependent on, and at what cost. Edin and Lein (1997) found that, to support their family on a minimal budget, single mothers have to rely on additional strategies whether they are on welfare or low-wage work. In fact, to last in the work force, *they must have some extra support*, whether it is in the form of child support from fathers, affordable and reliable childcare provided by family or friends, or employed boyfriends. Single mothers and their children remain the poorest demographic group in the USA. Stagnant wages and modest government support contribute to this situation (Edin and Lein 1997). However, even when more long-term reliable government cash assistance was provided, prior to 1997, single mothers were not often consistently dependent on it – rather, a majority left the welfare rolls within two years, and very few stayed on for more than 8 years continuously (Pavetti 1992; Harris 1993; Edin and Lein 1997). Dependence on government is less of a concern in my estimation than the consequences of single mothers and fathers being dependent on a precarious labor market or exploitative domestic partners.

Young Moms

"Teen moms" have been castigated by some policy commentators for being rational actors who calculate the benefits of receiving welfare without having to work, and thus choose motherhood (Luker 1996). Going even further, anti-immigrant commentators have claimed that Latina mothers come to the USA with the express intention of becoming pregnant and having their babies on United States soil as a way to "anchor" themselves in the country – part of their argument for greater immigration control and to justify harsh family separation tactics. In other accounts, teen moms are castigated for the opposite: failing to act rationally and, in effect, dooming themselves to a life of hardship by having a child so early (Luker 1996). In the 1970s, teen pregnancy was offered up as a major cause of poverty in the USA. In the 1980s and 1990s, teen mothers were recast by conservatives as exploitative, and teen motherhood was discussed as an epidemic. African American adolescent mothers, in particular, were viewed as a major cause of urban poverty. In the 2000s, reality television shows spectacularized teen motherhood as a matter of bad behavior and character. Luker argues that, behind these representations in the public realm, concern over the sexuality of adolescent women ruminated. In effect, teenagers became the focus, or front, for various concerns and discomfort regarding sexual liberation in society (Luker 1996).

Recent research has cast doubt on the notion that early childbearing is a cause of poverty. The direction of causation appears to be the other way around: poverty is more likely to lead to early childbearing. Moreover, when girls from impoverished families become mothers early on, they are not significantly more likely to remain in poverty than their counterparts who are also growing up in poverty (Furstenberg 2007). As Erdmans and Black (2015) point out, early childbearing may be a rational life-course strategy in poor communities with few marriageable men or jobs. Many of the adolescent mothers they studied who went on to struggle as low-income parents had already had problems before their first child was born. They had in many cases already given up on high school and often had experienced trauma of some kind, or significant family neglect. For some, pregnancy and the prospect of motherhood gave them a reason to desist from self-destructive behaviors. For the few young mothers in the study whose families were supportive both financially and emotionally, they were neither living in poverty nor on a path to poverty. For these young women, early parenthood did not mean they had to sacrifice any hope of a career. This does not mean teen motherhood is a picnic – one can wave good-bye to a carefree and liberatory youth. What these results do mean is that teen or single motherhood need not doom a family.

The teen pregnancy literature is a good example of how research that does not explicitly use a culture of poverty framework (discussed in the next chapter) may still encounter some of the same hazards. Furstenberg (2007:3) writes that "the causes and consequences of early childbearing . . . have been misunderstood, distorted, and exaggerated because they are refracted through a peculiarly American lens strongly tinted by our distinctive political culture." Furstenberg identifies the problem more in the interpretation of the research than in the research itself. Many earlier studies found that families in which the mothers began childbirth in their teens were more likely to be poor. Such results are easily overinterpreted in a context of general misunderstandings of the family lives of poor women (Furstenberg 2007:4). Moreover, early childbearing and childrearing – without a partner, in particular – were considered problems with Black family life in the mid-to-late twentieth century (Moynihan [1965] 1967; Wilson 1987). Black families were viewed as pathologically matrifocal, with childbirth out of wedlock reinforcing poverty and deviancy. Charles Murray (1984) even argued that young women saw a viable lifestyle in having children out of wedlock and relying on welfare. This negative view of the effects of young single motherhood became commonsense knowledge, and research showing correlations between adolescent childrearing and poverty was comfortably interpreted as confirmation.

Furstenberg (2007) relies on a more comprehensive, prospective study of early childbearing to cast greater perspective: a comparison of young Baltimore mothers' life experiences with those of their counterparts who postponed childbirth. The longitudinal and comparative aspect helps us separate correlation from causation in a way that the multiple cross-sectional studies do not. Although teen pregnancy – viewed as a major social problem by many – became an explanation for why so many of the poor did not succeed, this is not altogether true. It is a marker of marginality and inequality, but the impact early childbearing has on the life chances of poor women has been greatly exaggerated (Furstenberg 2007:5). Ultimately, we must be careful to refrain from confusing the consequences of decision-making by the poor with its many precursors. Furstenberg shows that the literature on the effects of early childbearing for the next generation (i.e., the children of teen moms) has made this mistake, and studies that compared children born early and later in parents' lives failed to account for preexisting differences (Geronimus and Korenman 1992; Furstenberg 2007). Mothers who give birth early are poorer and have less access to prenatal care and health services overall, compared to those who either do not give birth at all or do so later in their adult years (Furstenberg 2007). The health risks associated with early childbirth are largely due to inadequate prenatal and postnatal care (Luker 1996). (For various reasons, pregnant teenagers are less likely to seek out medical care.) The exceptions to this are very young mothers, under the age of 15, whose pregnancies are often due to involuntary sexual activity. We do find more health risk associated with childbirth of mothers under the age of 15, even controlling for access to healthcare. But these very young mothers account for a very small percentage of all teenage mothers. In 2019, the birth rate for females aged 10–14 was 0.2 births per 1,000, compared to 16.7 births per 1,000 females aged 15–19 (Martin et al. 2021).

Children are often highly valued among people who do not have many social roles to choose from, and who see their children as their chance to make an impact. Edin and Kefalas ([2005] 2011), Duncan (1999), and Fitchen (1981) found in their different studies across rural and urban places that children are highly valued among their research subjects who have few life options. Erdmans and Black (2015) find that pregnancy is a more appealing option for young women *after* they have dropped out of school. Edin and Kefalas ([2005] 2011:31) also suggest that the poor place "extraordinarily high social value" on children, and "eagerly anticipate" them. Having children is a more realistic goal that these young people can not only envision, but understand, unlike going to college or getting a career, which remains mysterious. They also have considerable experience being around children and having to care for children. The role of caregiver is a familiar one.

In Edin and Kefalas's ([2005] 2011) study, most research participants did not plan to get pregnant when they did, but there were notable exceptions. Sometimes, it is a way to escape a troubled home life. Childbirth provides love and intimacy not found elsewhere. The isolation of the poor is exacerbated for adolescents, and they do not have many people they feel they can trust in their life (Edin and Kefalas [2005] 2011; Erdmans and Black 2015). They may want somebody to take care of. More often, the pregnancy is not planned, but neither is it actively avoided. It may be passively allowed. Edin and Kefalas argue that, in their study, unplanned pregnancy is not due to a lack of understanding of the "facts of life" or access to birth control; rather, the lackadaisical use of birth control is due to the lack of cost associated with having a child for this demographic. While their young research participants realize there is some stigma with teen birth, and they do not wish to acknowledge actively seeking pregnancy, they also do not view it as something they will gain much by delaying. As Edin and Kefalas ([2005] 2011:40) put it, the "vigilance and care that most birth control methods require are hard to maintain when women like Tasheika see so few costs to having a baby." Some simply have stopped caring about their future altogether. And in these cases, the baby may be a turning point for them. There is also a religious fatalism among some of the women, viewing the conception, and therefore parenthood, as meant to be. It is important to note here that many young people from this demographic may feel very differently from these particular research participants about having children young, as this sample is of course selective. Those young residents of these neighborhoods who have not had children may have a very different outlook.

Many of these young women view the call to parenthood that comes with conception as a call to duty which they have a moral responsibility to answer (Edin and Kefalas [2005] 2011). Abortion is often viewed as reprehensible, even though many of them have had previous abortions. Apparently, if the young woman feels she is able to be a parent, then the abortion is wrong, but if it is the wrong time or circumstance, it is justified. Refusing to have an abortion also indicates that one is now mature. For instance, Antonia Rodriguez, a young, single mother in poverty, told Edin and Kefalas that she and her partner had intended to wait another year or two at least, but Antonia described the choice to keep the baby as "facing reality," or, the responsible way, as Edin and Kefalas summarize it. It's a hard life, but they find a lot of solace and meaning in their children (Edin and Kefalas [2005] 2011). And they do not necessarily have much to lose by having children early.

Of course, family planning and reproductive healthcare are shaped by one's intimate relations, including sexual empowerment relative to one's partner, parental/familial relations, access to affordable healthcare, religious beliefs, the education system, and peer knowledge and support. These relations are all heavily patriarchal in most respects, or at least persist within a largely patriarchal culture and society. Young women thus face fraught choices around sexuality and reproduction. Adolescent and young women are frequently shamed for planning for sexual activity by acquiring contraception, shamed for not doing so, and generally shamed for any decision made about pregnancy. Thus, poor women from conservative families – in rural areas, especially – are in some of the most difficult positions when it comes to sex and reproduction. Reproductive rights of poor women are in general a low priority for the USA. We do not provide universal prenatal care or guarantee drug addiction treatment for pregnant women. In fact, the patriarchal tradition that a woman's body is not her own is nowhere clearer than in the lack of reproductive rights.

Sexuality education is fragmented and haphazard across the USA. Though federal statutes discourage government involvement in prescribing schools' curricula, the federal government allocated millions of dollars to abstinence-only education from the 1990s through the 2010s, effectively manipulating state sex education policies (see the Adolescent Family Life Act 1981 and the Personal Responsibility and Work Opportunity Reconciliation Act of 1996). This policy strictly required that schools accepting federal money institute a sex education program that has "as its exclusive purpose" promotion of the benefits of abstinence. Moreover, 35 states and Washington DC allow parents the option to remove their child from instruction (Guttmacher Institute 2022a). Hence, young women who grow up in conservative families or go to rural schools with fewer resources are less likely to get a full sexuality education.

Many of the women in my family planning study experienced mental health issues, physical health issues, or mild disability, which complicated their reproductive options (Seale 2017). Accessing contraception was not easy for them. Accessing abortion is even more difficult for women in poverty, women in abusive relationships, and those who are raising children alone (Dickey et al. 2022). Since the overturning of *Roe* v. *Wade* by the Supreme Court decision *Dobbs* v. *Jackson* in 2022, research suggests women in poverty fare the worst from the restriction of abortion and closing of clinics in conservative states. Not surprisingly, maternal mortality and severe maternal morbidity have increased, as research has consistently shown these outcomes are directly related to access to abortion (Gerdts et al. 2016). Furthermore, Dickey et al. (2022:1) found that social support and social capital "were key facilitators of both abortion access and parenting, but participants often experienced barriers to economic support within their social networks due to poverty, unstable partnerships, structural inequality, and abortion stigma." Whether a young pregnant woman decides to get an abortion or bear the child, she faces a tough decision that will be heavily influenced by her social relations at the micro and macro levels.

Telling young people that having children early is a bad idea does not seem to work (Erdmans and Black 2015). Neither does penalizing them for having children early. Teens who go on to give birth are mostly disadvantaged in life beforehand and discouraged from pursuing education long before the child comes along (Erdmans and Black 2015). Middle- and upper-class women benefit from delaying childbearing and childrearing as they have the options to focus on career goals and/or personal fulfillment. Young women in poverty do not have the same set of trade-offs.

When examined carefully, postponing childbirth for most young people who have children early has not been empirically shown to provide anything but a very modest benefit to the child (Luker 1996). The problem, in short, is poverty, not early childbirth. A high number of pregnancies in the USA are ended by abortions, most of which occur for women over the age of 20. Unintended pregnancy is generally common, regardless of age (within the 15–30 range) and marital status – but carrying to term is more common for young women who do not have rosy career prospects (Luker 1996). Birth rates among youth are actually down from the 1990s, not due to an increase in abortion but to higher use of contraception (Wald 2014). After childbirth, the issue reverts back to the fact that many mothers are unwed – single motherhood is the situation these women end up in, a result of both choice and circumstance. More and more women across classes are choosing motherhood without marriage, though not always for the same reasons.

The outcome of early childbirth happens in the context of a variety of relations, including relations to school, education, and healthcare, and relations to family and intimate partners. Lack of better relations with kin may impact childbearing – specifically, in those cases where the mother is most vulnerable to poverty. For many young women who grow up in loveless or deeply troubled households, intense relationships that last and are rewarding can only typically be found with one's children (Erdmans and Black 2015). While this outcome may not be a major cause of poverty, it also does not improve their situation. Having more options for love and life beyond having children would be a far more desirable set of conditions for these young women.

Child Maltreatment

The worst parenting outcome is the neglect or abuse of a child. Among the categories of child maltreatment, it is child neglect that is most associated with poverty. Child neglect is also the most common reason for child maltreatment that ends in fatality. Occurrences of child maltreatment are influenced by the relations a parent has with their children; the relations they have with their own parents; the relations parents have with institutions, including the labor market, religion, social services, schools, and healthcare; relations with significant others; and family relations more generally, including between the two legal parents. (The relations the child has with others also matter, but we will focus for now on the parental role.) Generally, American society views child well-being as the responsibility, ultimately, of the parent or guardian. And, certainly, we need to put much focus on the parent or guardian in understanding child well-being. But we will better predict and understand negative outcomes by considering the relations the parent has with their child and these other people and entities. Let's consider some general findings before looking at specific problems.

Research on maternally inflicted child maltreatment finds the amount and quality of social support, the presence of depression and other forms of mental illness, intimate partner violence, a history of being abused, access to childcare, and substance abuse are all important factors (Assink et al. 2018; Ayers et al. 2019). But even among those parents who are raising children in poverty and have been found wanting as parents, it is important to recognize their strengths as well as their faults. In a narrative analysis of "bad" mothers by an attorney who worked in child abuse cases in the Chicago area, Appell (1998) contends that courts and caseworkers overemphasized the weaknesses of impoverished mothers, failing to recognize their love for their children and their strengths as parents. The mothers' conduct and psychology were identified as the problem to be fixed, and their situations were ignored. In reality, however, an "ideal" mother is a relational product that requires certain structural and cultural arrangements that provide social support, financial stability, healthcare, decent childcare, and protection from abuse and high levels of chronic stress. Interventions that focus on providing education on infant development and access to social support and social services, and that are prolonged (starting before childbirth and continuing for two years after birth), are most effective in preventing child maltreatment among at-risk mothers – specifically young, low-income mothers (Levey et al. 2017). Cases of abuse are not always explainable, but courts and caseworkers too often fail to distinguish between mothers who do not care and then those who do care but, due to social- relational constraints, simply do not or cannot meet the middle-class standards for ideal motherhood. As a result, their children may enter a foster care system that often introduces them to even worse experiences, in addition to the trauma of separation.

Meta-analyses of the research have identified several relational factors in child maltreatment (Stith et al. 2009; Assink et al. 2018).

Even the anger/hyper-reactivity of a parent – which, not surprisingly, is highly correlated with abuse and neglect of one's children – is a matter of how the parent habitually relates to others (Stith et al. 2009). Stith et al. also found that the amount of family conflict and measures of family cohesion are factors for physical abuse. The parent–child relationship is a significant factor for neglect, as is also the parental level of stress, self-esteem, and perception of the child as a problem (Stith et al. 2009). Assink et al. (2018:142) found that, though poverty itself was identified as a risk factor in this meta-analysis, "supportive relationships with non-abusive adults both in childhood and adulthood . . . may buffer against intergenerational transmission of child maltreatment." Social isolation, stress, mental illness, and substance abuse of parent are all independently associated with child maltreatment (Assink et al. 2018). These issues either occur as a result of the individual's relation to others, or have their effects in the context of social relations. When relations demand more than they give, in aggregate, for an individual, stress results.

In *Scarcity: The New Science of Having Less and How It Defines Our Lives*, Mullainathan and Shafir (2013) examine studies that show how dealing with scarcity – be it financial scarcity like poverty or scarcity of time, energy, or some other resource – consumes a significant amount of mental energy, making it discernably difficult to focus on other things. Psychological experiments in which the subjects are given *less of some thing* clearly demonstrate lowered concentration and task performance. Mullainathan and Shafir argue that it takes mental bandwidth to accomplish a lot of daily routine tasks adequately. This means people in poverty are not just short on money, but short on mental space or energy. Overtaxed bandwidth means a greater tendency to forget, less tolerance for frustration, and less self-discipline (Mullainathan and Shafir 2013). But this is not to say that the poor are less self-disciplined than other people: it is to say that *the poor have their self-discipline tested more intensely* than other people. When one can afford so little, so many more things need to be resisted, and self-control is repeatedly needed. Thoughts of scarcity erode sleep, which further taxes one's bandwidth. Noise can tax bandwidth. And any form of skill acquisition takes bandwidth. Parenting, to say the least, is a great user of one's bandwidth. This fits in with the more relational notion of precarity (Trachtenberg 1982; McNay 2008; Lemke 2016). Precarity refers to a situation of ongoing insecurity and deprivation, one that is rooted in unbalanced relationships involving dominance or dependence (Lemke 2016:14). Precarity is important because it can show how "Social oppression not only deprives individuals of the material resources that enable autonomous agency, but it may also deprive them of fundamental emotional resources" (McNay 2008:281). The bandwidth-taxing scarcity explanation is a very useful metaphor, however. As Mullainathan and Shafir (2013) point out, taxed bandwidth explains several things about programs that serve people in poverty, such as why reliable and safe childcare provision does so much more than just free up a segment of time, why missing one class in a training program ends up causing the person to drop out, and why penalties fail to motivate. Such an explanation also suggests that anger management training involving coping strategies should perhaps be integrated into childhood and early adult socialization. After all, many Americans have bandwidth scarcity problems. It helps to remember when working with people in poverty, however, that their bandwidth may be taxed in even more profoundly problematic ways.

An example that relates to parenting can be found in Joshua Phillips's (2016) description of a homeless mother reacting to stress. Phillips (2016:103) notes that the actions of a homeless person can seem grossly irresponsible to an outsider until one finds out what is happening in their lives, as he discovered in the case of a woman named Becky with four young children:

> Becky then left the building and spent the next hour smoking cigarettes at the picnic table out back. The longer she was gone, the more furious I became with her behavior. First, it looked that her children were well-behaved and did not warrant the types of public lashing she had given them so early in the morning. Second, it seemed wholly inappropriate of her to leave her four young children alone in the common area of a homeless shelter while strangers wandered in and out of the shelter all morning. As a staff member, it was my responsibility to confront her about her irresponsible behavior, and as a researcher, it was of interest to figure out why she had engaged in this type of behavior. When the situation had calmed down enough to approach Becky, I walked outside and simply asked, "What do you have going on today?" Distraught and exhausted, Becky quietly remarked, "Everything."

Becky went on to list several issues: two job interviews on the other side of town; a rash on one of the kids, who now needed to see a doctor; the father of another is supposed to see his son on the weekends, but Becky doesn't have any way to get him over there; and a job-related test given in Marion where she can't get to today, so she'll have to wait another month before the test is offered again (Phillips 2016:104). Phillips at that point began to understand where her callous behavior derived: "Becky's day was full, chaotic, and uncertain. To top it off, she was living in a homeless shelter with her four kids, no job, and no idea where she was going to once her 30-day stay was up. Without a car, no employment, little money, and four children, the pressure of her situation was simply overwhelming" (2016:104).

When it comes to child abuse and neglect, race plays a role in several ways: (1) to the extent that racial inequality increases the stress and challenges associated with parenting and poverty; (2) in how Black mothers in particular are viewed in the United States with greater suspicion and criticism, thus eliciting greater surveillance and punishment; and (3) through limited networks and support systems. Some research does find higher odds for Black parents and children being identified with child maltreatment (Ha et al. 2015; Kim et al. 2017), though other research does not find any difference once other variables such as mother's age and marital status are factored in (Maloney et al. 2017). In some cases, racial minority neighborhoods may receive less attention from child protective services, as found in southern rural counties (Smith et al. 2018; Smith et al. 2021). However, large-scale and meta-analytical studies find that experiencing major stress and a lack of social support combined is a major determining factor for predicting child maltreatment (Kotch et al. 1995). To the extent that this combination is more likely for a given racial minority or any other group of people, we might expect to see greater odds of child maltreatment.

Relations of Support

Childcare burden – the amount of childcare a parent has to do entirely on their own – is associated with child maltreatment among low-income families (Ha et al. 2015). Ha et al. (2015) find that the number of childcare providers since a child's first birthday was positively associated with likelihood of physical aggression on the part of the mother, even when taking work status, marital status, and various risk factors into account. The mental health of the child was associated with the likelihood of the mother engaging in physical or psychological aggression and neglectful behaviors like leaving the child at home. Also related to neglectful behaviors is not having someone reliable for emergency care. Here again we see that not having *support* – specifically, relations with people who can provide a cushion against emergency situations and everyday problems – leads to acts of neglect, not just how much, or whether, the mother cares for her child or children. This study also found that reports of psychological aggression toward a child were associated with the cost of childcare relative to income and the number of special child-care arrangements having to be made. Interestingly, the frequency of missing work or school due to childcare problems was *negatively* associated with psychological aggression – missing work but being at home with the child or children did not increase aggression but actually decreased it. These data are based on self-reported behaviors of mothers. But a larger limitation is the lack of comparative data – does the childcare burden have the same effect on mothers at higher income levels? We simply do not know. However, these results do clearly indicate that child maltreatment on the part of low-income families is related to problems in provision of childcare.

It makes sense that not having a support system is going to make leaving the children alone more likely. And aggression is more likely to occur – losing one's temper, for instance – when parenting comes with added stressors. Research by Kotch et al. (1995) supports this, and their data are based on the number of social services maltreat-ment reports for a cohort of newborns, occurring within the first year of life. Specifically, they found an interaction between stressful life events (including financial, employment, parenting, or interpersonal problems) and social support (measured in terms of networks, social contact, and quality of intimate relationships) such that stressors were most likely to impact maltreatment when social support for the mothers was lesser. They note that "the group with the higher level of social support and the lower number of life events had the lowest risk of a child abuse or neglect report in the first year of their infants' lives" (Kotch et al. 1995:1126). Even research looking at the effects of parental substance abuse on neglect has found that the impact is mediated by social support (Lloyd and Kepple 2017). One study found that single mothers with other relatives in the home (especially grandmothers) are at lower risk of child maltreatment, whereas single mother households with unrelated men were at a higher risk (Zerr et al. 2019). Additional life stressors of women who are raising children alone or before they have any work experience can also contribute to the risk of child maltreatment.

As unemployment rates increased during the COVID-19 pan-demic in 2020–1, child abuse became another major concern (Lee et al. 2022). Survey results suggest that a parent's perception of social isolation during the pandemic was associated with greater use of corporal punishment with children, verbal aggression, and physical and emotional neglect (Lee et al. 2022). Job loss and depression were also associated with child maltreatment during the early days of the pandemic (Lawson et al. 2020).

Social isolation certainly plays a role in the perpetuation of violence for people in poverty. But social isolation does not just mean exclusion from other people – it also means exclusion from people who are supportive and people who have the means, and not just the desire, to provide support. Neglect from mainstream institutions filters downward. How people relate to one another is also affected by cultural factors. This is illustrated by research on gender, culture, and violence.

Gender and Coupledom

Causes of father-perpetrated child maltreatment are not as well studied or understood, despite the significant proportion of severe cases of child abuse that are in fact perpetrated by fathers and other men in the household (Stiffman et al. 2002; Guterman and Lee 2005). Research finds that, for physical and sexual abuse in particular, male adults are more likely perpetrators than women, such that the likelihood of child maltreatment is found to increase with female employment but decrease with male employment (Lindo et al. 2018). This is consistent with the fact that the most likely form of child maltreatment perpetrated by mothers is neglect. However, because mothers are considered to be the primary caregiver, child welfare workers tend to focus on the role of the mother, and fail to engage the father (Scourfield 2014). Major correlates for father-inflicted child maltreatment include substance abuse, battering of the mother, unemployment, age of the father, and experiences of childhood abuse (Guterman and Lee 2005).

Intimate partner violence is a strong predictor of child maltreatment. Pregnant women with few resources are particularly vulnerable. Bhandari et al. (2011) suggest that there are multiple reasons why pregnant women will endure abuse – for instance, for the sake of the family and for survival. Physical and social isolation, a lack of resources, and a culture of male dominance all limit the options of rural, low-income pregnant women and affect their coping mechanisms. Their research found that protection of the unborn baby figured most highly for these women, but that did not always mean escaping from the abuse or the ability to make good on a desire to escape. The relationship between the mother and father or adults in the household is itself an important area for future research (Guterman and Lee 2005).

Mothers in poverty are faced with several no-win situations. First, they must confront the fact that inviting a male into the household could lead to danger (personal, relational, and to the children). But, second, they know that being single and unable to call on the father for childcare support increases the odds of child neglect and maltreatment (often at her own hands). More scholarly attention to the role of fathers and men in the household could lead to a decrease in child maltreatment. Rather than disenfranchise fathers, it would make sense to reach out to them, while also recognizing that they need help with healthy relationships as much as – or more than –anyone.

Cultural Factors and Violence

Early experiences of abuse not only lead to trauma and mental illness, but are also themselves associated with early childbearing and child maltreatment (Erdmans and Black 2015; Espinosa et al. 2017). Haugen and Boutros (2014:xi) argue that violence is "*endemic to being poor*," and, moreover, is a major obstacle to escaping poverty. Violence extends beyond monetary costs, leading to PTSD, substance abuse, mental illness, and all manner of adaptations that make it difficult to thrive in a non-violent context (for example, being unable to trust people). Researchers have suggested that service providers who serve the poor or the most disadvantaged need to assist clients with issues with violence (Surratt et al. 2004). Low-income individuals are more vulnerable to violence, and violence is more common when people are more vulnerable. For instance, consider that violence in urban neighborhoods is not always about gangs or drugs. Sometimes it's about protection, territory, and survival. Harding's (2010) book, *Living the Drama*, points out that for many boys in the impoverished neighborhoods of Boston, they had to be tough and protect their fellow neighborhood members at all costs, or else leave themselves as well as their neighborhood vulnerable to crime and victimization. Individuals are subject to their neighborhood's reputation for toughness and retribution, whether they like it or not. If a neighborhood does not maintain a reputation for being tough, then individuals from those neighborhoods are viewed as easier targets, and the neighborhood itself might be subject to invasion and additional crime (drugs, car theft, vandalism). The social context of neighborhoods and violence may in certain cases transfer to violence against children.

Child maltreatment is, unfortunately, fairly common. Across social classes, parents often try their best and fall short for various reasons. Kim et al. (2017) estimate that as many as 37.4% of all children experience a child protective service investigation. This is not just a poverty issue. Yet, child maltreatment is consistently found more often in families in economic distress (National Research Council 1993; Slack et al. 2011; Lloyd and Kepple 2017). Poverty compounds the stress of parenting. Poverty may also render the children more vulnerable (Erdmans and Black 2015). It is worth remembering that, for so many young people, home is not a safe place.

Conclusion

Obligations and Expectations

Social relations are clearly important to family planning and parenting. Relations with intimate partners and potential partners, with one's children, with other family members, with the labor force, with the state, and with the wider community and social networks all profoundly shape parenting outcomes. Let us consider what obligations and expectations affect parenting decisions and outcomes, and how these obligations and expectations are shaped by structural and cultural arrangements. Individuals' expectations for their future certainly affect family planning and the likelihood of becoming an adolescent mother. A lack of love from others can make early childrearing far more desirable to a young person. Levels of social support from kin and community contribute to parents' ability to cope with the demands of parenting, especially if they are also struggling financially. More general social relations matter as well. The efforts of parents in poverty to command the resources their children need from society is an ongoing battle. African American parents have long had to actively and persistently fight for their children's education. Moreover, the conditions of poverty challenge parents' abilities to take care of their children when they must choose between work and family, between keeping the family together and giving their children the necessaries, between trust and risk, between love and stress, and between hope and reality.

Relations are often gendered, with mother–father and mother–partner dynamics predominant. Cultural ideology around parenthood and marriage affect family-related choices. High standards for marriage increase the likelihood of single motherhood. First of all, there is the burden of childbearing that women carry, with the added likelihood of bearing the burden of the majority of childrearing. Fathers can more easily escape the consequences of childbirth – although, at the same time, they face less reward for being involved in a child's life, and substantial risk and expectation in accompaniment. Patriarchal expectations of men and women contribute to distrust and relationship instability. Distrust is a major feature of the lives of men and women in poverty, at least for many low-income families living in metropolitan areas. Marriage is less common among people in poverty compared to the upper and middle classes, but especially in cities. Levine (2013) suggests that is not the meaning of marriage that differs so much between classes, but the opportunities associated with it. Both men and women in relationships find it difficult to balance the expectations for them as parents and their economic realities.

Furthermore, there is not much in the way of sources for self-esteem, or any reason to walk the line, for young people who do not see bright futures for themselves. A desire for meaning and purpose makes becoming a parent attractive to many young people. These are also the very individuals most likely to be extremely vulnerable regarding education, employment, and intimacy.

Romantic or domestic relations can be either supportive or extraordinarily draining. This is true in the financial sense and in the emotional sense. Sometimes, the balance between these two possibilities shifts regularly over time, thus leading to general uncertainty. Sometimes, such a relationship can be supportive in some ways, draining in others. This variation has been found important for explaining low-income mothers' decisions about potential sexual or domestic partners in a variety of ways (Edin and Lein 1997; Edin and Kefalas [2005] 2011; Levine 2013). Research has also suggested that decisions are affected by the perception of the "market" supply of potential partners. Some individuals may be willing to pay a high price to have a domestic partner, even – or especially – if one also has children. For many people, poor and nonpoor, the importance of companionship is such that even harmful relationships are viewed as better than nothing.

One's employment and income support options are also important relational matters that structure unwinnable choices for raising a family in poverty. As Edin and Lein (1997:5) describe it, the dilemma for single mothers is that they must not only ensure "their children are sheltered, fed, and clothed, they must also see that they are supervised, educated, disciplined, and loved," and these goals conflict. Moreover, mothers:

had to choose between a welfare system that paid far too little to provide for their basic needs and a labor market that offered them little more than they could have gotten by staying home ... mothers who choose work over welfare often had to trust their family's medical care to county hospital emergency rooms and their children's upbringing to the streets. (Edin and Lein 1997:5)

Research has even found that additional income has a beneficial effect on the mental health of children in a household (Costello et al. 2016; Akee et al. 2018).

Finally, relations with the state matter as well in terms of what people can expect out of life. We should look to encourage relations characterized by options and opportunity versus dependency and distrust. Social policies affect the likelihood of a single mother household living in poverty, even when controlling for individual characteristics of the mother (Brady and Burroway 2012). Statisitical modeling shows that expansive and universal welfare states substantially reduce the poverty rate among single mothers (Brady and Burroway 2012). Moreover, there is no evidence that more conservative welfare-stingy policies discourage teen or unwed birth – in fact, quite the opposite. England saw a quadrupling of out-of-wedlock births under the Conservative Thatcher administration (Luker 1996). Teen or single motherhood may encumber a number of different disadvantages, but many current disadvantages can be addressed through social policy that would in fact improve family life for many. Social policy, specifically as relates to employment, childcare, and education, is a central issue.

Players and Power

Who are the relevant players in affecting familial outcomes? Certainly, other family members on both parents' sides matter, as do relations with the state and community. The number one factor for child neglect involves the resources individuals have to support the raising of children. Mothers have some power relative to fathers because the mother typically controls access to the child. Importantly, non-married women have more power relative to intimate partners than they would have if married – at least, that is their perception. It is probably correct, since many romantic partners do not have assets or income for which to sue. When it comes to child support arrangements, there is little incentive for mothers to sue for it, though fathers fear it. Fathers prefer to provide informally, as they can. The state decides whether and how much to assist single mothers. What this has meant in many cases is that single mothers are often dependent on family/kin to help out. Reciprocity is expected. This can trap a mother into a never-ending struggle to keep her head above water, never quite able to find a foothold in security.

In governing women's bodies, the state shapes reproductive options. In 2022, the US Supreme Court overturned the *Roe* v. *Wade* court precedent, thus allowing states to enact their own laws restricting abortion and contraception. Women in poverty are more likely to seek an abortion than the nonpoor, though there is not a large difference. The Guttmacher Institute (2022b) reports that 49 percent of abortion patients live below the federal poverty line, and 59 percent are women who already have children. Women in poverty are also more likely to say they are anti-abortion. Yet, when a woman already has children she is having a hard time taking care of, having another child is not something she can easily afford. A *New York Times* article (Williamson 2022) reported on a woman's inability to get an abortion under Texas's enacted laws against the procedure. T., as she is called in the article, was rejected at a clinic. She had not been told about medication abortion. Distraught, she was directed by an anti-abortion activist ("sidewalk counselor") to an anti-abortion pregnancy resource center, which assisted her by finding a place that helps pregnant mothers with bills and provides job training for pregnant women who already have children. The program helps for only up to a year. The article quotes T.:

> "The pressure is really on," T. said on a Thursday, four days after she gave birth to Cason. "I have one year to rebuild my life while my body heals, and four kids to take care of at the same time. It's scary. I try not to think about what will happen when I leave the program. I know I can be a great mom, it's just, can I provide for my children, keep the kids healthy and safe and have a roof over our head, and food?"

As Williamson points out, Texas has one of the harshest conditions for mothers, with one of the highest maternal mortality rates in the nation. Prenatal care can be difficult to access for low-income women given the state decision to opt out of Medicaid expansion. For many women in poverty, there is no real choice between abortion and having a(nother) child:

> For the past half-century, the US has fought over abortion in rhetorical terms that, upon scrutiny, are hollow. We speak of "choice" and "life"

as if they reflect women's actual experiences when opting for or against having an abortion. To examine the role poverty plays in abortion and mothering decisions is to give the lie to this framing of our discourse. What we learn from those who seek abortions is that the decision to terminate a pregnancy is not so much a choice as a response to the ways in which poverty inscribes itself onto our bodies. (Oberman et al. 2018:670)

Whatever one's position on abortion, it is clear that the relations of women in poverty to their health providers and family members are shaped by government policy at the state and federal levels in ways that undermine their health and the well-being of their family. As T. is quoted as saying: "Women, all we really have is our dignity and our voices . . . And you're taking them away" (Williamson 2022).

Family law also plays a role in shaping family outcomes for people in poverty, affecting the rules of the game for child maltreatment, foster care, custody and visitation, escaping domestic abuse, being accused of domestic abuse, and child support. Family law thus structures our relations to family, defining who is family, and what family should look like. Family separation is a major source of trauma and despair among people in poverty. Family separation happens as a result of a parent's inability to care for their children, often due to lack of income or mental illness; the incarceration of a parent; the military service of a parent; the deportation of an unauthorized immigrant parent; guest worker programs that allow parents to migrate, but not bring or visit their children; and even through a failure to protect mothers from domestic violence. Sometimes, family separation is unavoidable or for the best, as in extreme cases of child abuse and neglect. However, foster care brings its own trauma and challenges. Sometimes, the abuser you know is better than the one you don't know.

Being a good parent is not without major costs itself, often posing difficult dilemmas. As Edin and Lein (1997) discovered, mothers in poverty often had to hustle, adopting risky strategies to take care of their children adequately and keep child welfare investigators from knocking on their door. Since neither welfare nor work provides enough income to live on, single mothers had to engage in other "income-generating strategies" for economic survival. They struggled to be good mothers to their children, and faced tough choices. They believed that good mothers treat their children once in a while, and so some would forgo necessities in order to afford the occasional treat – typically a movie rental, a cable TV subscription, a trip to a cheap restaurant, new clothes for the first day of school, or name-brand sneakers. Edin and Lein point out that these "luxuries" often serve additional purposes as well, such as keeping the kids off the street and away from crime. Yet many families "regularly went without items that virtually every American would consider necessities" (Edin and Lein 1997:47). One mother indicated she had to keep her children home from school on really cold days because she didn't have sufficiently warm clothes for them (Edin and Lein 1997). Another mother indicated that she feared if she did not purchase some name-brand clothing for her son, he might be lured into selling drugs. As a result, she takes on side jobs to afford these extras. One mother said that to buy shoes for her child, she ate only one meal a day for a month. Sometimes, the choices these mothers made appeared irrational at first. For example, maintaining a telephone might be considered more important than a few meals: "some mothers from our sample who had children with asthma saw the lack of a phone as potentially life threatening and considered a few missed meals at the end of the month less serious" (Edin and Lein 1997:57). Maintaining a telephone was often necessary to access job prospects, such as getting a call for an interview, and when mothers had to leave their children home while they worked, it could be used to reach them in an emergency (Edin and Lein 1997). It is worth suspending judgment when it comes to scrutinizing the parenting of people in poverty until one knows a little more about the situation.

Other relations matter immensely for family planning and parenting, including relations with employers, with social services, and with the institution of education through relationships with teachers and peers. Many researchers of poverty have called for education programs to transition young people into the workforce; better healthcare; legal aid to assist with a number of issues commonly faced by people in poverty, such as housing and family conflict; better housing options; and improvements in social services to better accommodate and inform families poised for economic mobility (McNichol and Springer 2004; Barnes 2008). Lack of opportunity is also a central condition of poverty and violence. Hence William Julius Wilson's (1987) argument for the creation of national performance standards for public schools and federal support for low-income schools so that high school graduates will be better equipped to find a high-skilled job or continue their training. Improving family support systems – such as childcare, parental leave, and support for single mothers – would also alleviate many employment problems. We also need an adequate supply of employment that provides decent earnings.

The relationship between employer and employee is a social relation of high importance for understanding poverty and is discussed in Chapter 6, "Opportunity and Personal Autonomy."

The education system, while unable to solve all the problems of inequality that persist in society, is nonetheless one of the major forces in the lives of people in poverty. Although teen parenthood may not be the great problem we once thought it, life chances remain better for young men and women who put off childrearing until their twenties or thirties. Rather than just focusing on preventing pregnancy, however, we should provide youth with visible and concrete life opportunities. For Erdmans and Black (2015), the best teen pregnancy prevention program is a good educational system. Their research suggests that education and teen pregnancy are intricately related – from residential dislocation and unresponsive schools that push out failing students, to the use of rigid and exclusionary policies, to a lack of adequate staff or resources among low-income community schools, including undertrained counselors and an inability to meet the needs of ESL students and other challenged youth. Such conditions make high school drop-out more likely, and pregnancy a more appealing option (Feldman et al. 2017).

Overall, institutions such as education, the labor market, the law, the military, and the state more generally are critical touchstones for understanding family and poverty. Gender relations also play an important role in the options, opportunities, and cultural contexts for family-related decisions. Culturally available meanings of motherhood and fatherhood combine with structural constraints to shape the ways in which so many children in poverty grow up. Many parents in poverty wrestle with the choices they have to make between working more and being with their children, between keeping the family together and giving their children the necessities, between trusting potential intimate partners and the considerable risk involved in giving such trust, between expressing love and coping with nonstop stress, and between maintaining hope for the future and living the ongoing reality of never enough.

4

Culture

Once, while teaching a class the different explanations for poverty, I explained the culture of poverty explanation as the notion that people in poverty adapt to their circumstances in ways that help them cope but that do not help them in other social contexts. A student haltingly raised her hand. "Isn't that the case for all of us?" she asked. Well, she had me there! Of course, the issue is that the culture of poverty thesis, as it became known, was rather more than that.

Concisely put, the culture of poverty thesis is the claim that there is a subculture among the poor that serves to reinforce their position in society. Although the term "culture of poverty" is attributed to Oscar Lewis, showing up in the title of his 1959 book *Five Families: Mexican Case Studies in the Culture of Poverty*, the thesis is related to a larger set of claims about, and approaches to, poverty that go far beyond (and precede) Lewis's work and intentions. Many scholars have considered the idea that people in poverty develop certain behaviors and values that may help them adapt to everyday situations while simultaneously cementing their lower position in society. The issue is whether this amounts to a subculture that can be generalized across groups or used to explain poverty. In short, we can appreciate how all people adapt to their circumstances in ways that tend to keep them in those very circumstances. However, the jump to theorizing a single culture, or even a set of behaviors and values, that explains poverty not only is flawed, but actually leads to the misunderstanding of poverty.

The culture of poverty thesis is used by many social scientists, government officials, teachers, social workers, and other gatekeepers. An online search for "culture of poverty" will reveal it in the work of social scientists working in developing countries, in the early education literature, and, to a lesser extent, in the field of psychology and development (Long 2006; Vu and Austin 2007). Ruby Payne's (1995) work on "the hidden rules" of people in poverty continues to be an influential guide in public education training of administrators and teachers. As an explanation for poverty, culture has become compelling and persistent. Many people continue to view the poor as self-defeating or irresponsible. But even variations of culture of poverty ideas that are intended to avoid victim-blaming can be problematic because of overgeneralization and a failure to understand how the behaviors and ideas of people in poverty develop in complex ways out of sets of circumstances. Many such applications are well meant, and perhaps even helpful in some ways, for developing a better understanding of people in poverty. But if not properly qualified and contextualized, use of culture of poverty notions exacerbates a negative and mistaken view of the poor. In this chapter, I consider "culture of poverty" in historical context and alongside similar ideas in sociology and US policy. After addressing some of the main critiques of culture of poverty, I'll discuss more contemporary work on culture and poverty.

Lewis describes the concept of a culture of poverty more extensively in his book, *La Vida: A Puerto Rican Family in the Culture of Poverty – San Juan and New York* (Lewis 1965). He identifies four main aspects of the culture of poverty:

1 Lack of participation and integration in larger society. This can involve a critical attitude toward major institutions. Although those in poverty may claim middle-class values, Lewis warns that does not mean they actually live by them.
2 A low level of organization beyond the family in the community.
3 Absence of a protected childhood, the prevalence of free unions, female-centered families, authoritarianism, and lack of privacy.
4 Individual feelings of marginality, helplessness, dependence, and inferiority.

Although questionnaires were filled out by 100 families in San Juan and New York City, Lewis focuses on one family in particular – the Ríos family. Lewis does not indicate what proportion of the questionnaires fit these four characteristics, nor does he provide any analysis at all of the questionnaire data. Instead, portions of field notes are edited into a narrative and biographies of members of the family. These chapters are extremely detailed, but there is no attempt to analyze these data or compare with the other data. After describing the Ríos family in what seems to be a picture of extreme pathology, describing the women as violent and promiscuous, men as dependent, and both men and women as lacking control over desires and emotions, Lewis then claims the Ríos family is by no means an extreme example because they are not addicts or career criminals. He then lauds their strength and their "own sense of dignity." Lewis's contradictory and confusing depiction of Puerto Ricans in poverty does more to stereotype and obscure the processes by which the study participants live in poverty than it does to explain the processes by which people adapt to their circumstances.

Furthermore, if we examine the four characteristics of a culture of poverty, these appear as much structural as cultural. The lack of participation in larger society, as Lewis describes it in some places, is not so different from the notion of social exclusion, except the culture of poverty version tends to focus on the individual and the social exclusionist version places the onus on society. Second, reference to a low level of organization certainly evokes the notion of social disorganization that became central to understandings of urban poverty in the early twentieth century, and this notion remains a critical approach in criminology. But whether "level of organization" should be viewed as culture or structure is a matter of quite lengthy debate among academics. Number 3, especially absence of a protected childhood and a lack of privacy, again describes realities that are imposed upon people in poverty. They may shape culture, but they are not conditions desired by the people experiencing them. Finally, individual feelings of marginality, inferiority, dependence – these traits are certainly not generalizable to people in poverty, and may or may not be relevant in a given scenario. Lewis would probably agree with most if not all of these assessments, but because his analysis was not very clear about these realities, it made it easier to misuse his work.

Indeed, many social scientists expressed skepticism toward Lewis's work (Valentine 1968; Leacock 1971). They feared it would encourage the tendency to overgeneralize and to assume all the poor held the same values and acted similarly. There was concern that culture of poverty ideas polarized differences between the poor and nonpoor, such that researchers would focus on the differences between classes, as opposed to seeing the similarities and overlap. And reservations were expressed about the tendency of the culture of poverty thesis to ignore variation not only among the poor but even in the behavior and experience of an individual (Valentine 1968; Leacock 1971). In usage, "culture of poverty" was often empirically blind (Leacock

1971). For instance, Leacock notes that the "irony is that while teachers attend workshops to learn the reasons for the seeming apathy of ghetto children, black parents are beginning to beat down the doors of the schools to gain some say in the educational process" (Leacock 1971:189). Front-line workers and other non-social scientists also saw problems with the culture of poverty thesis. Patterson (1981:121) cites a social worker named Elizabeth Wickenden who said that, though there are ways in which poverty discourages and isolates people, it is dangerous to suggest that such qualities are intrinsic to the poor, rather than a result of the social conditions they encounter. Others questioned whether the culture of poverty was supposed to be geographic, personal or familial culture (Patterson 1981:121). They pointed to evidence that the poor wanted work and that they were realistic, not apathetic.

Nonetheless, several stereotypes derived from culture of poverty explanations stuck with the public as a result of scholars such as Charles Murray and George Gilder, who were not so cautious in their generalizations. In *Losing Ground*, Murray (1984) argued that the war on poverty exacerbated the situation of the poor, inviting them to remain dependent and squashing any ambition. Others agreed that there is a culture of poverty, it is highly problematic, it is worsened by the welfare state, and that the poor ultimately are hindered by their own behaviors. Gilder (1981:12; cited by O'Connor 2001:226) wrote that poverty "is less a state of income than a state of mind . . . the government dole blights most of the people who come to depend on it." Both Charles Murray and George Gilder were known to be major influences on the presidency of Ronald Reagan (O'Connor 2001). Many sociologists who take issue with culture of poverty approaches see this view as the inevitable outcome of the culture of poverty thesis, especially as it spoke so well to middle-class fear and desire – and political expediency.

Certainly, the notion that poverty is caused in part or on the whole by irresponsibility and wrong choices of individuals is widespread among the middle class (Sweeney 2012). Such ideas would no doubt exist without" culture of poverty" as a coined term, but they would not have the same veneer of academic credibility. For instance, Ladson-Billings (2006) discusses how novice schoolteachers use the word "culture" loosely to refer to the problems of students they find different than themselves. Culture of poverty thus lives on, in both hidden and open forms.

Historical Context

The historical importance of the culture of poverty thesis in the evolution of our thinking about poverty in the USA can hardly be overstated. Culture of poverty has ties to several different sociological avenues, and intersects with early scholarship on crime, juvenile delinquency, nation-building, and racial inequality in the United States. Late-nineteenth- into early-twentieth-century scholarship on poverty recognized diversity and heterogeneity in terms of culture and experiences of the impoverished (W. E. B. Du Bois in the USA; Charles Booth in the UK). This coincided with the Progressive Era in the United States, when many activists and reformers organized to improve social conditions for some of the most vulnerable members of the society. By the mid twentieth century, however, much of the scholarly and political interest in poverty focused on deviance, and favored the broad notion of *social disorganization* as the main explanation. Social disorganization refers to the lack of neighborhood-level mechanisms of social control and/or integration, particularly the means whereby group-level needs and desires are met, such as reducing crime or enforcing commonly held values (Barnett and Mencken 2002; Lee et al. 2003). Social disorganization is often thought to be a structural feature of a neighborhood in that it is most often measured through the amount of population turnover and heterogeneity – basic organizational features. However, the theory has cultural implications in its emphasis on norms and values.

Early American social scientists such as Du Bois ([1899] 1967), Jane Addams (1910), and Chicago School theorists Robert Park, Ernest Burgess, and Roderick Mckenzie (1925) analyzed the social organization of disadvantaged communities. *The City* (Park, Burgess, and Mckenzie 1915), as a collection of works, helped launch the Chicago School's approach to understanding urban life. These scholars advocated for immersion in the social worlds of the city in order to better understand social problems and social change. Both structural and cultural elements were described as part of the organization – and, hence, disorganization – of impoverished parts of the city. The disorganization in city slums or ethnic enclaves was viewed as a problem to be solved or a stage in the process of assimilating to American urban life (Wirth 1928). Thus, the Chicago School approach emphasized the internal dysfunction of poor neighborhoods, rather than the external factors of wider social functioning such as industrial capitalism, politics, and exclusion.

Following them, Shaw and McKay (1969) developed the theory of social disorganization in their study of high-crime urban communities. For Addams and fellow Hull House investigators, disorganization referred to the lack of political and social organization (Lengermann and Niebrugge-Brantley 2002). Many disadvantaged neighborhoods lacked access to the middle- and upper-class institutions that were often highly organized and effective, such as schools, law and security, homeowners' associations, clubs, and so on. They lacked the kinds of group networks that would facilitate organized demands for better resources and living conditions from local government. Shaw and colleagues focused rather more on the internal conditions from a social control perspective. The implications of this slight difference in approach, however, were profound.

The settlement movement, associated foremost with Jane Addams, used social science as a tool to improve conditions in urban neighborhoods in the early twentieth century. They wanted to distinguish their work from charity work, which they interpreted as attacking symptoms not causes (O'Connor 2001). Causes were identified as low wages, the exploitative factory system, and the lack of political and social organization in working-class neighborhoods. They couched their work not as "helping the poor," but as addressing issues of work, community, and ethnic relations. Their main tool was the settlement house – like Hull House – which provided a place for people in a disadvantaged neighborhood to access resources, arts, culture, and education. But, more importantly, the settlement house operated as a means to connect people. Lengermann and Niebrugge-Brantley (2002) interpret social disorganization as used by settlement sociologists to mean disconnection from each other and between social classes. The settlement sociologists viewed this as a responsibility of, and dependent on the actions of, the upper classes as much as of the poor. Hence, we see evidence of a relational sociology applied to understanding poverty as early as the second decade of the twentieth century.

And even earlier: in *The Philadelphia Negro*, Du Bois ([1899] 1967) described his study of the African American community living in Philadelphia in 1896–7. Like the settlement sociologists, Du Bois did not frame this study as about poverty per se, but it is one of the earliest examples of an empirically thorough examination of the lives of people in poverty. Social disorganization for Du Bois refers to a situation in which individuals become disconnected from important institutions such as work and family. He identified forced transnational migration and later rural-to-urban migration as major producers

of social disorganization among African Americans. The displacement of these migrations disrupted the institutions and norms that
previously structured daily life. The influential Chicago School of
sociology later incorporated these issues in their analysis of city slums
without acknowledging Du Bois. Du Bois views social organization
as key to the well-being of a population, and the church – while
not ideal – serves this role in the African American community in
a promising way. Unfortunately, at the time, his work was either
entirely ignored, or praised for its honest portrayal of the faults of
Black people without recognizing the political economic factors that
Du Bois emphasized (O'Connor 2001; Morris 2015).

As may be evident by now, early approaches to the issue of
lower-class life and values often focused on the Black poor. This
approach has implications for how American researchers thought
about poverty and the culture of lower-class communities (as argued
by Valentine 1968; for examples, see Frazier 1950; Moynihan
[1965] 1967; Murray 1984). In fact, the culture of poverty thesis
became, for some, code or veil for *the race problem* – that is, African
Americans as a population of political concern due to their poverty
and their potential for resistance. Culture of poverty is also used
explicitly to describe the White poor experience – specifically the
isolated, rural White poor (e.g., Pilisuk and Pilisuk 1971). However,
early scholarship on values and lifestyles among the lower classes
often focused on African Americans, particularly the matriarchal,
disorganized family structure in Black communities. Some scholars
were eager to change the discourse about biological inferiority by
pointing to "social" reasons for Black disadvantage. In this context,
scholars including Frazier and Myrdal produced their influential
works on African American poverty, contributing to the rise of
such ideas as the vicious circle, the Black matriarch pathology, and
disorganization.

E. Franklin Frazier (1937) identified "the Negro matriarch," later
adopted by prominent race and poverty scholars (Myrdal 1944;
Moynihan [1965] 1967), as a feature of Black families. The matriarch was considered an effect of Black male joblessness and a legacy
of conditions imposed by White American enslavers. Frazier also
claims that social and familial disorganization occurred with migration to urban areas, where men faced racial discrimination in the
workforce and children born to an unstable family then had problems
assimilating with modern culture. Scholars could have viewed the
strong maternal role as adaptive and beneficial. But because it devi-
ated from the White middle-class model, many scholars portrayed it

as evidence of disorganization. The Black family model thus became pathologized.

Gunnar Myrdal's *An American Dilemma* (1944) furthered this double-view of Black lower-class culture as about both deviance within and racism without (O'Connor 2001:94). Racism prevented assimilation. Lack of assimilation maintained Black cultural deviance, which further disadvantaged the Black lower class and fed White racism. The "vicious circle," as he called it, became a staple of social science. Historians and race scholars argue that the vicious circle was often used as a convenient explanation for the troubling behavior of young, Black individuals, signaling a failure to grapple with the complexity of the lives of the Black poor (see Dickeman 1971; Leacock 1971; O'Connor 2001; Raz 2013).

In the field of criminology, Shaw and McKay (1969) are well known for the notion of social disorganization as a major feature of urban neighborhoods with high crime. They viewed social disorganization as a breakdown in neighborhood structure and concomitant lack of attachment to traditional mores, leading to anomie and marginality (Bursik 1988; Lee et al. 2003; Marwell and Morrissey 2020). This notion was very similar to the Chicago School ideas, especially the focus on the ability of people to regulate themselves at the neighborhood level (Bursik 1988). Such regulation would entail formal or informal cooperation among neighbors that instilled a sense of the permissible and impermissible across residents – basically social control. One of their primary insights was that weak networks, owing to population turnover and the heterogeneity that formed in inner-city areas, directly induced social disorganization (Bursik 1988). This is considered more of a structural than a cultural theory, but it has been developed in ways similar to culture of poverty approaches. Subsequent social disorganization researchers departed from the original Shaw and McKay model, confusing cause and effect or correlation and operationalization (Bursik 1988). For instance, using crime rates as indicators of social disorganization confuses the cause, social disorganization, with the hypothetical outcome, crime. Scholars began to use low socio-economic status and minority demographics as proxies for social disorganization, muddling the issue further (Bursik 1988).

Deviance-focused approaches to low-income communities became dominant in scholarship and the popular cultural narrative throughout the twentieth century. Reliance on subculture explanations for poverty and crime – which often boiled down to the notion that deviance causes more deviance – proliferated in the second half of the twentieth century. The focus on structural causes for the deviance and various cultural outcomes that were so carefully detailed by prior scholars were often lost in the shuffle from theory to practice. Halpern (1995) provides an extensive examination of the use of social disorganization theory by activists and reformers who wanted to improve the inner city, including the programs operated through the Office of Equal Opportunity. Halpern argues that proponents of social disorganization theory often encouraged physical improvement as part of general community improvement because they thought it would enhance residents' sense of control over their lives. He notes that, in such cases, they rarely pressed for improved city services. Rather, solutions assumed that the residents were responsible for the conditions of their own neighborhood, and factors such as landlord neglect and redlining were not addressed (Halpern 1995). By World War I, Progressive reformers were becoming disillusioned and apathetic. Failing to see how extreme resource scarcity makes it difficult to volunteer time and trust for some abstract benefit, some reformers concluded that the poor just did not care (Halpern 1995:43).

From the 1960s until the mid-1970s, a new culture of poverty approach became popular in the poverty remediation work at the sub-neighborhood level. The concept of "cultural deprivation" was used to explain and address the effects of poverty, and shaped the discourse of mental health and child development (Raz 2013). Raz argued that "theories of deprivation as developed by psychiatrists and psychologists became the leading framework by which to evaluate the lives, needs, and abilities of low-income children and adults of color" (2013:5). By "culture," these scholars and experts often meant external stimuli of various kinds that were thought to be crucial for development, and sensory deprivation research was used to justify many claims without actually illustrating direct deprivation in the lives of poor children (Raz 2013). As Drucker (1971) pointed out, much of the interpretation of class or race differences in intelligence or development among children did not actually reflect difference in their ability to abstract or conceptualize. For instance, presented with an apple and a peach, the lower-class child might comment on them both being round, or both being good to eat, whereas the middle-class child might say that they are both fruits. This was interpreted as evidence that the lower-class child operates primarily on the basis of sensory features of the world, whereas the middle-class child is more "symbolic" in thought processes (Drucker 1971:42). Drucker argued that such results do not reflect difference in level of abstracting or conceptualizing, but are arbitrary, with many possible interpretations.

Critics also saw cultural deprivation theory as devaluing the culture and family life of largely non-White groups (Dickeman 1971; Wax 1971; Raz 2013). Applications of maternal deprivation depended on the race and class of the family. For instance, Raz (2013) writes that, whereas low-income and racial minority children were assumed to benefit from being separated from mothers and put in daycare programs, middle-class children were viewed as better off at home with the mother. At the time, this notion of cultural deprivation was considered an improvement over biological explanations for the troubles of racial minorities (Raz 2013). Cultural deprivation is now generally recognized as highly problematic, and is no longer accepted as a term in mental health and public policy. But culture of poverty in its various forms did not disappear forever.

For instance, if culture of poverty is taken to refer to social pathologies of communities in poverty, then William Julius Wilson in 1987 turned our attention again to the culture of the Black poor. This time, however, urban poverty was explained in terms of externally produced and concentrated disadvantage. Wilson identified the effect as the creation of an "underclass." The underclass thesis, as it became known, is the argument that joblessness under deindustrialization in the inner city, combined with middle-class flight, produced social isolation that compounded social pathologies of single mother households, welfare dependency, and other problems of poor people of color. *The Truly Disadvantaged* (Wilson 1987) was very influential on the study of urban concerns and race, especially the idea that the concentration of poverty had devastating consequences as residents became increasingly isolated from job networks, role models, influential institutions, and mainstream behaviors. *The Truly Disadvantaged* heralded a new wave of research on neighborhood effects, including social capital and networks. This has been highly influential on policy as well, especially in terms of advocating mixed-income housing and the placement of people in more advantaged neighborhoods.

Alternative explanations and critiques of the underclass thesis were quickly forthcoming (Jencks and Peterson 1991; Massey and Denton 1993; Wacquant 2008; Gans 2010; Theodore 2010). Notably, some scholars viewed the underclass thesis as another manifestation of culture of poverty, with similar problems, including the erasure of diversity among the urban poor (Jencks and Peterson 1991; Jargowsky 1996). Gans (2010) also argues that many of the so-called effects of concentrated poverty are better explained by the fact that the households themselves are in extreme poverty, rather than by the concentration of poverty. Perhaps in response to some critiques, Wilson's 1996 book, *When Work Disappears*, emphasizes structural factors – namely, the causes of high rates of unemployment in the inner city. He locates the problem in a global economy jobs shrinkage that polarizes wages for low-skilled and high-skilled workers. Crime, welfare dependence, family dissolution, and social disorganization continue to be viewed as the negative side effects of concentrated unemployment, but his policy proposals focus not on the behavior of the poor, but on what he sees as ultimately responsible for their predicament, such as failing schools, poor returns on low-wage work, lack of childcare. Therefore, while Wilson's underclass thesis was critiqued as stigmatizing the inner-city poor, he did take pains to refocus attention on the structural causes of their disadvantage. Yet, O'Connor (2001) surmises that the notion of Black lower-class culture was so entrenched in mainstream scholarly understanding that it simply lived on despite obvious faults. Black lower-class culture was viewed as both adaptive and pathological, a product of internal and external forces, transitional, yet seemingly permanent (O'Connor 2001:94).

Notions of lower-class or minority communities as disorganized or dysfunctional have been a major feature of the social science of poverty for a long time. However, the degrees to which this dysfunction is viewed as structurally induced, culturally perpetuated, and relevant for alleviating poverty have varied. Du Bois, for instance, viewed the dysfunctions of Black communities in Philadelphia as structurally induced, an effect of historical disadvantage. Lewis recognized structural factors, but emphasized the cultural factors as perpetuating poverty.

This is a far cry from the previous chapter's assessment of parenting. The culture of poverty thesis fails to acknowledge the choices people in poverty face. Considering social relations first reveals how that which looks like undesirable behavior to outsiders, such as early childrearing or harsh parenting, is not explainable by a culture of poverty. Rather, such behavior is a more complex reaction to the sets of conditions people face, structural and cultural, formed by and forming their relations to other people and institutions. Single mothers do not remain single because that is just the thing to do as learned from their community. In-depth research demonstrates that, in fact, many single mothers in poverty in the study would like to get married, if circumstances differed. Although there is a cultural component to their singleness, it is certainly not best explained by the culture of poverty thesis.

The larger problem, however, is the tendency of audiences to focus on the cultural dysfunctions described by scholars such as Lewis, Frazier, and Myrdal. Descriptions of cultural dysfunctions have been taken by policymakers and other elites as indication of the inferiority of people in poverty, used to identify their behavior as being in need of change, and to dismiss the ability of people in poverty to act as their own advocates. In the United States, race is never too distant from people's perceptions of poverty. In no place is this clearer than the realm of politics and social policy.

Culture of Poverty and Policy

In 1964, President Lyndon B. Johnson declared war on poverty. The US War on Poverty subsequently involved the largest concerted effort in American history to address the lack of economic opportunity and social inclusion for people in poverty. The poverty rate cited at the time was an astounding 19 percent. Media representations of people living in a culture of poverty enflamed the public's concerns. And the Civil Rights movement took the White establishment to task for unemployment, poverty, and job discrimination (Halpern 1995). Michael Harrington's 1962 book *The Other America*, widely read, acclaimed, and believed to have helped inspire President Johnson's War on Poverty, argued that poverty is a persisting blight deserving of our attention. As a political scientist and activist, Harrington used the notion of a culture of poverty to reveal the desperate life circumstances of the forgotten and neglected people at the bottom of American society. A complex and sometimes contradictory notion of poverty developed as part of the vision for the War on Poverty and its many manifestations in policy and practice. This notion began with the recognition that economic opportunity was the problem, but focused on individual and neighborhood processes as the solution (Halpern 1995). Poverty was viewed as a pathology – like a sickness of the community or the individual – even as it was recognized as structurally induced. Nonetheless, the federal position of the 1960s – that poverty is a problem, that it is a product of the workings of society, that it can and should be eradicated, and that the federal government will devote millions of dollars to this objective – stands as a remarkable political moment.

Though a rise in the militancy of Black urbanites may have incentivized an expansion of social programs in the 1960s, Johnson lost little time upon assuming the presidency in announcing the War on Poverty. In 1966, concerns raised about pockets of deep rural poverty led Johnson to charge a committee to investigate. In 1967, the President's National Advisory Commission on Rural Poverty released their report, titled *The People Left Behind*. The Commission found that rural poverty was worse than urban poverty, and that the rural poor were almost completely overlooked by federal authorities. In this report, they note that the rural poor experience health problems such as infant mortality at higher rates, and that unemployment and underemployment remain intractable issues given rural economic realities. Over time, however, attention was redirected toward inner-city Black poverty. "The Moynihan Report" was, in at least a small way, responsible for this shift (Pilisuk and Pilisuk 1971). "The Moynihan Report" (Moynihan [1965] 1967) brought public attention to the notion that underclass family life – in this case, "Negro American" family life – should be targeted for intervention. Perhaps precisely because of the intractability of employment issues in rural areas, in addition to concerns about urban unrest, little attention was given to rural areas (where almost 40 percent of the poor lived in 1965) or the south-to-north migration that continued to add pressure to the urban context (Patterson 1981).

President Johnson's "war" was waged with the passing of the Economic Opportunity Act (EOA) of 1964, which involved the formation of the Office of Economic Opportunity (OEO) to oversee local community action agencies that would address poverty and racial inequality. Many of the programs created during this time – such as Medicare, Medicaid, Job Corps, HeadStart, and VISTA – remain in place in the 2020s. There were and are many criticisms of the War on Poverty (which is used synonymously with the EOA of 1964) from both the left and the right. It seems, however, undeniable that the programs created through the OEO lifted millions of people out of poverty.

Yet the War on Poverty did not end poverty. Researchers provide a number of different explanations for why the OEO programs did not fully succeed. Patterson suggests in his historical review that, despite officials' realizations that structural forces such as technology, low wages, and racial discrimination prevented many willing workers from getting out of poverty, they "drew back from these facts and placed their faith in extending opportunity . . . [their programs] never seriously considered giving poor people what many of them needed most: jobs and income maintenance" (Patterson 1981:136). Similarly, O'Connor (2001) points out that community action programs often used ideas of cultural deprivation and other conventional ideas of the poor, focusing more on disorganization and inadequate social services than on structural inequality.

Ultimately, it seems, there was some conflict of interest – what O'Connor refers to as "the question of whether community action could happen without a challenge to authority" (O'Connor 2001:136). Indeed, Patterson (1981) writes that there were multiple anti-OEO parties, including especially state and local politicians, that were inherently antagonistic to the sorts of community action supported by OEO. One of the central principles of OEO was this concept of maximum feasible participation by the poor. Patterson suggests this was not supposed to lead to a challenging of local authorities, though arguably some local authorities were the problem. The actions of local authorities often reinforce the disadvantage of people in poverty, including allocation of funding, in laws and policies that criminalize poverty, and efforts to support and recruit the middle class while discouraging settlement of people with less money (Chablani 2016; Geraghty 2016; Edelman 2019; Herring 2019). In addition, maximum feasible participation was difficult to define, and difficult to put into practice. Some of the poorest of the poor, Patterson notes, were not prepared to participate; some were unattached transients; and some were divided by ethnicity and race. The main participants in and leaders of community action tended to be the upwardly mobile and/or near-poor. The community action programs were a "safe and inexpensive alternative to massive commitment of federal funds" (Patterson 1981:150). Patterson suggests that, in fact, community action is inherently limited in its ability to transform wider economic and structural factors. I would add to this the more proximate social relations that people in poverty face.

The mixed success of the War on Poverty was thus due to a number of factors. Poverty proved to be more difficult to eliminate than expected. The programs were a mixed bag – at times misinformed, underresourced, or undermined by other social elements, and in other regards fairly successful. Some of our most important contemporary social programs were developed under the OEO and the War on Poverty, such as the educational and economic advancing programs HeadStart and Job Corps. But its limited success and premature elimination occurred alongside a far more harsh view of poverty and a vicious backlash against social spending on the poor.

Many became convinced that dependency on social welfare programs created an "underclass," despite evidence to the contrary. Patterson asserts there is no evidence to suggest that Aid to Families with Dependent Children (AFDC) created a welfare class of dependents in the late 1970s; AFDC served families in acute economic distress, typically early in their lives. The average time on the rolls was 44 months (Patterson 1981, citing Rein and Rainwater 1978). Nonetheless, by 1980, there was pressure to reduce so-called "welfare" spending. And much disagreement remained as to how to address poverty, even in the OEO.

As Janice Peterson (2020:380) notes, it is instructive that "'welfare' has come to refer almost exclusively to programs for the very poor, most particularly those that serve poor single mothers and their children." "Welfare" simultaneously became unpopular. During his election campaign, President Ronald Reagan success-fully tapped into and exacerbated the growing concerns of White working-class and middle-class voters about government spending on Black mothers in cities, citing unfounded examples of fraud and excess (Quadagno 1995). After his election, he began dismantling the War on Poverty. But the ideas about Black women especially taking advantage of welfare stuck. Indeed, "The pejorative meaning of 'welfare' is steeped in views of the appropriate roles and behaviors of women and in racism" (Peterson 2020:379). We see this again, as Peterson argues, in the Trump presidential administration's call to increase the work requirements of "welfare" programs. The Trump administration declared that poverty has been conquered in the USA, drawing on a report by the Council of Economic Advisers (CEA). "In a somewhat novel twist, the CEA (2018) report attributes both some of the decline in material hardship as well as the increase in welfare dependency to increases in federal spending on social welfare programs" (Peterson 2020:380). The problem stated by the Trump administration is individual and household dependency on govern-ment, not more general economic and social precarity. Yet an ever growing body of literature documents increasing economic insecurity and precariousness of work and life for many Americans (Pugh 2015; Kalleberg 2018; Hacker 2019). Researchers have also argued that welfare reforms since the 1980s have been especially detrimental to the deep poor (Peterson 2020).

By the mid-1990s, however, welfare had such a bad name that even liberals wanted to get rid of it. Hence, President Clinton, a Democrat, overhauled social welfare for the poor, ending the ability of people to in any way "depend" on welfare. O'Connor (2001) suggests that this occurred after culture of poverty ideas had been mostly discredited by experts, but elements of culture of poverty were revived by the focus on the chronically poor. Bane and Ellwood (1994) found that most people on welfare remained on it for a short time, as a stopgap during a time of serious crisis. But they also identified a small group of welfare clients who were "dependent" on government assistance for a much longer period of time. Researchers focused again on single motherhood, proposing a number of negative effects of growing up in female-headed households (O'Connor 2001). O'Connor argues that single motherhood and especially "dependency" were increasingly ideological terms in the argument against welfare, but that this notion of dependency was inaccurate. In reality, welfare recipients have overwhelmingly relied on other sources of income, including the formal workforce, informal work, social networks, and other income-generating strategies (e.g., Stack 1974; Tienda and Stier 1991; Edin and Lein 1997; Edin and Shaefer 2015). Nor does employment bring independence from government aid (Edin and Lein 1997; O'Connor 2001). O'Connor (2001:254) writes that "to learn this, however, poverty researchers had to look beyond the official statistics to speak with welfare recipients themselves."

Concerns about welfare dependence won out. In 1996, AFDC was eradicated and replaced by TANF, Temporary Aid to Needy Families. The number of people on TANF plummeted in the following 10 years. These are the welfare reforms Peterson (2020) references, and the rules of eligibility have for the most part only become more restrictive since 1996. The irony is that social welfare programs that serve the middle class – such as old-age insurance, first home-buyer's assistance, and financial aid for college – though largely very effective in supporting the middle class, are far more expensive than TANF, or even AFDC. Tax incentives, corporate bail-outs, direct subsidies and credits – these are not policies we tend to think of as "welfare," but they are essentially government-provided financial assistance to the middle class or the already wealthy. But it is the poor's dependence on government aid – the specter that they might depend on this in lieu of working and develop a culture of dependency – that dominates concerns about welfare in American politics.

Problems with the Culture of Poverty Arguments

The impact of culture of poverty ideas on poverty is problematic because there are fundamental problems with the wider notion. I have already touched on many of these issues here (and elsewhere: Seale 2020), but, before moving on, I want to reassess exactly what is wrong with culture of poverty ideas as they have been used in the past. Then, we can better determine what is worth keeping. Ultimately, four main problems reoccur in the use of culture of poverty, contributing to the overreaching and misinterpretation of poverty scholarship during the twentieth century. These include: (1) the lack of empirical support, especially for assertions of difference; (2) failure to recognize diversity and mobility among the poor; (3) conceptual issues with the notion of culture; and (4) oversimplification of causal and behavioral pathways.

Empirical Issues

Commonly used variations on the culture of poverty thesis suggest that the subculture that exists among the poor involves dependency on government assistance rather than work, and the intergenerational transmission of these values (see Ludwig and Mayer 2006; Evans and Anderson 2013; Baron et al. 2015). A wealth of research exists, however, that suggests that concerns over the intergenerational transmission of a culture of dependency are overblown, if not completely false. Even with AFDC, welfare dependence equated to considerable hardship. Edin and Lein (1997) found that the wage-reliant single mothers in poverty in their study spent almost 50 percent more than the welfare-reliant mothers, especially on housing, medical care, clothing, transportation, childcare, school supplies, and miscellaneous expenses. Mothers who grew up in households receiving welfare were not more likely to be on welfare themselves, and did not seem to find it any less stigmatizing (Edin and Lein 1997). Racial minority mothers on average spent less than White mothers (Edin and Lein 1997). There is also not much evidence to suggest that welfare-reliant mothers prefer welfare over work. Despite the hardship of welfare-reliance, work came with special difficulties that simply made it unfeasible for some mothers (see Chapter 6). Low-wage work does not pay much better, and costs much more, than not working.

Explicit comparisons between the poor and nonpoor continue to be lacking in much of the culture and poverty literature, with the notable exception of Lareau (2003), whose work is discussed later in this chapter. Thus, it is not clear that the views, habits, strategies, etc., of the poor do actually differ significantly by social class. Actually, much research finds that the beliefs, values, and goals of people in poverty are the same as those professed by the wider public (Rank 1994). Researchers frequently find that subjects in poverty believe hard work begets success, desire stable family arrangements, and view education as the key to their children's future. In addition, we tend to focus on the problems of people in poverty and assume any problem must be related to the poverty. But anytime we take a microscope to human lives, regardless of class background, we will find *something* that could be considered pathological. Often, it is a matter of perspective. For example, is the lack of autonomy of a young woman in poverty who passively accepts early childbearing different from the lack of autonomy of a young woman of the middle class who passively accepts going to college because that is what is expected? For these reasons, it is important to be careful not only in generalizing about the poor, but in assuming people in poverty are different than the middle class.

Social disorganization models also come in for their share of criticism and empirical challenge. For instance, Sánchez-Jankowski (2008), in his work *Cracks in the Pavement*, argues that his research shows how some of the very same indicators used for disorder are in fact ways of building order. One early critic who stands out in his appraisal of the organization of the slum is William Foote Whyte (1943) in *Street Corner Society*. Oft-cited as a rejoinder to social disorganization theory, Whyte argues that the impoverished Italian neighborhood in his study is actually a well-ordered organization that differs from more economically secure communities. He describes how the "cornerboy," unemployed, apparently idle, actually has a well-defined role in relation to his community. Groups of men who hang out on the corners form important ties of mutual obligation. Loic Wacquant (1997:346) asserts that "the ghetto" is not disorganized, but rather organized *differently* in response to "unique structural and strategic constraints." Jencks and Mayer (1990) review the quantitative literature on neighborhood effects published prior to 1990 and conclude that, when it comes to crime, evidence that neighborhood affects juvenile delinquency *above and beyond* family circumstances is surprisingly thin. Yet much research does point to a number of disadvantages associated with living in certain neighborhoods.

For nearly any assertion about people in poverty and behavior, one can find empirical publications that claim the opposite. For instance, as many scholars bristle over the portrayal of single motherhood among Black Americans as pathological, there are scholars who bristle over implications that growing up in single mother households is acceptable (Farber 1997). I think it's important to recognize both views, in that, maybe for some families, single parenthood is the far preferable option, and for other families, the children do suffer as a result of growing up in a single parent household. But whether single parenthood is acceptable or not is really not the most important point. The point should be to identify the source of disadvantage. Single parenthood may be more of a symptom than a cause. This is another reason for centering social relations. In Chapter 3, we learned that doing so reveals why single motherhood can be problematic. But centering social relations also reveals why single motherhood is so often preferable to the alternatives. The problem is not located in single motherhood. It is located in the social relations that lead to single motherhood for those who might wish it otherwise, and the social relations that make being a single mother so difficult.

The tendency to view traits among disadvantaged groups in negative ways is common. If one is studying juvenile delinquents, for instance, any commonality they share is likely to be viewed as a problem – including, for instance, single mother households and teen pregnancy. Snow et al. (1994) cautioned researchers against the tendency to over-pathologize the homeless because it is too easy to see signs of mental illness when we are expecting it, or when we already view someone in a disadvantaged position as different from us.

An obvious but persisting fault with culture of poverty is the assumption that what is true for one group of people in poverty – or, indeed, one person in poverty – is true for others. This is especially problematic since people in poverty are so incredibly diverse. Yet overgeneralization remains a hazard (Seale 2020). Even Lewis's data show a wide range of situations and behavior among the poor, "the majority of whom do not appear to be in the culture of poverty at all" (Leeds 1971:235). Overgeneralization is one of the problems that can occur with interpretation of qualitative research. Most qualitative researchers are appropriately aware of this limitation of method, but consumers of the research, particularly second- or third-hand consumers, may not be. By necessity, qualitative research is often focused on a small, historically and/or geographically specific, group of people. This allows for in-depth, holistic understanding, but not generalization beyond the people in the study. This is one of the typically unavoidable trade-offs of social science. No single study can provide a complete or definitive answer to the research topic of interest. It is only in relation to other studies, using different samples or methods, that we can interpret the particular study to make more definitive statements about human behavior. Qualitative research should lend itself to a more multifaceted and nuanced understanding, especially of social processes. Social processes are not about specific people but about how, under certain circumstances, social interaction unfolds, and thus can be generalized with less risk of stereotyping. For instance, Lareau (2003) finds that, when parents from a low-SES background do not have much education and feel insecure interacting with teachers and other school officials, they are less successful in obtaining benefits for their children and less able to offer their children helpful advice about how to solve school-related problems. Properly interpreted, this does *not* mean that a majority of lower-class parents therefore are unable to interact with school officials in beneficial ways, and that is why their children perform less well on average. What it *does* mean is that, *when* lower-class parents do not have certain skills and insights, they are likely to be disadvantaged when it comes to the workings of schools. However, in my experience, readers of Lareau's work often take her to mean the first interpretation, and the distinction between the former and the latter interpretation is lost.

Finally, poverty demographics do not line up with a culture of poverty explanation for poverty. For instance, concentrated poverty is the exception, not the norm. People in poverty at any given point in time face odds of roughly one in three of leaving poverty the next year (Bernstein et al. 2018). One or two years in poverty is certainly not long enough to develop "a culture." We also learned in Chapter 2 of the variation across the poor in people's experiences and problems. And even among the chronically poor specifically, immense variation exists in the sorts of problems they face, the behaviors that characterize individuals, and the social relations that perpetuate their poverty.

Conceptual Issues

One of the most immediate critiques of culture of poverty was the use of "culture." One thing most culture scholas agree on is that culture, by definition, is a group-level phenomenon. To be "culture," it must be shared. But at what level and by whom is the culture of the poor shared? Is it national, regional, community, or familial? This is never clearly addressed. To be a culture, it must be specific to a time and place and population. Lewis also cannot clarify why some of the poor do not have a culture of poverty. Leeds charges Lewis with having nothing more than a collection of traits with no real explanation for how they are related and how they constitute a culture.

Even more problematic are how culture is used to refer to values and norms, and the lack of relational and dynamic components. Behaviors cannot be used as direct indicators for values or motives because behaviors are heavily influenced by opportunity structures and internalized expectations (Vaisey 2010).

Rao and Sanyal (2010) contend that culture "is not, as we are often told, a primordially fixed, historically endowed, explanatory variable that is highly resistant to change" (169). Their definition makes it explicit that culture is relational, happens at multiple levels, and is a major part of domination: "Culture is concerned with identity, aspiration, symbolic exchange, coordination, communication, and structures and practices that serve relational ends, such as ethnicity, ritual, norms, and beliefs" (150). Culture must be seen as something that is complex and dynamic, as opposed to coherent and fixed. Culture affects our understanding of reality and allows human communication to occur (Swartz 1997). Think of a few of the words we use to refer to people and positions: race, Black, White, cultured, Latinx, dumb, trash, boy, girl, tomboy, sissy, gay, and on, and on. This is culture. It changes daily, though never completely all at once. Given that, we would not expect to find a single culture for any group of people, let alone one for a population that is as dispersed and variable as people in poverty.

It is not just "culture" that is problematic conceptually. The terms "underclass" or "concentrated poverty" carry problematic baggage as well. Gans (2010), for instance, questioned the notion that concentrated poverty is somehow different from the fact that there is just too much poverty. A focus on concentrated poverty has resulted in policies that break up neighborhoods rather than addressing the root causes of poverty (Gans 2010). It has justified the tearing down of public housing and various dispersion programs that have been controversial. The problem with concentrated poverty and the underclass is that it not only stigmatizes people – it tends to draw the focus toward the actions and characteristics of people or neighborhoods in poverty, as opposed to the actions and characteristics causing the poverty in the first place. Social relations of importance are ignored in favor of scrutiny of the behavior and culture of people in poverty. The cause of the problems in inner-city neighborhoods or public housing is not that there are a lot of poor people living together. The problem is that residents are isolated from basic services, decent living conditions, and employment (see the informative documentary by Friedrichs [2011] on one of the most famous housing projects in American urban history: *The Pruitt–Igoe Myth*).

It is common to confuse condition and culture. But this is extremely problematic for allowing us to justify the conditions other people live in. Rank (2004:48) argues that "Too often we look at the issues . . . and blame the poor for bringing these on themselves, while losing sight of the fact that it is the condition of poverty that results in much of the stress and frustrations that we have seen." Stoll writes that "we will fail to ask the right questions if we are deceived into thinking that some people have no history, that their poverty is inherent, its causes self-evident" (Stoll 2017:31). We have made these mistakes in terms of views and myths about Indigenous Americans (Mann 2006), persistent public misperceptions of the people of Appalachia (Stoll 2017; Catte 2018; Hazen 2018), and repeatedly in terms of African American urban communities, especially the designation of an underclass (Gans 1967; Wacquant 1997; Gans 2010; Raz 2013). In many cases, we engage in circular and essentialist reasoning, assuming that the results of conditions of living are the cause of those conditions, and that any group of people are the way they are because that is the way they are. However, *the conditions in which we find people at one point in time are not the causes of the condition in which we find people.*

One of the most important pernicious legacies of the culture of poverty thesis – although it certainly has other antecedents – is the ideological distinction made between the deserving and the undeserving poor. It might seem an expedient way to solve the problem of serving a diverse population, especially if an institution has few resources. This binary logic is prevalent in American attitudes and policy around poverty, but should be resisted for a number of reasons. First of all, we cannot trust our evaluations of people, as we tend to judge people on the basis of bias and unexamined expectations. As demonstrated in Chapter 3, we do not always understand people or know what they're going through. Furthermore, to identify someone as the undeserving poor is to blame them for their poverty, and justifies society's abandonment of them. We should distrust such a tendency on the principles of its temptingness, the inordinate amount of harm that can result, and the probability that we are not being just. In many cases, the acts we view as evidence of undeservingness may in fact be the result of the poverty itself. We tend to apply standards to the poor that we do not apply to ourselves or others. Why should someone in poverty have superhuman strength to resist all temptation all the time, stay hopeful and upbeat, and always act meek and polite? Binary logic can be dangerous; it restricts our ability to see complexity and context. None of this is to say that people in poverty can do no wrong. In fact, quite the opposite. People across social class do wrong things for which they should be held reasonably responsible. But when we view unethical or harmful behavior as a reason for poverty to exist for *anyone*, I think this is where we cross over into dangerously unjust territory.

Contemporary Research on Culture and Poverty

The problems with the culture of poverty thesis do not mean culture is irrelevant to understanding poverty. Culture is vitally important to understanding inequality, poverty, and social behavior. It helps, however, to think of culture as more an *effect* than a *cause* of poverty. In this section, recent influential studies, both quantitative and qualitative, are discussed, including work by Cynthia Duncan, Annette Lareau, and others. These works demonstrate careful, rigorous research that largely avoids the mistakes of culture of poverty approaches. They also illustrate some of the enduring challenges in researching people in poverty, including the need for comparison and contextualization. These newer takes on culture and poverty differ in key ways from earlier attempts, especially in how they define and operationalize culture. These researchers recognize the dangers of overgeneralization and are far more likely to view culture as dynamic, as opposed to static or independently coherent. Hence, culture, because it is about how we interpret ourselves and the world and provides meaning, is essential to an understanding of poverty.

Pierre Bourdieu is one of the more influential theorists of the late twentieth century. Bourdieu developed a theory of social reproduction that included culture because he recognized that the structural does not impose behavior upon people in direct, deterministic ways (Swartz 1997). Moreover, why do people accept the ways in which structure constrains and advantages people differentially? Inequality must be legitimized somehow, or else face constant challenge. For Bourdieu, legitimation is achieved through culture. Culture is how inequality is reproduced without the conscious recognition of individuals. People do not just develop shared meanings, however, but come to embody their roles in the hierarchy. We often act without rational calculation, depending on our own habits and strategies, although we develop such strategies and habits as a reflection of what is in our basic self-interest (Bourdieu 1990). The problem for the individual, of course, is that what is sometimes in one's best interest is not so in other contexts. Bourdieu's concepts have proven useful for studying the disadvantages that people in poverty face in relation to others, as well as in particular situations. Critically, this theory recognizes that the perpetuation of inequality for people in poverty does not simply operate through structure. We need to acknowledge the ways in which positions at the bottom are legitimated, and this happens in part through restrictions on personal development, the development of semi-strategic action, and unconscious processes, all of which occur through habitus.

Bourdieu's notion of habitus encompasses how individuals respond to their environments in ways that become encoded bodily and cognitively, from how we hold ourselves and make eye contact in interactions with others to our knowledge, worldviews, and ideas of what is possible. Although our individual habitus is durable, it can and does change. However, Bourdieu (1977) used the notion of habitus to explain how the social structure is reinforced through action, even when individuals do not wish to reinforce the structure or have objective interests in resisting power. For instance, educational choices are dispositions, not calculated choices. Aspirations are not always in alignment with real chances. Habitus is a mechanism that can be adapted to different circumstances, but "it always addresses present situations in terms of past experiences" (Swartz 1997:213). Bourdieu also recognized that lifestyle characteristics are not intrinsic to any class or group – they obtain significance only in relation to one another (Swartz 1997). Hence, his social reproduction theory is a deliberately relational theory.

Bourdieu discussed social capital as another key factor in social mobility and reproduction of class relations. In sociology, social capital is frequently used to explain a variety of outcomes at the individual and group levels, from health outcomes to economic development. Social capital refers to the resources provided by relationships (Agnitsch et al. 2006:36). It is sometimes referred to as a property of individuals; in other cases, it refers to a group-level phenomenon such as levels of trust or capacity to work together (Fulkerson and Thompson 2008). *Who one knows* influences access to opportunity; access to knowledge, including cultural styles; and our sense of how the world works and our place in it. For people in poverty, social capital is crucial. It has implications for the amount of social support they can draw upon, both tangible and intangible. It has implications for employment opportunities and schooling.

Researchers often distinguish between two main types of social capital: bonding ties, such as between close family members and friends; and bridging ties, such as professional connections or acquaintanceships. Research on bonding and bridging social capital among the poor has yielded interesting results. In one unique study of suburban Australia, Browne-Yung et al. (2013) found that if one is low-income in an advantaged neighborhood, one tends to do better with bridging than with bonding forms of ties. If low-income in a disadvantaged neighborhood, one tends to do better with bonding than with bridging forms of ties. But research also finds that friends may be a luxury for many people in poverty (Callan and Dolan 2013; Stacciarini et al. 2015). Bonding social capital can also be negative in some respects. Garcia (2010) found that heroin use is not associated with isolation from family, but that in fact it often occurs or is managed within the family. However, oftentimes, without these social ties, the individual would be even worse off. Case studies of successful upwardly mobile families suggest that both bridging and bonding ties are needed, and neither are sufficient in and of themselves. For instance, supportive social networks are found to work best when they include *both* formal government support and kinship ties (Mammen et al. 2015).

Religion can be a powerful source of both bridging and bonding social capital. Williams and Kornblum (1994:55) suggest that key figures in churches, schools, and other organizations in low-income communities help create "safe spaces" for the youth. Smith (2001:302) notes that scholars have identified religion as a positive force in poor urban communities, especially important for the "facilitation of safe, constructive spaces." Religious groups may provide resources, may recruit members in poor communities, or attempt to empower poor communities, as did the urban faith-based group in my dissertation study (Foley et al. 2001; Seale 2013). However, Smith also notes that the role of the church for the urban African American poor has been troubled by culture clashes and class differences, for example, during mass migration of poor Blacks from the south and resulting increased social service demands on northern Black churches. Among White churches, their involvement with minority urban poor has been primarily one of social service provision, and they sometimes resist neighborhood influx (Smith 2001). Foley et al. (2001) suggest religious-based organizations are very much important conductors of social capital in poor communities, but that this role is not activated as much as it could be on the behalf of those in poverty.

Where someone lives makes a difference to their social connections, as shown in Duncan's (1999) study of three rural communities. In the Appalachian county, Duncan found small-town patronage does not work so well for the poor. Duncan wrote, "The body politic in Blackwell has been corrupt since the turn of the century when coal operators seized control. Elections have been declared null by state officials . . . the area's violent reputation dates back to political battles over school trustee positions" (33). Civic institutions do not always serve the powerless. In her study of Dahlia in the Southern Delta, Duncan noted that it is not only racially segregated, but is purposely maintained that way: "Land is notoriously hard to buy in Dahlia – partly because it has high value for farmland, but also because controlling land is crucial for maintaining segregation" (81). Community divisions are stark, even though – or perhaps because – White residents depend on Black residents for labor. There is almost no middle class, particularly among the Black population, because the Black middle class tends to move to the cities. But not all rural areas have such a divided populace by class and/or race. Duncan found that the community in Maine made less of class distinctions and people interacted more across the class continuum. As a result, poverty is not as much of a struggle, and escaping it is easier.

Mario Luis Small has been an active proponent of a return to culture. In an article on social organization of a Latinx housing project, Small (2002) suggested that structural interpretations of poverty, particularly the social disorganization theory of urban poverty, are incomplete. Structure here refers to institutional and demographic realities that create the conditions under which people live on a daily basis. Structural conditions, Small pointed out (2002), may provide limits to possibilities for social organization, but do not lead to changes directly. For instance, the lack of a local school does not directly determine whether people organize or not on behalf of some issue. For Small, the culture-as-values paradigm is defunct. Instead, the concept of *frame* involves the cognitive aspects of culture while downplaying the normative aspect. He noted this is similar to what Bourdieu's concept of habitus does, although habitus is often an unconscious process, whereas the use of a frame to motivate or justify action is often conscious. I would add that frame also differs from habitus in that it can be more dynamic and changeable than habitus. However, both Bourdieu's habitus and the concept of frames as Small used it also refer to the importance of one's experiences (Small 2002), which are in turn affected by structural conditions. What is important to me about both Small's and Bourdieu's approaches is that they keep structure and culture distinct, though they recognize how they are very much intertwined in terms of experience.

Also influenced by Bourdieu, Annette Lareau's (2003) study of Black and White families across class positions greatly influenced the sociology of inequality, contributing to something of a revival of interest in culture and poverty. She finds key class differences in how families interpret situations and how they subsequently act. For instance, middle-class parents and children in her sample expressed more comfort with major institutions, including education. Working-class and poor families lacked information about how schools work.

Interactional approaches to gatekeepers such as school officials and doctors differed by class, with more comfort and willingness to challenge authority among the middle class. Project researchers observed less trust and openness among working-class – and especially poor – families when interacting with resource gatekeepers. Language use also differed: more discussion and development of conversation and argument occurred among middle-class families, as did more scheduled activities. In contrast, the "accomplishment of natural growth" approach to parenting favored among working-class and poor families may have its benefits, but did not adequately prepare the children to compete in middle-class institutions. As a result, Lareau suggests, over time a sense of entitlement became instilled in the middle-class children, versus a sense of constraint among the working-class and poor children. The study thus illustrated how structure (as institutions) and culture (as language use and interactional dynamics) interact in our daily lives. This is critical because Lareau identifies relational processes that draw on both structure and culture. How the children relate to others and how they develop power in relations occur in interaction with their material and their cultural realities.

Other empirical critiques of culture of poverty ideas that maintain the importance of going beyond structure include Stack (1974) and Levine (2013). Stack (1974:22) specifically critiqued prior scholarship on the Black family, including culture of poverty scholarship, saying that too few pay much attention to "the adaptive strategies, resourcefulness, and resilience of urban families under conditions of perpetual poverty or the stability of their kin networks." The explicit or implicit comparison is the White middle-class model of family. Stack (1974:22) writes that, throughout the 1930s to 1960s, most studies reinforced popular stereotypes of the lower-class or Black family – particularly the Black family in poverty – as deviant, matriarchal, and broken. Few attempts have been made to view Black families as they actually are, recognizing the interpretations Black people have of their own cultural patterns (Stack 1974). Furthermore, Stack sees the trend of her day as increasingly racist in the sense that ideas of racial inferiority were becoming more prevalent. Indeed, theories of cultural opposition, cultural deprivation, and so on were in their heyday in the 1970s. She also points out that many studies neglect the external factors that shape conditions in the ghetto, such as exploitative capitalism, welfare, and the law and institutions that shape cultural patterns and interpersonal relationships among the poor. The distrust that Levine (2013) found among mothers in poverty, as discussed in other chapters, prevailed despite race, ethnicity, age, education, employment history, and time period. Levine (2013:16) indicated that low-income women find themselves in contexts that "are structured in ways that promote the untrustworthiness of others." Thus, the target for intervention should not be the women themselves, but their "interaction partners" (16). Levine was clear that her research suggests not that distrust is an individual trait, but rather that it is something people learn from experience. As such, she views it as counter to the culture of poverty argument. Moreover, the women were not *uniform* in their distrust. These are not cultural values that were passed down intergenerationally or socialized, as many indicated they were trusting in their early relationships. Their experiences produced the skepticism.

Culture can be targeted for positive change, but it has to be thought of in terms of culture as process and as related to experience. Rao and Sanyal (2010) found that public action can influence cultural processes to improve the voice and agency of the poor. In one study, villagers in south rural India created a deliberative, participatory culture with some success (Rao and Sanyal 2010). In another study, Sanyal et al. (2015) describe a microenterprise poverty alleviation project in rural Bihar, India, where they attempt to change women's access to symbolic resources, such as identity references, and physical resources such as credit, and to develop an institutional environment conducive to "new cultural competencies and capabilities." They are in effect trying to change the culture of gender norms in the target villages, and they report a high level of success. Interventions involved changing the physical and spatial mobility of women in the village by bribing them, with offers of financial help, to attend meetings that then opened them up to different ways of living. The meetings also fostered alternative identities and reference groups through deliberate and often physical means, including games, songs, and narratives. Over time, the women took it to the next level, becoming involved in community affairs and politics, where before they might have rarely left the house. Hence, gender norms can be changed relatively quickly even without alleviating the poverty, and despite resistance. This happened through a focus on regularity norms: changes in what the women *did* happened before changes in what they were *supposed to do*. Critically, the authors wrote that this is "not just a matter of nudging individuals to move towards new forms of behavior. Simply tricking the brain into behaving differently cannot result in long-term change" (Sanyal et al. 2015:53). Nonetheless, sustained behavioral change can occur before changes in beliefs, and can have a powerful impact on belief. This is a fascinating example of how situational changes can produce cultural change more quickly than targeting beliefs directly. In addition, we have a view of culture as relational (Rao and Sanyal 2010:149–50), and as relevant to agency, but not assuming agency. In other words, they recognized the constraints the women faced in moving around outside their homes, but also recognized that the change would have to come from actions the women took themselves. As the authors argued, "processes that equalize voice and agency are necessarily cultural; they are relational and communicative, creating the capacity for the disadvantaged to cross over from being passive recipients of public largesse toward becoming active participants in determining their own destinies" (Rao and Sanyal 2010:169).

These more nuanced approaches demonstrate that certain ways of looking at the world can develop among people facing economic constraints, but that these are neither inherent nor inflexible. Ways of viewing and interacting in the world change in reaction to people's experiences. Intervention from outsiders would do better to target those experiences, as opposed to focusing on the behaviors and views of people in poverty. These approaches also have the potential to recognize the positive aspects of people's approaches to interacting in the world. Not everything about the lives of people in poverty is necessarily bad. Some of the best art in the United States has developed from people who lived under severe economic constraints, including blues and bluegrass.

A Culture of Dependency or a Culture of Blame?

My grandmother was not a highly educated woman, but she told me as a small child to quit feeding stray animals . . . You know why? Because they breed. You're facilitating the problem if you give an animal or a person ample food supply. They will reproduce, especially ones that don't think too much further than that. And so what you've got to do is you've got to curtail that type of behavior. They don't know any better.
(Lieutenant Governor Andre Bauer, South Carolina:
Montopoli 2010)

In spite of an overall shift in favor of greater government help for the poor, a large majority (69%) of the U.S. public now agrees that "poor people have become too dependent on government assistance programs," although that number has declined from 79% who took that view in 1997. The belief that poor people are overly reliant on government aid peaked in July 1994, when 85% felt poor people were

too dependent . . .. Blacks and whites are more divided over this issue
than they were in 2003 and the partisan gap also has grown slightly and,
at 23 points, is now wider than at any time since 1992.
(Russell Heimlich, The Pew Research Center, July 21, 2007)

Due to COVID-19 concerns, homeless men were moved to a hotel
in a mainly white, liberal neighborhood in the Upper West Side of
Manhattan.. . . A private Facebook group – Upper West Siders for
Safer Streets – was created by residents who were up in arms.. . .
[One commenter] described the men as "subhuman," while others
called for "the National Guard" or "animal control" to clean up the
neighborhood.
(Daniel E. Slotnik, *New York Times*, August 18, 2020)

I want to consider this idea that a culture of dependency exists
among people in poverty. This is a very common notion, and I
think we should spend some time considering it. One of the more
important and influential examples of such an argument comes from
the highly acclaimed *Hillbilly Elegy: A Memoir of a Family and Culture
in Crisis*, by J. D. Vance (2016). The book was even made into a
movie directed by Ron Howard and starring Amy Adams and Glenn
Close. Vance takes a very individualized approach to understanding
the actions of family members in Appalachia, concluding that they
will have to pull themselves out of their own cultural mindset of
poverty and dependency. However, Vance's conclusions are based
on a very limited understanding of poverty. A relational approach
that takes into account historical, contextual, and place-based factors
is far preferable for understanding Appalachian poverty. This is not
to say that Vance's work completely lacks merit, but that its lack of
attention to social relations clearly hobbles Vance's ability to make
sense of the behavior and perspectives of the people he discusses in
his book.
Vance wrote:

Whatever talents I have, I almost squandered until a handful of loving
people rescued me. That is the real story of my life, and that is why I
wrote this book. I want people to know what it feels like to nearly give
up on yourself and why you might do it. I want people to understand
what happens in the lives of the poor and the psychological impact that
spiritual and material poverty has on their children. (2016:2)

Vance discussed the lack of agency among co-workers at a warehouse
as life experience that showed him how changing people's economic

opportunities is not enough. Rather, he argued, the poor lack a sense of agency; they accept their helplessness and, when offered a decent job, squander their chance. He also wrote that this culture is "distinct from the larger landscape of modern America" (7). This is important to consider, because I do not think his experience is unique. But I do take issue with many of the conclusions he drew from this experience.

For instance, Vance (2016) presented problems and trends in Appalachia as exceptional, when in fact they apply throughout America. Vance defaulted to – as many of us do – an ideology of the American middle class, and did so in order to juxtapose that with a portrayal of the hard lives of some of his friends and family. This relies on a fictional version of the American middle class that is widely shared but distant from the reality. The middle class may be better equipped to hide problems, but dig deep into just about any-one's family experiences and one will hear stories about their family involving substance abuse, mental illness, the laziness of some young relative, ruined prospects, debt and other erratic economic behavior, and even abuse, violence, or crime. These issues may appear more prevalent among people toward the bottom of the economic hierarchy because they have less capacity to address and to hide such problems.

Vance's (2016) overarching conclusion is that "society" is not responsible for these problems and cannot solve them. The lack of his-torical context for such a claim leads us treacherously astray. In *Ramp Hollow*, Stoll (2017), a historian of Appalachia, traced the region's poverty not to a development of a culture of dependency, but to very concrete actions taken by absentee landowners and policymakers. In West Virginia and Virginia, wilderness grantees – who were absentee owners and investors and owned most of the arable land west of the Blue Ridge – used their influence on state legislators to maintain the lack of political organization and general development in the mountain counties. Stoll wrote that even though schools, roads, etc. would have increased land values, they would also have increased property taxes, and were therefore suppressed. "Virginia's patrician class continued to regard the mountains as their private tax shelter" (Stoll 2017:133). The people actually living in the mountains lived in a patronage system that emerged from linked households in a context of few formal institutions. Corporate interests conspired with local elites and, by the early twentieth century, the peasant economy and the ecological context of the home that the people depended on was destroyed (Stoll 2017:140). The Appalachian life of self-sufficiency was thus no more, leading to impoverishment. This ultimately occurred as a result of four processes: population pressure, the loss of the homeplace, ecological destruction, and decreased value of mountain commodities (Stoll 2017). The forest was destroyed by coalmining. As the commons were undermined, many tried to make a living on them anyway. But they struggled to do so, hence the stereotype of the "hill"-billy.

It was not just industrialists who invaded Appalachia. Government "experts" arrived as well, but Stoll (2017:235) pointed out too many were too reliant on false assumptions: "Some of them gathered data reliably, and their conclusions could have shaped a progressive and empathetic public policy. Others relied on false assumptions rather than their own eyes and ears. They misread the people and the landscape." The portrayal of the region as stagnant and helpless persisted.

Since Vance's book was published, Appalachia has been portrayed in the media as a White working-class enclave of conservative racists. Elizabeth Catte, a public historian, wrote *What You Are Getting Wrong about Appalachia* (2018:22) to counter presentations of "Appalachia as a monolithic 'other America' that defies narratives of progress." She challenged the portrayal of Appalachia as "Trump Country." Catte pointed out that, while Trump did have broad support among Appalachians and West Virginians, and his supporters expressed alienation from both political parties along with White racial anxiety and failed expectations, these sentiments were not unique to these areas. Catte noted that economic strategies pursued by both Republicans and Democrats put the flow of capital in the hands of businesses, as opposed to people. Stoll also noted that political leaders offer citizens false choices between jobs and health. Catte argued that those candidates who are more committed to the interests of the people (and thus labor and environmental regulation) do not succeed *not* because there is no support from the public, but because the public are only offered choices between moderates who prioritize business interests over residents. The truth, Catte argued, is that we are all living in Trump Country. And of the 17,508 registered voters in McDowell County (sometimes used to represent "Trump Country" in the media) in West Virginia, Trump received 4,614 votes and Clinton received 1,429. Only 27% of McDowell County voters actually voted for Trump. This narrative of Appalachia as Trump Country also obscures its diversity and its historical role in a variety of progressive and radical movements, including the grassroots prison abolition movement in eastern Kentucky, the Highlands Institute, and the Appalachian Queer Film Festival in West Virgina (Catte 2018:52).

I do think Vance (2016) is right about one thing: we should respect the autonomy of people in poverty. We should not treat them as dependents. To me, this indicates that we should concern ourselves with improving education, social services, and employment prospects, and that we should ask people what it is they need and how they might achieve it. We can hold individuals responsible for the decisions that they make without punishing them out of all proportion to their mistakes. The evidence that people end up mired in poverty because they develop a habit of depending on other people and institutions is paltry at best. To the extent that impoverished people in Appalachia live in dependence on government assistance, it is not attributable to culture so much as the structure of economic and political relations that punish individuals harshly for any mistake, and offer few options and little dignity. In the next chapter, I explore the role that structural factors play in people's lives and examine how well structural explanations help us understand people in poverty. Following that, I pull from a large number of empirical studies to examine in depth exactly how people in poverty encounter opportunity, including such opportunities as those Vance claimed were squandered by working-class people encountered in his youth.

Conclusion

Culture is important because all people need meaning in their lives and they rely on culture to understand and act in their world. Moral hierarchies reflect what is available, but people do not always just accept what they are told, as Dodson's (2007) research on defiant mothers reminds us. While broader culture apparently cannot agree on whether the poor are defiant and deviant or overly accepting and dependent, social scientists demonstrate that there is in fact much diversity in how people in poverty experience and respond to conditions of poverty.

The relational framework allows us to make sense of this diversity by considering the social relations that apply to a given situation. Culture does matter in this, but not because there is a single culture that develops among people in poverty and that explains their poverty. Culture tells us how to relate to others. In a sense, it is the wider culture that has the greater impact on the experience of poverty, as opposed to any culture specific to a group of people in poverty. At the same time, local context matters as well. For instance, in some rural places, independence is so highly valued, and the stigma of relying on "welfare" so great, that people in dire straits will see it as in their interests to forgo social service assistance (Sherman 2006). And, as the student in my class suggested, all people adapt to circumstances in ways that may later work against them under different circumstances. People in poverty are often forced to act against their own long-term interests in order to survive on a short-term basis. Some cultural adaptations may develop in response to structural conditions. Ultimately, the examination of cultural factors is best applied in combination with the examination of structural factors, and, as we will see in the next chapter, with social relations to connect these multidimensional factors to our immediate experiences.

5

Structure and Social Relations

Unlike the hypothetical Kiz and Phan from Chapter 1, people do not have a clean slate on which to form relations with others. Instead, we operate within the ongoing effects of multiple social relations and webs of institutions, resources, policies, built environments, and technologies. Structural factors are less about our perceptions and more about the forces we navigate.

The term "structure" in sociology most commonly refers to the social organization of resources as operating through institutions, such as the various spheres of law, the marketplace, and public institutions such as education. Sociologists also insist that structure should be viewed as particularly durable forms of social action. This latter perspective often involves critique of the use of structure as a concept, instead calling for deliberate reference to processes and action. The claim is that reliance on structure in causal explanations denies agency, and fails to reflect society as an ongoing human construction. In examining the uses and critiques of structure, it becomes clear that we need some way of talking about how human action constitutes our political economy and institutional operations. I propose we think of structure as the durable and material outcomes of social action. There are four characteristics of structure to keep in mind:

1 Structure involves both intended (e.g., monopolization of wealth and income) *and* unintended (e.g., certain technological) outcomes.
2 Structure is difficult to change immediately merely with changes in intent (e.g., school segregation).
3 Structure affects material distribution (e.g., government taxation and spending).

4 Structure interacts not only with culture, but with external forces (e.g., pandemics).

But there are limits to a purely structural approach. Thus, I argue for incorporating culture and the notion of social relations into a larger conception of how society operates to provide the fullest understanding of poverty.

I first examine how attention to structural factors illuminates the understanding of poverty. Researchers have demonstrated, through the study of large-scale political economic processes and in the study of institutions, that conditions of poverty are created and maintained through societal structures resulting from prior actions. Then, I address social policy specifically, finding a two-sided reality of welfare that both helps and punishes people in poverty. Finally, I address some limitations of structuralism and identify how we can incorporate structuralism into a framework of culture, structure, individuals, and social relations.

How Structure Creates Poverty

Political Economy and Labor

In most sociological conceptualizations, the structural dimension is the set of opportunities for choices and constraints imposed by the *organization* of individuals (who are interchangeable under the logic of structure), institutions, and interactions. Structure also refers to material conditions, including the availability or scarcity of key resources, durable forms of distribution, and use of these resources. At the largest scale, the evidence shows a growing global divergence in wealth, such that the most affluent are claiming more of the world's resources for themselves (Milanovic 2016). But class advantage works in many different ways, throughout different social institutions. A review of the general ways in which sociologists have documented structural features of poverty in the United States illustrates the compelling strength of this literature. I address four processes of critical interest: the monopolization of wealth, labor markets, spatial processes, and institutional discrimination. Brief examination of these processes suggests they are both compelling and contingent.

In 2014, the *New York Times* ran an article on the difficulty of making ends meet in a low-wage job (Greenhouse 2014). One of the people they featured was a White man in Tennessee named Nick Mason.

> Nick Mason earns $9 an hour as an assistant manager for a Domino's, overseeing a crew of six. "I don't think $9 is fair – I've been working in the pizza business for 19 years, since I was 15 . . . I just wish we could have our home, but I can't afford to," said Mr. Mason, father of 7-year-old Halle and 5-year-old Eli . . . "We've had to sacrifice a lot of things," he continued. ". . . As a single father, it's impossible. I put my kids in karate about a year ago. They loved it, but I got to the point where it was a choice between paying for a cellphone or karate, and as a manager, I need a cellphone for people to keep in touch with me." Mr. Mason has heard the criticisms: Stop complaining about your pay; just go back to school and that way you'll find a better-paying job. "I would love to go back to school," he said. "It's easy for people to say that because they haven't been in my shoes. I'm already busy every minute of the day. I already don't get to see my kids enough. I doubt I'll be able to afford school, and I don't know where I would find the time."

Mr. Mason is talking about the structure of employment and how it affects his options. The issue is not just having a job, but having a job that is good enough. There is also the matter of being able to keep that job, which is in some senses a luxury for the poor. Certain people have major employment barriers, including various sorts of disabilities, illnesses, domestic violence issues, and financial constraints. A structure that would not induce poverty would have to provide enough jobs, good enough pay, good enough benefits, and affordable childcare, transportation, and healthcare. In addition, it would mean having jobs with flexibility for those with disabilities, public support for those who simply cannot work at all, and adequate education to provide the right skill sets. This is not the structure we have, and the reasons for this have little to do with the individual initiative of people in poverty. It is the result of structural dimensions of the political economy.

For instance, we do know that levels of income inequality have increased in the United States since 1975, much of it happening in the 1980s (Gottschalk and Danziger 2009; Chetty et al. 2014; Mather and Jorosz 2014). Primary reasons given by social scientists for the increase in inequality include:

- downward pressure on wages due to increased trade and immigration (Sassen 1998)
- capital-biased technological change, favoring high-skill workers (Sassen 1998; Gottschalk and Danziger 2009)

- increasing monopolization of the economy, particularly in the financial and energy sectors (Gottschalk and Danziger 2009)
- the decline in trade unions (Munck 2004)
- a shift toward plutocracy in government (Milanovic 2016:75)
- monopolization of wealth through the intentional coding of capital (Pistor 2019).

Market features such as global trade arrangements have major effects on labor opportunities. The labor market is considered the primary institution through which poverty is sustained. Lack of access to jobs with living wages and of possibility for advancement is the most commonly referenced reason people remain in poverty in the empirical literature. Technological changes involving automation contribute to the insecurity of low-skill jobs (Mason and Salverda 2010). As demand for higher education and skill levels has increased, paradoxically, so has the demand for low-wage workers (Bernstein 1999). Hence, sociologists and economists talk of labor market polarization as the reigning trend. High-skill jobs require more education than people currently in poverty can reasonably aspire to, and many of those jobs are highly competitive. Service jobs requiring affordable levels of training, such as that of Certified Nursing Assistants, offer low wages and little security or advancement (Mason and Salverda 2010). Another labor market development that concerns sociologists is the growing preference among employers for part-time, temporary, and subcontracted employees (Nickell et al. 2019). Although technological changes and skill requirements of the economy are often viewed as inexorable structural conditions, there are policy options to provide better support for less educated individuals (Gautié and Schmitt 2010). Racial minorities, women and immigrants are hurt the most by these trends (Mason and Salverda 2010; Méhaut et al. 2010).

Entrenched institutional processes continue to statistically favor certain kinds of people over others in ways that may have little to do with the main institutional goals. Institutional discrimination is most manifest in the perpetuation of racial inequality, known as institutional racism. Charles Mills (1999) in *The Racial Contract* argues that American society is built upon White supremacy. We have developed a system of governance that justifies racism. Although interactional discrimination occurs, such that people with resources or power favor White individuals over people of color, much racial inequality is attributable not to individual bias against people of color but to institutional processes that systematically favor Whites. These processes occur across a number of institutions or fields, including the criminal justice system, banking and loans, economic algorithms, civil law, primary education, healthcare, and more. For instance, much of the education gap between Whites and Blacks in the United States may be due to differences in quality of schools and family resources, but there is also evidence of discrimination in school discipline and in tracking (Corra et al. 2011; George 2015). Another example of institutional racism that directly affects the pocketbooks of people in poverty is the prevalence of Alternative Financial Services (AFS) in racial minority neighborhoods. AFS include a number of financial services that take advantage of people's poverty – offering high interest rates or other penalties – such as payday loans, pawn shops, check cashing outlets that charge fees, rent-to-own stores, and certain credit cards. AFS form a multibillion-dollar industry that is used by almost a quarter of the American population (Faber 2019). They cost people more money in the long run than similar services that people with greater financial stability can access, such as checking accounts, savings accounts, and bank loans. However, Faber (2019:817) found that such AFS businesses are more common in racially segregated metropolitan areas, suggesting that "racial segregation creates easily identifiable markets for institutions to avoid, target, and exploit." All of this is to say that joint actions or patterns of social relations that make up "structure" may be deeply embedded.

Globalization, particularly involving immigration and trade liberalism, is also a structural factor affecting low-skill workers. However, the impact of globalization for low-skill work is complex. Trade protections, for instance, tend to benefit low-skill workers significantly less than mid-skill workers (Bradford 2019). When it comes to immigration restrictions, Clemens et al. (2018) find little positive impact on labor market conditions in US agriculture. Robertson et al. (2009) find that even low-income countries have some control over their economic structure upon further opening of their borders. Capital mobility, however, has tended to undermine employment in middle- to higher-income countries (Vallanti 2018). Although globalization may sometimes appear inexorable, the extensive literature on the effects of policy decisions suggests that states retain some initiative and control over dimensions of globalization such as labor markets and trade. States retain the option to enhance education, health services, and social welfare programs. Moreover, through unionization and other worker actions, laborers are not completely helpless. They can and will organize against poor working conditions.

Another disturbing feature of late capitalism pointed out by social scientists is the combined trend of increasing commodification and greater wealth inequality (Christiansen 2017; Grusky et al. 2019). Increasingly, everything costs money, including the skills needed to get ahead. In the USA, this can be seen with education. To find a decent school for their children, parents shop around by neighborhood (Grusky et al. 2019). One must afford to live in the right neighborhood to have one's child go to a decent public school, or send them to private school. Thus, the issue is not only income or wealth differences, but the fact that these differences, such as they are, have an even greater impact because there is a greater need for money. A society can be structured by more or less need for money. The more we commodify public services, such as education, access to water and sewage, transportation, etc., the bigger the impact of inequality is for quality of life and for the ability to escape poverty within or between generations.

Spatial and Global Factors

Structure has a spatial and geographic element, meaning that location near certain structural features – such as intensive resource extraction – environmental problems, local politics, and population densities continue to matter. Not all structural features are equally spatial or geographic, though arguably the effects of *any* structural feature are *both* time and place dependent. What happens in one place can jump geographic distance to affect another place, as occurs with production outsourcing, international trade, or colonialism. Yet the process by which structure has its effects on people works through place-based infrastructure such as urbanization or broadband access.

Spatial factors also play a major role in poverty. Access to jobs and resources requires spatial proximity and/or transportation. Types of jobs available vary by place. Investment, disinvestment, and gentrification patterns affect where people can live and what resources their neighborhoods can offer. Resource extraction and tourism contribute to problems for the rural poor by shaping the resources available and the operation of local governments and organizations (Pickering et al. 2006; Stoll 2017). A low tax base and lack of investment in some places can result in fewer services in emergency, healthcare, education, community development, and social support. In both rural and metropolitan locales, capital accumulation and accompanying impoverishment produce places with deep poverty and community deterioration. Thus, poverty has been identified as not only macro-institutional, but geographic and historical (Falk and Lobao 2003; Lobao 2004). Uneven development continues to play out in terms of places and labor forces that have been exploited and then abandoned upon resource depletion or economic restructuring (Mirza et al. 2019). Rural places subjected to energy extraction may face resource depletion and the boom–bust cycle that perpetuates inequality both within and between places (Fulkerson and Thomas 2014). Less populated places have become sites for prisons and nursing homes, offering some economic opportunity, but largely failing to reduce poverty (Bonds 2009; Genter et al. 2013). Many community institutions have also been adversely affected by withdrawal of private and public resources from the cities (Crookston and Hooks 2012; Sheely 2012). However, some scholars have argued that the distinction between rural and urban is increasingly blurred as we grow more spatially interdependent (Lichter and Ziliak 2017). Spatial interdependence has only been intensified by the COVID-19 pandemic, with effects for inequality that remain to be seen.

Neighborhood inequality has been extensively studied in terms of academic achievement, health, and a host of other outcomes (Fryer and Katz 2013). While people can and do move, they often sacrifice as much as they gain in the course of moving (e.g., finding better schools or a safer environment, but leaving friends and family supports behind). The social relations that determine who lives where and how those places form are profoundly important. This is a class and a race issue. It is well documented that African Americans have been discriminated against in the housing market for many decades now through institutional practices such as redlining, whereby financial loans and other services are withheld from individuals and businesses in neighborhoods marked as high-risk due to high poverty or racial minority rates. Stark residential and home ownership segregation has then restricted access to good schools, jobs, and wealth (Massey and Denton 1993; Rugh and Massey 2010; Krysan 2011). Risks, opportunities, institutions, and peers are all key elements affected by neighborhood of residence (Sharkey and Faber 2014). Where someone lives has implications for the quantity and quality of services, jobs, and resources available.

At the same time, it is important to look beyond what occurs within specific spatial boundaries in order to understand how places are constituted. The development of places is traceable to organizational decisions that occur outside of that place. Marwell and Morrissey (2020:236) wrote:

A shift to considering how cities are organized not only by informal social relations but also by formal decision-making allows us to consider the many other fields that structure cities. In doing so, we can see that a much wider set of organizations are relevant to urban poverty, since they are key actors constructing social order in those other fields. Thus, we have fields such as subsidized housing, health care, eviction, banking, social services, and incarceration. The configuration of incumbents, challengers, and rules of the game in all these fields have impacts.

Marwell and Morrissey cited a number of examples of external players affecting impoverished inner-city communities, including decisions of mortgage lenders regarding foreclosures, real estate processes reinforcing racial inequality, and how the incorporation of immigrant or Black populations in city politics is associated with lower crime. Even cities' use of financial technologies such as tax increment financing may lead to spending patterns that disadvantage certain populations. In addition, they argued that nonprofit organizations play a major role in allocating funding for housing, jobs, and social services, and operate as a critical link between people in poverty and government. Thus, by considering governance, we discover that neighborhood conditions are profoundly affected by the actions of nonresidents and the nonpoor who act through organizations (Marwell and Morrissey 2020:246):

> Governance draws our attention not simply to the observed conditions, but rather to the organizations whose practices produced those conditions – e.g., gun retailers or local political party organizations (Vargas 2016) for neighborhood violence; police, courts, or prisons for incarceration; or paint manufacturers, property owners, or building inspectors for lead levels. When organizations become the object of empirical analysis, we confront the human agency underlying the conditions of urban poverty – and recognize that much of that agency is enacted through organizations.

The focus can be zoomed out to the global. Although we live in geographic space, all the people of the world are interconnected and interdependent. Capitalism operates globally as well as locally; the goods we rely on and the labor involved in producing our world come from all over the globe. Those who control the resources control the rewards. There are a variety of ways in which our national poverty situation is related to the situations and doings of people in other nations. Such global processes include both formal, and the less visible, practices of political economy.

For instance, the global shadow economy consists of businesses and transfers of money that occur outside of legal regulations, including tax havens, money laundering, and illegal industries such as human trafficking. The global shadow economy is also sometimes called the poverty creation industry for allowing the mega-affluent to avoid paying taxes, make money from illegal industries, and concentrate more and more money into fewer and fewer hands (Brewer et al. 2013). Tax havens, also known as offshore jurisdictions, are places where capital is taxed at significantly lower rates, and are thus used as a method of tax evasion. A global industry of lawyers, accountants, banks, financial experts, and real estate specialists knowingly enable the tax haven phenomenon (Haberly and Wójcik 2015). Aalbers (2018:918–19) has indicated that: "Tax havens, offshore finance and shadow banking were not only at the heart of the global financial crisis of 2007–9 but also of a range of corporate scandals, including those of Amazon, Apple, Google, Lehman Brothers, Starbucks and HSBC." At least 80 of the largest 100 publicly traded corporations in the USA have subsidiary companies operating in tax havens (Aalbers 2018). More than half of global trade and bank lending passes through tax havens (Aalbers 2018). As a result, elites who use government-financed systems in making money avoid paying tax, placing the burden of financing our global economy and redressing the environmental and social impacts of their businesses on the less affluent (Leaman and Waris 2013).

In terms of general political economy, sociologists suggest that economic growth comes at a price. That price manifests during recessions and downturns in particular. And when the bill comes in, it is the poor who pay, at the greatest cost to themselves. Much of the actual distribution of financial resources for the lower 90% of humanity occurs through the labor market. As we shift to a postindustrial society, jobs become bifurcated into sectors with two main orientations: service and information. The information jobs require high levels of education. Much that remains in the United States for those without (and even many with) four-year college degrees is service-oriented and offers little security (Albelda and Carr 2014). "Care work" is one type of labor that is in high demand but undervalued (Bennett 2014). Human beings need a lot of care, including care as children, healthcare, elderly care, maintenance of their surroundings, accommodation and food, and so on. As working-age adults spend more time working, they need more care for children, elderly family members, and themselves. People without high levels of education often do this work, much of it at low wages and at some cost to their own well-being (Linnan et al. 2017). It is no coincidence that immigrants, people of color, and women are more highly represented in lower-paying service and care-work jobs (Jacobs and Padavic 2015).

Understanding the unequal distribution of wealth and economic growth is critical for understanding why we have poverty in a wealthy society. While global elites are disproportionately responsible for conditions of inequality, there are ways that we are all implicated. People who struggle economically in the USA often view Wal-mart as a "life saver." Wal-mart offers goods and even services at the lowest prices, based in part on its ability to remunerate employees poorly, but even more in terms of its ability to dictate the supply chain. Amazon operates similarly as an online retailer, employing 1.3 million people globally as of 2021, with 950,000 in the USA (according to a July 29, 2021 press release by the company). Laborers in other countries are paid far less to produce clothing and goods that many Americans rely on being able to purchase relatively cheap. Meanwhile, job prospects for people without technical skills or upper levels of education in the USA are minuscule. We pay our cleaners, servers, cooks, eldercarers, child-carers, shelvers, warehouse workers, and many other providers of human services very little. To pay more would be to increase the prices we pay for just about everything. In a sense, all of America is addicted to cheap labor.

Social Policy: Punishing the Poor

Organizations that have developed to interact with, control or assist the poor in the United States largely punish people in poverty, adding to their difficulties and sometimes even contributing to their poverty. Relations between these organizations and people in poverty develop on the basis of the relative powerlessness of people in poverty, and in reaction to elites' notion that people in poverty are to be feared and controlled.

Social Services

Economic assistance to people in dire financial straits, sometimes called "welfare," is both critical and problematic. While welfare programs in America provide absolutely critical assistance to people in or near poverty, the programs also fall short in a variety of ways in the prevention of poverty. Many programs are administered with the conflicting mandates of help and control. Policymakers, officials, and funders worry disproportionately about clients taking advantage of these programs, and enact mechanisms designed not only to control costs and prevent abuse, but also to control behavior viewed as irresponsible (Seale 2013). These control mechanisms serve to punish those who rely upon the assistance.

In 1997, Aid to Families with Dependent Children (AFDC) was replaced by Temporary Aid to Needy Families (TANF), a workfare program. Workfare involves requiring recipients of aid to work in some capacity or to demonstrate that they cannot work. Blau (2006) argued that TANF represents another move to workfare that serves employers better than it does people in poverty. TANF recipients are required to formally search for work or be in work of some kind, and states must document that at least 50% of the federal cash recipients engage in eligible work activities for a minimum of 35 hours per week. The exception is incapacitated clients – those who have insufficient income but are unable to work for some reason, usually due to a disability. These clients count toward the 50% in work activities rule, so TANF case workers have to limit their numbers. Basically, the cash assistance program run by states under these federal rules operates as a joint last-resort and employment service. Support services may include childcare, transportation, assistance for uniforms, job skills classes, résumé assistance, job search assistance, and referrals for domestic violence and mental health problems. States can provide some support services to help clients transition into a new job, but the federal funding for these services is extremely limited. Clients are sanctioned if they fail to meet one of the program demands, which means that their monthly allotment is reduced or cut altogether, although that month continues to count toward their 60-month total. Sanctioning and other discretionary practices vary widely by office, but are sometimes used quite frequently, especially in places with high caseloads (Schram et al. 2009; Monnat 2010; Taylor and Seale 2013).

TANF is a block grant program, meaning that states receive a certain amount of money and can decide how to spend it, as long as they remain "compliant" by documenting the meeting of certain federal rules. States do not have to use these funds. There is no guarantee that, simply because someone qualifies, they will receive cash assistance. This differs from the entitlement system of SNAP (Supplemental Nutrition Assistance Program) – more colloquially referred to as "food stamps" – which is guaranteed for those applicants who meet the qualifications and fill out the paperwork. Any adult receiving TANF cash assistance is limited to federal funding of

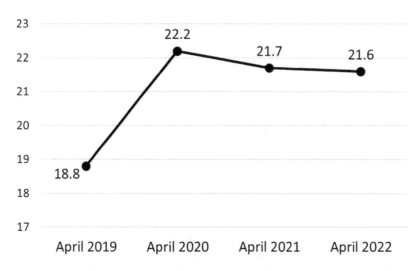

Number of recipients of Supplemental Nutrition Assistance Program, in millions, 2019–22

Source: data from the United States Department of Agriculture (2022b)

60 months in their lifetime, unless the county welfare office exempts them. Federal funding for exemptions is limited and comes at a cost for counties and states in terms of their official levels of compliance. States can impose stricter rules, such as additional time limits, but cannot relax the rules without ramifications.

The US Department of Agriculture administers the "big five" food assistance programs, which are among the least controlling of programs: SNAP, WIC (Women, Infants, and Children), CACFP (Child and Adult Care Feeding Program), NSLP (National School Lunch Program), and SBP (School Breakfast Program). In April of 2019, there were 18.8 million households receiving SNAP, and in March 2020, there were 19 million (US Department of Agriculture 2022b). This jumped to 22.2 million the following month (April 2020) as the COVID-19 pandemic took hold in the United States (2022b). The number has been slowly decreasing, at 21.6 million as of April 2022 (2022b).

At this rate, it may take a decade before levels return to pre-pandemic levels, though policy changes in eligibility could more drastically change those numbers. SNAP has been found highly effective in reducing food insecurity among Americans, and for general economic stimulus (Rosenbaum 2013). SNAP comes in the form of an electronic debit card which recipients can use in the supermarket checkout line to purchase food, and sophisticated computer programs monitor SNAP transactions for patterns suggesting abuse. SNAP can only be used to purchase food for home preparation and consumption – it cannot be used for tobacco, alcohol, or hot foods intended for immediate consumption (Congressional Research Service 2018). A good number of SNAP participants also rely on soup kitchens and food pantries. Nonetheless, the vast majority of food aid comes from government sources. This is due in part to a greater legislative and public tolerance for food aid, especially food aid targeted at children, as opposed to cash assistance.

A number of other programs and policies exist to assist people in or near poverty. The Earned Income Tax Credit (EITC) is an important source of assistance for low-income families. The United States federal EITC is a refundable tax credit for low- to moderate-income working individuals and couples, particularly those with children. The maximum amount of credit ranges from $1,502 to $6,728, depending on number of children. Despite the fact that housing is one of the main areas of crisis for people of low-income backgrounds, federal assistance programs remain modest in scope. The National Low Income Housing Coalition reported in 2014 that in no state can someone work full-time at the minimum wage and afford a one- or two-bedroom dwelling at fair market rent. The Department of Housing and Urban Development (HUD) is the main federal agency for helping the low income with housing. HUD's main approach today is the Housing Choice Voucher Program (a.k.a. Section 8). HUD funds local public housing authorities (PHAs) to administer the program. In many places, however, the waiting list is long and demand remains high. The federal government has not funded any new public housing development since 1994, and many remaining federal public housing units house the elderly or disabled. TANF, SNAP, HUD, Medicaid, and the EITC make up the majority of America's welfare program for the nonelderly and nondisabled. Social Security – including a number of programs for the elderly, people with disabilities, and unemployment compensation – is even larger in scope, providing income and healthcare access for tens of millions of Americans. Altogether, these programs keep millions of people off the street.

Yet these programs fall short of full poverty relief. Hundreds of thousands of people do live on the street, while many more make do with crowded housing, inadequate income, unsafe accommodation, unsafe jobs, and other consequences of the current political economy. And, often, these programs make people jump through multiple bureaucratic hoops in order to access the little they can receive. Expanding the social safety net is always contentious in US politics. Two concerns repeatedly undermine poverty relief: financing the programs, and whether the people on the receiving end really deserve and benefit from the assistance.

Moffitt (2015) examined who received what in terms of transfers (EITC, food stamps, TANF, etc.) between 1980 and 2004, and found that people in deep poverty have received less in government transfers over time. The trend in social policy has been to favor married couples over single parents, households with children over those without, and people in the workforce over those not formally employed (Moffitt 2015). As a result, transfers have shifted more toward these households, leaving those in deep poverty with fewer forms of assistance (Moffitt 2015). Men who are not attached to households with children or spouses are particularly disadvantaged by government policy, even if they have an advantage over single mothers in the labor market.

In addition to this shift toward the so-called "deserving poor," the bureaucracy involved in obtaining assistance can be overwhelming. Although application requirements for SNAP and Medicaid have eased up at the federal level, these programs tend to be more politically supportable than cash transfers. Any sort of direct financial assistance, including emergency cash, emergency bill paying, and long-term housing assistance, requires extensive documentation that can take days to complete (Seale 2013). Such a process discourages people from applying unless they truly have no other recourse. It also communicates to the public and funders that undeserving people are not taking advantage. And it serves to ration limited resources. This occurs not only in government offices, but among nonprofit agencies as well.

To receive virtually any services beyond the most minimal, including at nonprofits, one must first go to the local Social Service office. I have volunteered at more than half a dozen nonprofit agencies in North Carolina and New York, and nearly all of them required documentation from the Department of Social Services (DSS), indicating that the individual or household had applied for services at DSS, what services they were being given or not given, and why. This served as income verification – sometimes DSS would turn people away because their income was too high, though nonprofit agencies had more leeway in that regard. However, going to DSS posed difficulties for people without transportation, for those who had to work regular hours, or for anyone who had any obligations during the day. It might take all day in the waiting room to finally see a caseworker. Many people I talked to at these agencies indicated that they hated how they were treated at DSS – not just in terms of interactions with people, but in how the general atmosphere and process seemed designed to indicate their low status. By the time the individual received their documentation from DSS, they typically had to come back to the nonprofit agency the next day, and go through another long process of intake.

Many researchers have pointed out that the TANF cash assistance program in particular is about penalizing clients. Katz (2018) wrote about mothers being sanctioned by TANF caseworkers for failing to meet program demands while desperately trying to balance mothering and schoolwork in an effort to escape poverty. Workfare participants in Katz's study reported that welfare caseworkers in the San Francisco Bay Area, who were balancing high caseloads and dealing with computer program changes, would sanction participants for what were in effect computer glitches. Pickering et al. (2006) found that more families lose benefits due to administrative reasons such as missed appointments than to work-placement issues. In fact, many TANF participants were very eager to get full-time work (Pickering et al. 2006). They fully supported the ideas behind TANF (self-sufficiency and financial independence), but were frustrated by the lack of help and policies that impeded their ability to get work or get by. As Taylor and Bloch (2018) indicated in their volume on *Marginalized Mothers, Mothering from the Margins*, mothers in poverty are policed by the state in multiple ways, based on the assumption that care work is not work, and are required to work outside the home in order to deserve assistance, even if that work is unpaid.

Criminalizing Poverty

An extensive literature also documents how the relations between the criminal justice system and people in poverty are largely coercive and penalizing. Not only are the poor disproportionately likely to be arrested for a criminal offense compared to the nonpoor (Lofstrom and Raphael 2016), but poverty itself is criminalized. People in poverty are penalized in ways both carceral and financial through the criminal justice system, including by:

• vagrancy laws criminalizing activities that indicate poverty or idleness, including loitering, begging, sleeping in public, and even "having no visible means of support," for which people could be arrested and forced to work (Kerber 1998; Glenn 2002)

- mass incarceration, as the USA incarcerates a greater proportion of its population than any other nation, at 639 per 100,000 in 2019, and spending on incarceration has increased at a much higher rate than spending on education (Stullich et al. 2016)
- incarceration for administrative reasons, such as violation of parole or probation supervision, or ineligibility for bail even for a minor infraction. The Council of State Governments found that one in four state prison inmates were there as a result of supervision violations in 2019 (Sawyer and Wagner 2020).
- the criminalization of homelessness, and punitive interactions such as move-along orders, citations, and destruction of the property of the homeless by police (Herring et al. 2020; Goldblum and Shaddox 2021)
- criminal monetary sanctions, such as Legal Financial Obligations (LFOs), which keep indigent defendants under the thumb of the criminal justice system, often for the rest of their lives, as legal debtors (Harris 2016)
- the bail industry for defendants who cannot pay their bail and which subsequently charges non-refundable premiums (Page and Soss 2020)
- the consequences of a drug conviction, which may include denial of TANF, SNAP, public housing benefits, and federal financial aid for higher education
- the exclusion of disability due to drug or alcohol use from consideration for Social Security Disability Insurance, Supplemental Security Income, and potentially Medicaid.

Charges for loitering on public grounds (such as sitting or sleeping on the sidewalk) can bring fees that mount up, preventing people from saving up sufficient rent money (Goldblum and Shaddox 2021). The majority of people convicted of a misdemeanor or felony receive some type of monetary sanction. People in poverty are often unable to pay these upon release, and even small amounts add up with the interest and surcharges applied. They sometimes have to report regularly to court, and may not regain rights lost upon conviction, such as the right to vote, until their account is paid. In 44 states and DC, judges are allowed "to incarcerate people for unpaid or delinquent LFOs" (Harris 2016:50). Debtors cannot be cleared through bankruptcy, cannot have their records sealed, receive pardons, or request deferred prosecutions. Debtors remain singularly powerless in relation to the criminal justice system. LFOs directly sustain poverty by rendering the poor poorer and even more vulnerable to local government control (Harris 2016:156).

Goldblum and Shaddox (2021) argued in their exposé of the conditions of poverty that, every time they looked into a situation of supposedly "bad choices," they found people were making the only choices available to them. For instance: "We found more than a thousand examples of African American and Hispanic homeowners at risk of losing their homes, not because they were profligate with money but because their lender was unethical" (144). As they pointed out, these situations were due not to irresponsible spending on the part of the homeowners, or to accident or bad luck. Rather, this particular housing situation "is the direct result of government policy and of malfeasance by a financial industry that continue to discriminate against people of color without fear that anemic regulators will exact any meaningful punishment" (144). This attribution applies to many other situations discussed in this section: people in poverty are penalized for their poverty because they are vulnerable to exploitation by the criminal justice system and viewed as undeserving in the social welfare system. Even though penalties are often enacted after the person has made some sort of "mistake," such as missing a meeting with a social worker or a probation officer, using illegal drugs, or not paying rent, the consequences are much worse for the person in poverty than for anyone else. People in poverty have a relationship with the state that is largely punitive. I have touched on only some of those relations in this section.

The Limits of Structuralism

Sociologists argue that the foundations of how our society operates make poverty unavoidable. The global and local labor markets that provide our goods and services, the profit-based economic system that benefits investors over laborers, the tax and expenditure system that privileges top-down economic policy rather than bottom-up economic policy, and the competition over resources that disadvantages civic organizations and local governments all function in enduring ways. These would require fundamental transformation to begin working to the benefit of the most disadvantaged of society. The ability to acquire massive amounts of wealth on the part of a few individuals is systematic and closely protected in American society. Thus, structure is a powerful factor in creating and reinforcing poverty.

Structuralism is critiqued as having two main weaknesses, however. It denies human agency, and it fails to reflect society as an ongoing human construction. We need to account for both the compelling nature of factors of political economy and institutional discrimination *and* their dependence on actual social action. This provides an understanding of structure that is not just about how society is organized, but how it is produced and reproduced. To put this another way, we require a conceptualization of structure that recognizes society's stability as dependent on human action, while also recognizing the durability of certain outcomes of human actions and social relations. It would also be useful to have a way to account for non-human influences such as pandemics and ecological developments. Ultimately, what we want to understand are those durable and material outcomes, such as law, governmental processes, resource depletion, and so on; how they are created; and how they interact with culture and agency (Archer 1996).

It is necessary to acknowledge the ways in which people are spread out over space, for instance, including segregation, as something apart from the actions that produced such segregation. What we are talking about, of course, is primarily material and institutional outcomes of human action. Culture involves the reasoning we employ to make sense of segregation and what accompanies it. Structure and culture as thus defined are both implicated in the production and experience of poverty. These terms reference essential elements of the social experience that are distinct, yet intertwined. As Archer (1996) argues, it makes sense to study these as autonomous processes that interact. We need a concept or set of concepts to represent the durable and material outcomes of human action in social relations – to use Porpora's definition, "effects that have effects" (2016:440) and which are not merely a matter of ideology.

At the same time, these forces are not inexorable. Structural features rarely compel one specific decision or set of decisions. Nonetheless, they must be reckoned with. Social features such as labor market demand or legal allowances for capital represent outcomes of action that have widespread and persistent implications, and it would take enormous effort to change them. However, there are people who do intend for political economic and discrimination processes to occur as they do. These processes continue to occur because someone with power benefits from them.

In recent theory, structure has been reworked to take individual action and agency better into account (Giddens 1984; Emirbayer and Goodwin 1994). For instance, Giddens emphasizes the routinization of action as the key mechanism for the reproduction of structure, and argues that it endures to the extent that the particular forms of routinization do. I find the most useful conception of structure is provided by the critical realists Margaret Archer and Douglas Porpora. Material interest motivates behavior, and though it is certainly not the only motivator, many social phenomena cannot be explained without regard for material interests (Porpora 2015). Material interests involve access to resources. This notion of structure is distinct from that of Giddens. Both Archer and Giddens view structure as involving "conditions of action and . . . unintended consequences which form the context of subsequent interaction" (Archer 2010:226). But whereas Giddens characterizes the social system as a visible pattern that can be reduced to practice, Archer (2010:228) views structure as containing properties that are irreducible to practice alone. For example, Archer emphasizes the role of time in making structure. Structure involves the outcomes of human action, which have an effect on human action that occurs later in time. Consider residential segregation or law. Sometimes, the outcomes are intended. By viewing structure as more than just routinized action, we can better interrogate intention. Hence, the outcomes of human action develop an objectivity that then acts on human action, even though these outcomes may be changed or supported by subsequent human action.

The answer to the question of why people act as they do includes both structural positioning and the meanings that people create and navigate their lives by. In human behavior, what is viewed as possible, what is viewed as permissible, and what is viewed as valuable (i.e., culture) operates *in addition to* what is possible, what is permissible, and what is valued (i.e., structure). The two shape each other. Culture, therefore, never makes sense as the sole explanation for some social or group outcome. And might we not say the same of structure? What structure can hold up without *meaning* to legitimate and explain its existence and allow for the repetitive actions that must occur to sustain it? How do people in poverty interpret their institutional encounters? Or, perhaps, the presence of some opportunity may exist structurally, but remain unsupported by the cultural reality of an individual – for instance, when a young person simply does not believe they are capable of something or that something is meaningful, such as becoming a doctor, although financial support may exist. In such a case, the individual may be just as unable to take advantage of such an opportunity as in the reverse situation, in which the cultural reality exists but not the structural. For instance, when an individual desires to attend a particular school, but cannot afford it.

Archer (1996) suggests that we include both structure and culture into a larger analytical framework because, though distinct, they operate closely together. She assigns independence to each realm, in order to examine their interplay. A unified approach that includes agency also allows us to examine "how discursive struggles are socially organized and [how] social struggles are culturally conditioned" (1996:xxix). She sees both structure and culture as existing at a larger level than that represented by individuals and the momentary interaction between them. They can in turn "penetrate" the other at the interactional level. For instance, the explanations for the formation or success of social movements involve both material interests and ideas. While culture of poverty as an explanation for poverty has been discredited, culture still matters for understanding social outcomes.

I believe social relations may be the missing piece. As Burkitt (2016:333) wrote, "it is not others, as individuals or organizations, that constrain us but the nature of our relationship to them." Wealth accumulation processes, labor markets, and spatial processes are all examples of durable conditions created by prior social relations that then exert influence and compel other social relations. Sociologists have also identified objective realities which may be human-caused, but that play a strong role in social life once they are in play. As we have seen with the COVID-19 pandemic, the economy and people's quality of life are not just subject to human control and decision-making. While pandemics, ecological features, climate change, and natural disasters are generally not considered "structure," they do represent an externally imposed reality with which we must reckon when dealing with issues of poverty. These material realities exert effects on social relations.

A Relational Approach

How do social relations fill in the missing pieces of the *structure–culture–individual* triad? Social relations are the intermediaries between structure and culture on one end, and the individual at the other. Structure and culture create social relations and are created through social relations – that is, how people are connected to each other. We can think of a relation as a set of expectations and transactions between two or more actors, with organizations sometimes filling in as the "actor." A relation is transactional (Dépelteau 2008) and involves a set of expectations regarding rights, obligations, and value. Relation is a more general term. Relationship has more specificity; it is a relation or type of relation involving expectations that develop out of communication between actors (Fuhse 2013). A relation more generally does not have to involve any communication, or even knowledge of each other as individuals: "The concept only implies a basic relatedness in terms of positions somehow standing in relation to each other" (Fuhse 2013:184). This basic relatedness may involve being defined through each other (expectations) or involve negotiation or exchange of some kind (transactions). Transactions can include communication, financial transactions, exchange of resources or information, obligations, symbolic resources, or anything of social value. Expectations can be subsumed under transactions, but a set of expectations may be necessary to the existence of a social relation, above and beyond other forms of transactions. There must be some transaction, which may include just a set of expectations. "Expectations" sound voluntary, but generally are not. We are expected to obtain a professional degree before practicing a profession. We are expected to meet certain standards of parenthood in our interactions with and attitudes toward our dependent children, else we may face separation or other legal sanctions. We expect others to perform certain actions or symbolize certain meanings. Consequences for not meeting expectations of a social relation vary from trivial to fatal.

The context for each of these relations is drawn from the "structure" and "culture" previously formed by other social relations. Structure and culture are products of what is done through social relations. In other words, both the expectations and the resource or transactional differential that make up a social relation derive from products of other social relations. For example, housing problems consist of social relations between actors looking for housing and landlords who own the housing. These relations depend upon laws and understandings about the need for housing, the need to one's property, the issues around paying rent, the responsibilities and rights of each party, and the ability to enforce these rights and responsibilities, all of which in turn depend on past social transactions. "Actions are always chosen in a relational context, and the menu of available choices is influenced, but not determined, by the institutional frameworks and organizational fields in which actions are pursued, as well as the relative power of actors in those fields" (Tomaskovic-Devey and Avent-Holt 2019:226).

There is a middle way between the individualism that puts all of the responsibility on individuals, on one hand, and the pure structuralism that posits explanations that are indifferent to individual agency. That way is the relational approach. This is why I propose we reframe our understanding of poverty – its causes and its effects – by thinking in terms of sets of conditions and social relations. The processes contributing to poverty are not merely economic. In a relational framework, culture and structure together, as sets of conditions, provide context for the social relations that give meaning and consequence to people's behaviors and expectations. Thus, the social relations are what we need to focus on – not the culture of the poor; nor merely the structural arrangements that limit people in poverty. As the preceding arguments strongly suggest, inequality and poverty are products of both symbolic resources *and* material conditions and durable products of social relations. Poverty is plural in nature (Wolff and De-Shalit 2007). Many of those in poverty are not just disadvantaged by lack of money. To redistribute money, Wolff and De-Shalit (2007) have argued, will not end oppressive social structures, although it can make a difference for some individuals and probably alleviate many problems. The point is to conceptualize inequality as both a distributional (i.e., wealth) and a social (i.e., relational) problem. Material wealth is of course important, but so are the relations between people: social justice requires us to "create the right types of classless relationships between people; avoiding oppression, exploitation, domination, servility, snobbery, and other hierarchical evils" (5).

For instance, consider Bhandari et al.'s (2011) analysis of intimate partner violence and pregnancy among rural women. Bhandari et al. (2011:834) have noted that: "Among rural women living in Appalachia, Bailey and Daugherty (2007) found rates between 14.6% to 28% for physical or sexual abuse during a current pregnancy and rates of psychological abuse as high as 80%." These rates of abuse are linked to structural factors, including geographical isolation, lack of necessary resources such as education and employment, and gender inequality (Bhandari et al. 2011). These structural features affect social relations between men and women in intimate partnership such that intimate partner violence is more likely. The social relations of women's vulnerability and the lack of accountability for men allow such abuse to occur. Additional social relational factors may come into play, including substance abuse and the situation of unwanted or unplanned pregnancy. Thus, individual level behavior such as committing violence and the suffering of psychological abuse are made possible by, encouraged by, and/or permitted by structural and cultural features.

The application of a relational perspective along these lines to poverty studies has already yielded useful results. There are, in fact, a number of researchers across the social sciences who have declared themselves relational poverty scholars (Blokland 2012; Sharam and Hulse 2014; Elwood et al. 2017). I believe we can push the relational approach even further to encompass not only the view that poverty is not created by the poor but how the behaviors of people in poverty are relational achievements. Other scholars have also incorporated the power of relationality into their analyses or theories. Evelyn Nakano Glenn (2002:12) has defined race and gender "as mutually constituted systems of relationships – including norms, symbols and practices – organized around perceived differences." These processes occur at different levels. They are "relational concepts," by which Glenn meant that "race and gender categories . . . are positioned and therefore gain meaning in relation to each other" (13). The concept of relationality is useful because it points to the importance of the contrast – that the dominant category needs the subordinate category – and because it can be used to point out how group differences "are systematically related" (14). Differences do not exist merely in terms of experience; rather, the lives of people in the different groups are directly connected.

Combining an understanding of social relations and structure need not absolve people from moral responsibility for their actions. To understand is not always to justify or to forgive. Although the individual is always acting relationally, the individual still represents an agent with its own capacity and moral responsibility.

Wolff and De-Shalit (2007) addressed this issue in their book on poverty titled *Disadvantage*. They described how people in poverty face constraints and risks in their everyday lives such that mitigation involves them in greater risk and insecurity. For instance, in order to keep a job, a mother without childcare might leave her children at home alone. If we accept this, then how can we hold such individuals responsible for their actions and choices (Wolff and De-Shalit 2007)? As another example, to address the risk of hunger, one may take advantage of the vulnerability of someone else. Should that perpetrator be held responsible for their actions, or do we chalk it up to problematic effects of the structure? Of course, this is just another false dichotomy; the two are not incompatible. Structure does not determine the action of individuals, though it may constrain their options. Wolff and De-Shalit have suggested that, for purposes of policymaking, we should consider burdens as opposed to questions of moral responsibility. This involves asking *"whether it is reasonable to expect someone to act one way rather than another"* (Wolff and De-Shalit 2007:80). For instance, someone may have adapted to prior social relations in ways that make acting in new conditions difficult. And if taking advantage of an opportunity involves considerable cost, such as risk to other functionings, then Wolff and De-Shalit say we have to recognize that this cannot be counted as a genuine opportunity that the hypothetical person presumably threw away. The experience of indigence is typically complicated by additional dimensions of disadvantage that place the person in a structural position of vulnerability and irresolvable choices.

Relationality is not just about who you know or the strength of your ties. It references connections between people who do not know one another, such as a laborer and a stockholder for the same company. It is also about more than just the utilitarian benefit of social "capital." It is about the content of our interactions – how we relate to one another – as well as the positions of people in wider society. Yet there is real benefit from studying what is generally referred as social capital in the literature. For instance, Chetty et al. (2022) find that children from disadvantaged backgrounds who have cross-class interactions – measured by social media connections – are more likely to transcend poverty as adults than are their peers with fewer such connections. We just need to go beyond these notions of connections when thinking about what poverty involves more broadly. Fuhse (2013:181) writes that, although "social relationships [are] the constituent elements of social structure," we too rarely examine what social relationships are, how they form, evolve, and connect to other layers.

The relational approach is not a theory, but an analytic. Some theories are already relational; perhaps others would benefit from incorporating more relationality. It is important not to treat relationality as a theory because, by itself, the approach does not tell you *which* relations to examine. Logically, the relational approach is self-referential and circular: society is made up of social relations, so social relations are important to society and individuals. The relational approach, however, serves to remind us of the ways in which individual behavior is contextual and situational. More specifically, behavior is relational – we act in relation to others, and in the context of specific relations. There may be specific relations we want to examine. In the next chapter, for instance, I examine relations between individuals and the labor market, between individuals and employers, and between individuals and their peers, among others. This allows us to see that it is not just that the labor market is problematic – it is the relation people have to the labor market that is problematic. It is not just the employer or employee who is problematic; it is the relation between them such that the employee has no recourse. Highlighting these relations also points back toward structural and cultural conditions that support these relations. But the key thing is to change the relation.

Conclusion

Thus, structure is important, but it is not the only way to understand poverty. Thinking about the effects of structure and culture on social relations links the macro level of society to the micro level of the individual. The next chapter focuses on the structure of, and relations of, opportunity that individuals in poverty experience. We can understand the opportunities available especially as a matter of structure, but the individual's reaction to any opportunities that might exist occur in the context of social relations.

6

Opportunity and Personal Autonomy

Will people in poverty take advantage of opportunities that come their way? Opinions and impressions on this issue have influenced policy for decades. The research is divided on this because, of course, it depends. An individual's response to opportunity is shaped by social relations within a situation. A variety of social relations have been found to affect response to opportunity. I consider the literature on three major forms of opportunity as relevant for people in poverty: going to college; finding employment or better employment; and personal autonomy more generally. This is not an exhaustive list of the conditions people in poverty face; rather, the purpose is to examine the research around a few cases to illustrate the application of the relational framework and the light it casts on how people in poverty confront opportunity.

Going to College

The Macro View of Education

After beginning with a big-picture view, I will discuss the importance of relationships for young people's ability to complete high school and attend college. This approach in turn leads us into a consideration of how youth, especially those from low-income backgrounds, become disenfranchised from education. Since education, even a high school degree, is important for economic success, understanding these relations is useful for thinking about how to improve young adults' positioning relative to the labor market. And because education is also critical for a variety of other outcomes – health, arts and entertainment preferences, political and civil responsibility, general empowerment and quality of life (Perna 2005; Baum et al. 2013; Salazar 2013) – it is important for thinking about how social processes stratify people in non-financial ways as well.

Parental education and household net worth together are by far the strongest predictors for academic achievement (Conley 1999). Yet research suggests that young people from low-income families are nearly as likely as middle-income youth to aspire to higher education (Oyserman 2013). However, less than 10% of individuals from low-income families obtained a bachelor's degree by age 24 in 2010, compared with about 25% of those from middle-income families, and just under 50% for those from high-income families (Jeffrey 2020). About 47% of high school students from the lowest socioeconomic quintile enroll in any institution of higher education within a year of graduation (based on cohort data for ninth-grade students in 2009), compared to 88% of those from the highest quintile (Fain 2019). Researchers conclude that aspirations and expectations are necessary but not sufficient for college attendance (Oyserman 2013).

The entire process of education, from kindergarten to completing a bachelor's degree, is more challenging for children of low-income families. Roscigno et al. (2006) found inner-city and rural disadvantages in both family and school resources as compared to metropolitan and suburban districts. Rural public schools have limited resources with which to prepare students for college, such as limited access to college testing preparation (Whiteside 2021). Part of the disadvantage across place may also relate to the student composition. Peers have a major impact and set the tone for the classroom environment (Coleman 1966; Figlio 2005). Zimmer and Toma (2000) found that raising average ability in a classroom increased individual student achievement, especially for low-ability students. However, increasingly, private schools are preferred by those Americans who can afford them, leaving even fewer advantaged students in the public schools (Rooks 2017). Meanwhile, public schools reported increases in the number of homeless children (Edin and Shaefer 2015). The inequities in primary education for low-income and minority students lower their chances of attending and completing college. Applying for financial aid is a daunting process for many low-income families. Tellingly, even middle-income families experience serious difficulty in preparing their children for college (Napolitano et al. 2014). Attending college – especially four-year-degree institutions – is expensive, difficult, and time consuming, though the rewards are considerable.

The Importance of Relationships for Success

Going to college is not a discrete action. It is the product of steps taken over the course of many years. Low expectations among family, friends, and school officials impact an individual's sense of obligation to attend college. Non-academic obligations might interfere with making college attendance and preparation a priority. But expectations for oneself are also affected by a lack of confidence and adequate preparation, combined with the distant reality of college. This is reinforced by sets of conditions including the high costs of attending college, the difficulty attending college poses for earning money in the short term, and duties to family.

Parents and school officials play some of the most important roles in these situations at the micro level (Oyserman 2013). Positive interactions and close relationships with teachers, having a close family member who attended college, a mentor of some kind who has intimate knowledge of higher educational processes, or having close friends who plan to attend university play important roles for expectations of high school seniors and their ability to actually apply to and then attend college. Whiteside (2021) describes the challenges faced and supports required by first-generation rural students in college. Every one of the 20 students interviewed described taking unusual steps outside the context of their high schools to prepare for and attend college. One of the most critical elements for their ultimate success, however, was a long-term mentor-advocate. Julie Bettie (2003) found, in her in-depth study of a California high school, that the working-class young women intending to attend college as seniors had been heavily exposed to middle-class expectations. They may have previously attended a private school and/or seriously engaged in school extracurricular activities or athletics that middle- and upper-class students primarily participated in. Bettie (2003) also noted that the upwardly mobile Mexican-American young women intending to attend college often had older siblings who went to college.

Many studies on the transitions of young people from low-income backgrounds find the same thing in various ways: one's relationships with teachers, parents, siblings, mentors, extended family members, and peers often make the difference for a young person's educational aspirations, abilities, and knowledge regarding higher education. The exceptions tend to prove the rule: the successful students from low-income backgrounds always reflect the importance of who you know and having the right support from others. Unfortunately, a great many young people become disenfranchised from education before the senior year of high school, leaving them with even more diminished prospects for secondary school, and often even ending their high school career prematurely.

School Disengagement

Oppositional culture theory is one explanation for how young people from low-income or racial minority backgrounds come to reject the importance of education (Ogbu 1978; Ainsworth-Darnell and Downey 1998). This theory suggests that these young people develop and perpetuate a culture resisting mainstream values as part of how they maintain respect and a sense of belonging in their peer groups. This notion of an oppositional culture has been used to explain lower educational achievement among young African American boys and men in particular, who are thought to view academic success as "acting White." This theory has been challenged by research that finds most students from racial minority or low-income backgrounds do not reject the importance of education (Carter 2005; Diamond and Huguley 2014). However, research finds that many young people from disadvantaged backgrounds often disengage from school, finding it at odds with maintaining self-respect or self-affirmation (Morris 2012). Sánchez-Jankowski (2008), for instance, considers how low-income students do not so much resist or reject education as focus on that which provides affirmation. Many of the urban and minority youth he studied viewed high school as a temporary situation before real adult life began, and thus best used as a place for fun. Indeed, many of them may have viewed this time in their life as a last chance for any fun before a tough working life began.

In a classic study of working-class adolescent men in the United Kingdom, Willis ([1977] 1981) argued that the physical and social organization of schools often reinforced the position of the student as inferior and subject to the authority of the teacher. Some young men lose trust in the school as a result of their experiences, and there are many alternative authorities to switch allegiance to if one is working class. Teachers, in trying to maintain authority, sometimes give way to sarcasm and what are taken as class-based insults that can communicate a belief that the boys are incapable of learning. As a result, many of the male students from working-class backgrounds developed an oppositional orientation reinforced by the peer group. Willis called this peer group "the lads." As Willis's study suggests, gender plays a role in school orientations for low-income and racial minority youth. The pressure for working-class boys to prove their masculinity in delinquent activities versus the pressure for girls to conform and submit to authority actually confers an advantage on working-class girls over boys when it comes to performing well in school (Bettie 2003; Morris 2012).

Across studies, we consistently see examples of how protecting one's dignity in an environment where one is, or feels, at a disadvantage often reinforces one's marginalization. This has the additional effect of making it seem that they *choose* their place: to purposively fail, skip, or show up late to class, coming to school high, and so on (Willis [1977] 1981; Bettie 2003; Morris 2012). Rather than seeing themselves as inferior, working-class youth may develop an attitude that rejects bourgeois culture and lifestyles (Willis [1977] 1981). "The lads" believe the school makes false promises about the opportunities available to them should they conform. Moreover, it can seem disloyal to their family, peers, and general background to aspire to middle-class standards. Thus, Willis suggests, what seems on the surface irrational or illogical may be at some level quite rational and even "developmental," as opposed to "regressive" ([1977] 1981:120); in fact, this is another adaptation to their social relations. Yet, in rejecting bourgeois culture, the rejecters do not gain anything beyond a perhaps fleeting sense of dignity. By rejecting school norms, the lads rebel; by valuing working-class labor, they rebel; but the end result is that they actually conform to expectations for them held by wider society.

Finally, much research considers why some students exit high school before completion. Family support and privilege, of course, predict drop-out odds fairly well. Feldman et al. (2017), however, wanted to dig deeper in their study of high school "drop-outs" to learn the stories behind decisions to leave school. They found that many ex-students did not fit the stereotype of being delinquents from troubled families who did not care about school or learning. While delinquency and family crisis can both be problems, many of their issues started long before their last days of school attendance. Academic difficulties and the perception of being too far behind to ever catch up played a large role, but the researchers report a complex web of factors both school- and non-school-related. Problems usually started in middle school – the researchers were surprised to learn, however, that only a minority of drop-outs remembered elementary school as problematic. The disengagement began in middle school, worsened during high school, and then provided the context for failing to complete high school. Ultimately, a picture emerges of a lack of support in the school system for these students, for a variety of reasons. Many schools may not have had the resources to provide what these students needed, and could not address the social problems of peer influence, bullying, and the sense of not belonging.

It will be important to consider the disparate impact of the COVID-19 pandemic for students from different backgrounds. Access to technology during school closures and other attendance adaptations was a problem for low-income families (Shapiro 2020; Ford et al. 2021). Home environments for low-income families during the pandemic are thought to have been particularly disruptive due to stay-at-home orders, unemployment, and crowding (Johnson et al. 2022). Research has even suggested that, for advanced degree-seekers, familial support diminished for underrepresented students, causing more hardship for degree completion (Walsh et al. 2021). Educators and others are deeply concerned that this will worsen educational outcomes by social class and reduce upward mobility for years to come (Ali 2021).

Education is the best route to long-term security for Americans. Attending college, however, remains out of reach for many people due to the social relations of socioeconomic disadvantage. These relations are shaped by the institution of education, family circumstances, and neighborhood conditions, and include virtually everyone in a young person's network: family, friends, teachers, other school officials, police officers, and so on. These people and institutions determine whether a young person is prepared for college, and affect how a young person comes to see themself, their abilities, and options.

Finding (Better) Employment

But not everyone without a college degree lives in poverty. Given the constant flux of people in and out of poverty, how do we understand the factors involved in indigent status entry and exit? A number of social-relational factors affect this movement. While I discussed many of the structural factors responsible in the last chapter, here I look more deeply into some of the social relations that are affected by structure, and in turn affect income opportunity. I address two main issues: the reliance on work shaped by one's relation to the state, and that in turn profoundly shapes poverty in the USA; and the vulnerabilities derived from other relations that make this work reliance so difficult for so many. I then comment on a few related issues: the notion of work ethic that many view as a critical piece for contemporary poverty, the lack of opportunity, and the selling not only of one's labor but of one's life through military service.

Relation to the State and the Reliance on Work

To understand the relations of people in poverty to the labor force, it helps to understand their relations to the state, particularly in terms of social policy and immigration policy. Recall that Temporary Aid to Needy Families (TANF) developed out of legislation whose purpose was not to create jobs or improve job skills, but to promote immediate labor force attachment. TANF is based on the idea that if welfare clients were forced to take advantage of the opportunity of employment, they would be able to exit poverty for good and leave welfare dependence behind. This worked for some – mostly those who had the good fortune of adequate network support or some other situational advantage (Mammen et al. 2015). However, much empirical research reveals the insecurity of employment and the many obstacles to remaining in work. An absence of adequate training, education, or skills is exacerbated by the severe lack of decent jobs outside of those targeting particular kinds of skills. Other structural arrangements contribute to the difficulty of surviving in employment, including childcare difficulties – even when women could pay for childcare with assistance, they could not always arrange for childcare during their shift (Mammen et al. 2015). Place also matters. The lack of healthcare providers accepting Medicaid, along with the lack of public transportation, exacerbate these effects in many rural areas. The conditions that characterize high-poverty rural areas in particular, such as higher unemployment and lower educational levels, do not fit with workfare requirements.

Before welfare reform took effect in 1997, Edin and Lein (1997) undertook a study of the ability of single mothers to work their way out of poverty and to survive on extremely low incomes, whether welfare, work, or a combination of the two. In the context of single motherhood, their calculations of income and costs indicate that neither welfare nor work provides enough income to live on. And yet they survive somehow. Edin and Lein identified several "income-generating strategies" these single mothers engaged in for economic survival. The one mother in the whole study who did not engage in significant additional income-generating strategies – playing by the rules of the welfare agency – was *not making it*; she was in danger of losing custody of her children due to neglect. Three basic strategies were used to bring in money: work in the formal, informal, or underground economy; cash assistance from absent fathers, relatives, or boyfriends; and cash assistance from agencies. Across the four cities, however, single mothers faced desperate situations that they were unable to resolve. Even prior to welfare reform, this was a precarious existence.

For those mothers who were on welfare, most had held a job before, and their experience in the labor market taught them that the kinds of jobs they were likely to get would not do much for them financially or emotionally. Moving from welfare to work came with major risks. If the job did not work out, it could be months before they could get back on welfare. They also did not see much chance of advancing, no matter how long they stayed at a job. Training programs offered by the government added little to their earning power. Working could also jeopardize the safety and well-being of their children, if it subjected them to extreme hardship caused by losing the job or getting hours cut, or if it meant lack of supervision. This situation left some mothers feeling boxed in, forced to rely on welfare when they would much rather work (Edin and Lein 1997).

Nonetheless, most welfare-reliant mothers planned to work in the future. About half were working already in formal or informal jobs. Edin and Lein (1997:72–3) wrote that, in order to be successful, single mothers would need to get unusually lucky in finding a decent-paying job, have a childcare subsidy, and have very low housing or transportation costs. Yet they remained committed to employment as the solution, leaving welfare whenever possible. "Most mothers had moved from one job to another, always looking for some slight advantage – more hours, a better shift, a lower copayment on a health plan . . . without substantially improving their earnings over the long term" (Edin and Lein 1997:2–3). Only 14 percent of mothers interviewed had "no clear plans to leave welfare for work" (77). Some of these had a disabled child in the family. Of the others, half thought they'd be better off combining welfare with unreported income in order to keep their housing subsidies and medical benefits. A few were hoping to marry soon, and a very few simply felt their situation was too unstable to think about the future. Some mothers were using welfare as a way to get more schooling. One mother put it (Edin and Lein 1997:81):

This is what I call restructuring myself. Because really I worked for seven years and didn't accomplish anything. Living over here in the projects they took more away from me when I worked. As I was trying to struggle to get out, they was taking away from me, and I was losing ... So this time I said I was going to sit down and feel like I'm making a plan for myself, thinking about how I'm going to find some funds to go back to school.

Many of the mothers believed it was almost impossible to combine parenting, full-time work, and full-time school, whereas one could do schooling and parenting on welfare. Overall, cycling between welfare and work is a common pattern for single mothers, not a trap that keeps them dependent, although Edin and Lein say this may occasionally happen. But, more tellingly, low-wage work usually makes them worse off than they were on welfare, as it increased their vulnerability and dependence on a number of factors beyond their control (Edin and Lein 1997).

Relying on welfare in the ways that the women in Edin and Lein's (1997) study did is no longer viable. Since the 1996 welfare reform legislation, relying on government cash assistance is restricted to five years of an adult's life, and comes with many strings attached, primarily what are called work-related requirements. Nowadays, many in poverty assume that getting cash from social services is no longer an option (Edin and Shaefer 2015). Studies find that eligible individuals often do not even bother to apply, or are discouraged from applying by how social services are administered (Edin and Shaefer 2015; Lansberry et al. 2017). Welfare is now, at best, a short-term, last-ditch option.

An individual's relation to the state in terms of citizenship affects not only labor market opportunities and conditions, but the relational sacrifices they have to make in order to succeed economically. Some of the most poorly paid workers in the USA are unauthorized immigrants and guest workers. The experiences of immigrants not only direct attention to those who have already gone to great lengths to seek opportunity or survival, but can also illustrate the importance of macro-scale relations. As Cleaveland (2013:2) writes, "the global displacement of workers ... [is] facilitated by economic policies abetting deregulation of markets, diminution of the welfare state, and promotion of 'free' trade across borders (Sassen, 2002)." For instance, there are a number of different statuses that a foreign-born individual might have in the USA: naturalized citizen; legal permanent resident; refugee and asylum-seeker; legal resident on temporary visa, including guest worker; and unauthorized, also known as undocumented (Altman et al. 2021). Guest worker programs have been used for many decades as a compromise on the migration issue between those who fear a large influx and those who need workers brought from out of the country (Hahamovitch 2011). Unlike other immigrants, guest workers cannot bring their families or become citizens; they constitute "an especially vulnerable class of labor" (Hahamovitch 2011:backcover). Both authorized and unauthorized immigration have increased over the past three decades. Many migrants do not live in poverty, but we can identify certain risk factors. First-generation non-citizen children are at a high risk for (officially defined) poverty. Their poverty rate was 34.4%, averaged over the course of the last three decades, followed by second-generation children of two foreign-born parents at 28.6%, and first-generation citizen children at 17.5% (Thiede and Brooks 2018). The risk is compounded if one is Hispanic, which is also associated with greater odds of experiencing material hardships (Thiede and Brooks 2018; Altman et al. 2021).

Deciding to migrate is not an easy decision. Abrego studies the migration of parents to the USA from El Salvador. Many of the parents in Abrego's study only decided to migrate after a period of deep despair, in which they could see no other way. In the aptly titled *Sacrificing Families*, Abrego (2014) notes that transnational families face impossible choices – or, at least, choices that are difficult and costly even when migration is clearly the most viable option. Recent civil war, a weak economy, and highly structured inequality blocked access to the few positions of security. Furthermore, migration is sometimes effective for children's survival and/or advancement, but exacts a high emotional cost. The very restrictive paths to legal immigration mean that, in order to give their children a chance at survival, many parents must be "illegal." Illegality, or even the insecurity of a temporary protected status as workers, prevents visitation with family at home. Family separation takes a special toll, sometimes leading to despair when the length of separation becomes particularly long with diminishing hope for reunification. Having the ability to see each other in person made a big difference in terms of the well-being of parent and child, as did having a legal path to reunification (Abrego 2014). The punitive approach to unauthorized immigration – which is itself created by state policy that restricts legal immigration – has created an even more precarious situation for many undocumented immigrants. The threat and/or fear of deportation makes them vulnerable to criminals, to employers, and to abusers (Bacon 2008). Even legal immigrants are vulnerable and they may become illegal after their documentation expires (Abrego 2014). And there are no easy paths to legality – at least there were not for Abrego's research participants.

Citizenship is full membership in the society in which one lives (Glenn 2002). The lack of citizenship acts powerfully to limit access to certain material resources and opportunities to acquire material advantage, such as through education, healthcare, government assistance of many kinds, labor rights, and civil and legal protections. Citizenship is fundamental to a life of security. But it is no guarantee. The safety net for citizens does not provide much alternative to work. For those individuals with citizenship but lacking security, the granting of security to those without citizenship may appear contradictory.

Relations of Vulnerability

In addition to relations with the state, relations with employers, family members, and the general "other" shape the conditions of precarity within which so many people live. Vulnerability to even minor negative events is one of the main reasons it *appears* that a person in poverty fails to take advantage even when good things happen. In reality, they remain at a disadvantage for a long time in terms of their relations with employers, family members, and the wider world. Too much can go wrong before stability and security are attained.

The social relations between employees and employers or managers matter immensely. When employers are able to replace low-wage workers easily, or when employees are highly dependent on their employment, employees' work lives are often difficult (Zuberi 2006; Pugh 2015; Cassino and Besen-Cassino 2019). As Jacobs and Padavic (2015) found, low-wage workers commonly experienced unpredictable schedules, inadequate hours, time theft, and involuntary hours reduction as a means of control and punishment. One minor event, such as a short illness, can result in missed rent payments (Jacobs and Padavic 2015). Mammen et al. (2015) also found that health issues could and often did sabotage the ability of a low-income family to exit or stay out of poverty.

The first few months of a new job pose a particularly difficult time. Food stamps get reduced, but reliable income may not have provided a stable financial situation just yet (Edin and Lein 1997). Childcare becomes a new expense. Wage-reliant mothers sometimes gave up a higher-paying job for a lower-paying job that had better benefits (Edin and Lein 1997), but it is often some time before those benefits kick in.

Recent labor market developments have worsened employer–employee and employee–customer relations. About one out of four jobs pays poverty-level wages for a family of four (Edin and Shaefer

2015). For workers with little education, the service sector represents their best bet. Many service sector employers ensure regular turnover among employees to avoid paying benefits and raises (Edin and Shaefer 2015). The new "gig" economy is in some ways worse than the informal labor market, given that there is a "middle man" taking the biggest portion of profit. Edin and Shaefer (2015) discuss some of the techniques of the desperate in their study of deep poverty: prostitution; selling the social security numbers of one's children, and probably other people's as well; informal taxi services without any license, registration, insurance, or license plate. The development of a "shadow economy" – illegal or informal transactions that shadow a regular business or industry – further enables the exploitation of the most vulnerable.

Several factors influence exactly how difficult it is to make it on low wages, including obligations to very young children, the presence of a domestic partner and their relative contribution/obligation of support, and cultural arrangements that make employment nonetheless highly desirable for many people in poverty (Bennett 2014; Pendo 2016). The attractiveness of employment includes the pride in working, the opportunity to meet new people in a workplace, the desire to send a positive message to one's children, and the stigma of social service dependence (Hagler et al. 2015). Thus, we repeatedly hear people in poverty saying they want to work.

Work and Spending Ethics

Tienda and Stier (1991) found that only 6 percent of Chicago inner-city parents were voluntarily idle. There are those few who do wallow in poverty and unemployment – though I believe you'll find more of the idle among the middle class. But the vast majority of people in or near poverty work, and work hard. *No Shame in My Game: The Working Poor in the Inner City* is an ethnography of Harlem fast food workers and applicants (Newman 1999) in which researchers interviewed and surveyed over 300 people. These residents of Harlem and Washington Heights were African Americans, Puerto Ricans, and Dominicans. Newman (1999) shows how work experience often leads to a work ethic, not the other way around as many believe. Having a job makes a difference for young people – it provides structure, income, ambition, pride, and an identity as a working person. Many Harlem residents work despite many reasons not to: the job offerings pay poorly, offer little advancement, are often part-time – meaning workers make too much to qualify for Medicaid but often do not get health insurance – and some of the jobs carry a stigma. Like many other studies, these results attest to the endurance of the work ethic among the poor. Study participants say things like, "Having a job pushed me to go to school" and "There's a time for hanging out and a time for work. You know, you have to do something with your life, get some money, make something of yourself."

Flexibility in spending habits is necessary for coping with poverty (Fitchen 1981). On average, single mothers spend about 7 percent of their budget on what might be termed "nonessentials," such as lottery tickets, cable TV, restaurants, cigarettes, other drugs, movies, and other entertainment (Edin and Lein 1997). Spending small amounts of money on nonessentials such as cigarettes and soda helped the mothers avoid feeling completely hopeless or worthless. Spending money on one's looks, such as hair and clothing, might seem frivolous, but it can make all the difference to a person's motivation to job hunt, their confidence, and their success (Edin and Shaefer 2015). The lottery could provide a sense of escape for some, allowing them to fantasize a bit (Edin and Lein 1997). Spending on unnecessary items serves the purpose of keeping harmony in the family, while long-term saving goals are discouraging and often difficult to accomplish (Fitchen 1981). Newman (1999:258) found that none of the study participants was able to amass savings – "those who had something squirreled away ran through it rapidly." Familial expectations and networks of reciprocity make saving nearly pointless as the money will be used as soon as someone needs help. Stack (1974:128) similarly argues that the people in this study have a "remarkably accurate assessment of the social order . . . they can realistically appraise the futility of hoarding a small cash reserve . . . What is seen by some interpreters as disinterest in delayed rewards is actually a rational evaluation of need." Spending versus saving is another way in which people in poverty undermine their long-term interests in order to survive the short term.

What Opportunity?

To talk about opportunity in American society today is to talk about the opportunity to compete with many people for a small number of positions. Inequality of wealth and income have been increasing. Wealth is increasingly monopolized by the already wealthy. This leaves less for the rest of us. It is not a fair playing field. The privileged have and use the power to maintain and increase that privilege. Many of us are cut out from the beginning. Many others are cut out at every point along the way, and our individual actions often bear no relation to success or failure. Even when working, the jobs are often not sufficient (Newman 1999). Perhaps especially, the deep poor in Edin and Shaefer's (2015:xxiv) study "want more than anything else ... the chance to work." But will there always be situations where work is simply not a solution, as Edin and Shaefer argue (2015:xxiv)?

Let's consider the big picture in terms of movement across income divided into five levels, or quintiles. Intergenerational mobility is lower for those in the bottom quintile in the USA in comparison to other affluent nations, whereas it is about on par for the middle quintiles (Iceland 2013). Across rich countries, parents in the top quintile reliably transmit top-quintile privilege to their children (Iceland 2013). The biggest difference between the USA and other comparable nations, therefore, is among those at the bottom. Iceland identifies schooling, and the large variation in school quality across the USA based on race, class, and geographic factors, as likely culprits. Lower levels of social and health support in the USA, compared to other affluent nations, likely matters as well. There is also greater variation in American incomes, requiring a greater increase or decrease in income to transcend quintiles, even if one is actually better off than one's parents. There is still definitely mobility – slightly more than half of all children born to parents in the bottom quintile in prior years ended up in a higher quintile as adults (Iceland 2013). However, prior generational mobility patterns may not apply to young people today if income inequality and affordability crises continue to increase.

When encountering actual people in real situations, it nonetheless remains tempting to blame people's poverty on their own individual actions. But to understand the ways in which people in poverty attempt to escape poverty and variably succeed and fail, it is essential to refrain from committing what I call the Individual Blame Fallacy. Because all individuals make mistakes, one can always find a mistake on which to blame somebody's ill fortune. We need to think in terms of social relations instead, including those of race, gender, and disability. Why should some people's mistakes have so much greater consequences for their lives than others' for theirs? Why do we allow some people to face odds so much worse than others? This is not a problem that can be solved at the individual level or by targeting the abilities of people. When we consider the struggles of real people, we often discover what appears to be a futile effort to forever and completely escape poverty. Getting by day to day renders long-term planning difficult.

Edin and Lein (1997) discuss the typical situation of Brianna, illustrating how welfare usage is more of a cycle, not a dependence. Brianna had graduated high school and found a job as a clerk in San Antonio. She could not get full-time hours, tried to find another job, but was unable to in her town's depressed economy. When she discovered that she was pregnant, and although daycare fees would equal her whole paycheck, she decided to keep the baby because she planned to have children anyway. She did not see her economic situation improving any time soon. Right before giving birth, she quit her job and applied for welfare benefits. Brianna had been on welfare for two years at the time of the study interview, which was pre-reform. She had tried to make the most of that time by completing a training program, but it had been a "rip-off" program, leading not to a job but to $1,300 of debt. She then started another training course, this time paid for by the JOBS program, as a home health aide. Because she shared rent with her father and another couple, and received a daycare subsidy, Brianna expected to remain in work and off welfare for this first year. The next year, however, the daycare subsidy expired, and she would not be able to work unless the father of the child ended up getting a decent job. She would be back on welfare and in another training program.

A number of social relations and factors that are at first glance outside the realm of work affect one's relation to the labor market. The lack of affordable and adequate housing is one serious problem that must be addressed (Edin and Shaefer 2015; Desmond 2016). Adverse childhood experiences (abuse, trauma, etc.) increase the likelihood of mental illness, self-medication, and a variety of life course departures from upward mobility. Experiences of violence and lack of basic security that Haugen and Boutros (2014) argue are a major cause of poverty in the developing world also impact many American poor. Domestic violence, childhood abuse, the criminal activities associated with illegal trades, sexual assault, robbery, and physical assault disproportionately affect people in poverty, especially women and children, who are vulnerable to those who perpetrate violence as a way to get what they want (Haugen and Boutros 2014; Erdmans and Black 2015; Obernesser and Seale n.d.). These experiences have long-term impacts on the psyches of individuals, increasing the likelihood of depression, anxiety, panic disorders, substance abuse, suicide, and a variety of other problems. Even outside of direct violent assault, the toxic stress of poverty itself is traumatic and, in the long run, deadly (Edin and Shaefer 2015).

Getting out of poverty would seem to be a priority. But what is less recognized is that *success itself costs*, both in advance and afterward. Stack (1974) argues that the resilient strategies of Black residents of The Flats exacted a cost from participants. Attempting to move upward by marriage or employment entails drifting away from the kin network and the security that network ensures. In order to survive day to day, one must give up the chance of upward mobility. In taking the chance of upward mobility, one must give up a certain security and support structure. The pandemic has exacerbated crises that poor families navigate, which extends to the family members who are upwardly mobile (Purnell 2020). In April of 2020, Purnell, a Harvard law grad from a low-income background, published an opinion piece in the *New York Times* about how devastating the pandemic was for her family:

> I imagine that others like me feel immense amounts of guilt, pressure, relief and luck. I call this low-income plus. All in a day, we work, organize, write, shop online, donate to mutual aids funds, have Zoom happy hours, and share nostalgic Instagram photos from earlier beach moments – and – send groceries across the state or country, call health departments with the right voice and vocabulary to get testing information; bail family out of jail or put money on their prison books; and weep. I call this Tuesday.

Indeed, Chen et al. (2022) find that upward mobility for those from poor backgrounds comes at a measurable cost to physical health. Those who succeeded educationally measured worse on several physical health outcomes than their counterparts who remained in the poor neighborhood back home. Likely, this is due to the efforts of continually striving in an environment very different from prior experience, while meeting the sorts of competing demands that Purnell discusses.

Selling Your Life

For the able-bodied, the armed forces have long served as a real source of pride, of trauma, of social mobility, or of early death. Joining the military is a way for young men to escape small towns, dangerous peer groups, or general lack of opportunity, and is increasingly an escape for young women as well. The armed forces provide discipline, a sense of belonging, and skills. Military personnel do not just learn to kill, and they often serve in a peaceful capacity. They provide families with economic stability. (I myself was a beneficiary.)

However, this is a book about the relations of poverty: How does military service result from and affect social relations?

There are clear economic benefits to joining the military. The US Census Bureau (2020a) estimates there were 1.4 million active-duty service members in 2017. Their median income was $40,700, above the poverty threshold for a family of three. One-fifth of veterans receive Veterans' Affairs (VA) disability compensation (Giefer and Loveless 2021). Veterans are about as likely as nonveterans as a whole to have a college degree. Veterans are more likely than nonveterans of the same age to own a home and have health insurance coverage, which is likely a product of access to mortgage and health insurance options through the VA. People of color have always served disproportionately in armed conflict on behalf of the USA, although, among the poor and working classes, White men are the most likely demographic to enlist. Using the 1997 National Longitudinal Survey of Youth, Han (2018) found that Black men who scored low on standardized tests were actually less likely than White men who scored low to enlist – these Black men were more likely, however, to be incarcerated or face extended unemployment after high school. For women, military service can serve as an entry point to male-dominated professions (Laughlin and Holder 2017). Although, initially, incomes were higher for women veterans compared to their nonveteran non-college-educated counterparts, their labor market advantage declined sharply over time, for unknown reasons (Laughlin and Holder 2017).

Military service certainly affects familial relations, and may lead to family dissolution or family conflict as a result of separation, post-traumatic stress disorder, or enhanced aggression (Gerlock et al. 2014). Veterans are at higher risk for homelessness, drug abuse, mental illness, and incarceration (Schaffer 2014). Some research also suggests veterans are more likely to join far-right extremist groups. It is still not clear exactly how commonly people at risk for poverty before and after military service are recruited into extremist, White supremacist, isolationist, and/or violent resistance groups. Hall et al. (2021:226) go so far as to "argue that changes within the military resulting from the war on terror – namely, an increase in deployments and a relaxation of recruitment standards – provided an avenue for FREs to acquire military training more easily." Both Far-Right Extremist Groups (FREGs) and the military can provide a sense of meaning and belonging, as well as a network of support. When your relations are characterized by vulnerability, you are ripe for exploitation, especially when explanations are provided for your vulnerability *and* you are given a way to fight back (Simi et al. 2013).

The vast majority of veterans do not join FREGs, and military service requires sacrifice and discipline that individuals often turn to good effect. Armed service members and veterans are, of course, more highly represented among those who protect the country against FREGs than they are in those FREGs. We should be aware, however, of the ways in which people in poverty may be exploited and disproportionately used for their ability to give their lives because they have so few options. Although combat deaths in the twenty-first century for Americans have been quite low, nonfatal casualties in Iraq and Afghanistan were significant. Moreover, when a person joins the military, their life is no longer their own. One becomes government property, in a sense. Considering also the mental health issues many veterans cope with, it is not unreasonable to say that many have sacrificed something of their lives. Military service can be a boon for some individuals, but it comes with serious costs – and sometimes the highest cost.

Positioning in relation to the labor market is thus one way to conceptualize opportunity for people in poverty. Having the ability to develop valuable, well-paid skills, to travel, to stay away from home for periods of time, and to meet the physical and psychological demands of a job considerably improve one's options. Relevant social relations also involve what one has to give up in order to work, such as time with children or attending school. The need for some basic respect and dignity can also interfere with employment success. Overall, there are serious costs to doing what it takes to succeed in the labor market: to dignity, to family, to other social relations, to one's time and energy. And this is why sometimes people in poverty do not "take advantage" of opportunity that apparently comes their way.

General Autonomy

In my experience, human service providers who work closely with people in poverty often claim that these individuals lack a sense of autonomy and control over their lives. This is frequently mentioned in conjunction with concerns about addiction, suicide, tobacco use, unplanned pregnancy, abuse, and despair. The poor are sometimes said to lack self-esteem, a positive self-image, and motivation (Kim et al. 2018). But evaluating the poor as having these individual shortcomings is problematic, or at least insufficient, as it misleads us as to how to best address poverty, and may further stigmatize people. However, we can consider the social relations that limit autonomy and the ways in which people under severe constraints express and practice autonomy.

Autonomy refers to some level of independence and separation. It refers to the ability to make one's own decisions. It encompasses personhood, agency, empowerment, and self-governance. Feminists have used the term to refer to a more encompassing notion of freedom in which individuals are free from coercion. The sociological paradox is that there is no autonomy in society that is not defined by one's relation to others. Being uncoerced is a relational matter. Of course, we all experience limits to our own autonomy. To some extent, we are all conditioned and coerced by our environment in ways both conscious and unconscious. And I am not just referring to inter-personal relations, but the contextual relations and socially situated conditions as well. However, we tend to be blinded to the limits of autonomy because of our extreme individualism. If someone lacks knowledge of something or believes something false, it is viewed as a personal fault. If someone lacks the skills to negotiate or question or judge, that is, in many people's view, on them. Social arrange-ments, including insitutions of education and public safety, support the sense of competence held by many upper middle-class and elite people (Sherwin 1998). In turn, this sense of autonomy masks the privilege obtained from these structures and social relations.

But it is not only the privileged who do in fact practice autonomy. Obernesser and Seale (n.d.) find that people in poverty do, actually, practice agency under severe constraints, even though it does not always lead to desirable outcomes. In some cases, people will claim autonomy any way they can get it – even if it is to their own detriment. Levine (2013) found that mothers in poverty essentially want respect. Distrust served as armor against stigma and further hardship. This research suggests that, although individual-level factors may inhibit escape from poverty, it is also about relations of distrust. Much of this distrust is based on "direct experience undergirded by structural factors" (Levine 2013:205). As discussed earlier in this chapter, this distrust is not irrational – often these women's risks do *not* produce rewards. Some low-wage employees are quick to quit their jobs if they feel disrespected. This may seem odd or inappropriate, but Levine's research shows that one of the few areas of their life where they have control is in terms of how they are treated by others and what they are willing to put up with. Therefore, often at the slightest hint of disrespect or poor treatment, these mothers will assume the worst – that this treatment is a reflection of what is to come. Some of the research subjects were willing to take a drop in pay in order to work with people they felt would be respectful and fair.

Autonomy is limited in some critical ways for people in poverty. When people grow up with confined horizons, it affects what they can imagine and to what they can aspire. Many people prefer to stick to what they know. When it comes to relying on our own abilities, this is a common and smart strategy. But it sets severe limits for many people in poverty. Edin and Shaefer (2015) note that some people in extreme poverty have few opportunities to travel or see other places. They introduce Tabitha, in sixth grade, who had never left the Delta where she grew up. A few members of Teach for America (TFA) organized a trip for Tabitha's class to go to Washington, DC. But, first, they realized that few of the students had more than a change of clothes – a trip to Walmart was organized. The trip became the highlight of Tabitha's childhood. Many of the children had never seen an elevator before, thinking that the teachers were playing a trick on them "that the box behind the doors could actually transport them from one floor to another" (2015: 149). Then, as they got on the plane to return home, Tabitha told the researchers: "everyone was so mad at Mr Patten 'cuz we were like, 'You take us all the way out here, you show us *this*, and then you take us back to the Delta where there's *nothing*?'" Edin and Shaefer continue, "Once they were back home it would be back to 'waking up every day, not having enough food, sleeping with seven of us . . .'" (149). Tabitha's hunger – both literal and, figuratively, for what lay beyond the Delta – made her easy sexual prey for an unscrupulous teacher, who was reported but never charged or fired. With urging from a TFA teacher, Tabitha has a plan to go to college. But, she says, "I'm scared what if I don't make it in college? . . . Like, my sisters have always seen other kids who get up and fail. That's why they don't want to get up, because they always seen someone fail" (153).

A large body of research exists on the long-term effects of poverty, especially for children. This research demonstrates that there are negative impacts on average for economic success and general well-being, and that the impacts worsen with each additional year a child spends in poverty (Ratcliffe and Kalish 2017). This happens for several reasons, but, again, relations are key (Duncan and Magnusson 2013). Research especially implicates parent–child relations. Radey and McWey (2021) found that when mothers in poverty had less of an informal safety net in regard to their network, when they had greater psychological distress, and reported higher parenting stress, their children scored lower on the mental health appraisal. While the experiences of children in impoverished families vary, persistent poverty throughout childhood and especially in adolescence may compromise the ability to cope with problems and exercise autonomy. In Radey and McWey's (2021) study, 18 percent of the children from low-income families exhibited concerning mental health symptoms. In general, poverty appears to affect the daily well-being of children through what are called adverse childhood experiences (ACE), including child maltreatment or family dysfunction such as separation, mental health problems, addiction, parental incarceration, or domestic violence (Choi et al. 2019). As pointed out by Choi et al. (2019), ACEs are basically family relational problems that result from vulnerabilities related to poverty, and can be addressed through programs that improve parent–child relations. The stress of the parent devolves straight to children. Children in poverty are more likely to be exposed to more than one ACE, which seems to be especially detrimental (Choi et al. 2019). Even after following research participants for 12 years, those who experienced ACEs were significantly worse off in terms of behavioral problems than the young people from low-income backgrounds who did not experience ACEs. To the extent that it makes these ACEs more likely, poverty undermines individual development. The costs of these impacts for society are high, increasing issues associated with mental health, addiction, child abuse, crime, and individual autonomy.

Research suggests that having a sense of self-efficacy is necessary, but not sufficient, for improving the life chances of people in poverty. Individuals need to believe not only that they have the ability to succeed, but that they have the adequate support and opportunity to succeed in a particular domain. The vast majority of people in poverty still believe that hard work will lead to a better life in the end. Critically, examining interactions between people in poverty and authority figures illustrates the futility of self-efficacy. Power imbalances between criminal justice officials and people in poverty, between school officials and people in poverty, between medical practitioners and people in poverty, and between social services workers and people in poverty all play a part in undermining confidence in one's autonomy. Such interactions shape opportunity outside of or in addition to any sense of self-efficacy displayed by individuals in poverty.

Different conditions among the poor can lead to very different levels of personal autonomy, but the conditions that undermine personal autonomy are more common at lower socioeconomic levels, especially for those who have grown up in poverty. The experience of repeated obstructions undermines further perseverance (McLeod 1995; Edin and Kefalas [2005] 2011). There is also a strong element of chance here, as people in poverty may face circumstances in which perseverance can mean they prevail, whereas in other situations motivation does not matter. Earlier experiences of prevailing with perseverance may lead to a stronger self-efficacy, whereas early experience of the situations in which motivation has no effect may reinforce a lack thereof (Williams and Kornblum 1994). We tend to assume that personal autonomy is a good thing, but what if it leads – not to "hard honest work" – to a willingness to exploit others? What if self-efficacy is channeled into non-mainstream channels, from the wide-ranging possibilities of the drug trade to joining far-right movements? Far from suggesting a passivity in regard to opportunity, such paths can reflect great initiative and a willingness to grab any chance at bettering one's life (Preble and Casey 1969; Patton and Roth 2016).

Conclusion

This chapter illustrates two main themes of the book: the relations of vulnerability that characterize poverty, and the simultaneous need for dignity and meaning. Relations of vulnerability and the desire for dignity operate at cross purposes when it comes to taking advantage of opportunity. The level of belief in one's capacity to control one's life – what is variably known as self-efficacy, subjective agency, or personal autonomy – is undermined by relations of vulnerability. The threat to dignity that failure and ridicule pose means that certain opportunities appear more as a threat than an opportunity.

When one does not have many options, when one must rely on other people for every little thing, and when one lives in close quarters with those whom one relies on or takes care of, such a person is vulnerable in nearly all social relations. For instance, illegality is a relation that non-citizens come to have with the state and the citizens of that state. Abusive relations with an intimate partner further undermine success in the workplace. People who come from poverty or extremely vulnerable backgrounds have to pay more for their success in blood, in health, and in relationships. In serious conflict with this set of circumstances is the need for dignity – to be respected; to avoid risk, failure, and humiliation; and to exercise autonomy, even if it means rejecting "the beautiful people" before they reject you.

Wider social relations, such as relations between the rich and their subsequent political maneuverings, reinforce these vulnerabilities and indignities. For instance, the ability of the more affluent to avoid paying toward providing quality education for all is one of the most important sets of conditions to affect college attendance at the macro level. The dependence of K-12 public schools on local taxpayers creates a tiered system of public education that disadvantages rural and impoverished urban areas. Reduction in state spending on higher education further undermines the ability of people to afford a college education.

Thus, these difficulties that people in poverty find themselves in are not issues restricted to their own worlds. They are connected to the workplace and political economy that we all live by. The relations to the workplace of middle-class individuals may not be as dire as those of people in poverty, but positions in relation to the labor market shift. Those who want to choose to spend more time with family and caring for dependents have tough choices to face as well. The physical and psychological demands of employment are often immensely draining, forcing people to sacrifice their mental health. The problems of the poor are not so disconnected from the issues the majority of Americans face; conditions of poverty are simply at the worse end of the continuum, compounding issues, and signaling problems with the society we all live in.

7

Vulnerability and Dignity

People in poverty are just like everyone else, only closer to the cliff edge of economic privation, and the cultural quandaries entailed by society's refusal to recognize that cliff. I find the anthropologist Janis Jenkins's (2015) analysis of mental illness from a relational perspective illuminating. Jenkins explains the struggle with mental illness as "not just against an illness and its symptoms but also *for* a normal life, *to* make sense of a confusing and disorienting circumstance, *with* intimate others, and *in* a world characterized by stigma" (Jenkins 2015:261). Against a mere pathologization or medicalization of mental illness, Jenkins views experiences of mental illness as being on a continuum, writing that "those with mental illness are just like everyone else – only more so" (2015:260). She does not downplay the suffering involved, but rather situates the struggle as beyond one's internal feelings, in the realm of the social. This resembles my own view of poverty; poverty involves a different set of daily experiences than the nonpoor typically endure, but it originates in and is reinforced by the same social context we all live in. Our failure to recognize that social context and our insistence on individualizing responsibility stigmatizes people in poverty and undermines their struggle for meaning in the midst of privation.

In this final chapter, I reflect on the relations of poverty and what that analysis means for how we think about poverty and how we address poverty in policy and research. This book has focused on the context of the United States, but this approach is as relevant for thinking about poverty in other contexts and ultimately in a global relational framework. In other words, there is much more to understand about poverty by considering the global connections that affect living conditions across the world. I close by considering a few possible insights to be gained from applying a relational approach to understanding poverty internationally.

The Relations of Poverty

The relations of vulnerability of poverty and the human need for dignity conflict with one another, creating a variety of challenging situations and fraught outcomes. To the extent that these social relations exist throughout the lives of the chronically poor and other disadvantaged persons, cumulative disadvantage can make escaping poverty especially difficult. There is a role for the individual to play in their own life. But the continuation of the relations of vulnerability involve the consent, the complacence, and often the ignorance of other individuals. To understand people in poverty, we have to consider their relations with other people. Readers may be tired of seeing variations on the word "vulnerable." But it is so often the most apt word to use for the relations I describe. I have written less about the strengths of people in poverty, but the strengths of people in poverty are sometimes just the flip side of the vulnerability. The strength required just to survive day to day, and the love and care shown to others despite one's own suffering, are easy to observe once one has formed a relationship with someone in poverty. I recall the woman who brought lunch for me as we worked at the warehouse in a North Carolinian social program. I recall the many people who had kind words to say amidst their own crises. And I recall the many people who maintained their sanity and calm, even as everything in their life fell apart.

The poor value their dignity, just like everyone else. People need a reason to live and to strive. They need to feel good about themselves. They need some sort of comfort. Unfortunately, one way to do this is to denigrate or abuse others, thus sometimes creating a cycle of even greater vulnerability. In other cases, people will allow themselves to become more vulnerable if it gives them some sense of comfort or meaning. This need for meaning and dignity in one's life sometimes conflicts with actions that are necessary to escape poverty. As Stack (1974) discovered, escaping poverty for many of her research participants entailed leaving one's community behind. A parent wants to treat their children once in a while, even if they cannot really afford it. The comfort and sense of well-being and self-worth that opiate use can bring – however short-lived – may be a person's only source for such feelings. Sexual intercourse brings human connection, also short-lived, but again potentially a person's only source of such connection, or their only affirmation of their self-worth. These activities and examples are not unique to people in poverty, but poverty imposes greater costs.

As Mark Rank (2004:42) put it, poverty in the USA "is the paradox and humiliation of having to do without in a land of plenty." Relations with others can be warped by poverty. As one individual wrote in an op-ed (Hunt 2022), his coping mechanism to survive social situations as he grew up in poverty was to constantly lie to others about his reality. Many different individual survival mechanisms develop in interaction with others and in the attempt to reconcile one's position in the world with whom one would like to be seen as being. The desire for dignity can be exploited by predatory others, but it can also be a resource for personal transformation and agency. Even so, people in poverty have to pay more for their success in blood, in health, and in relationships. Consider the experiences of immigrant parents discussed by Abrego (2014) and their sacrifice of daily interactions with children to provide those children with a better future. Or consider the implications of joining the armed forces – both positive and negative. Even those who find success by attending college pay higher costs for their success in having to meet greater demands and in problematic health outcomes (Purnell 2020; Chen et al. 2022). Parents in poverty wrestle with difficult choices: between working more or being with their children, between keeping the family together or giving their children the necessities, between trusting potential intimate partners or avoiding great risk, between expressing love and coping with constant stress, and between maintaining hope for the future and living a reality of scarcity. How they respond to these dilemmas depends in part on the social relations they hold with each other, the state, community institutions such as schools, employers, other family members, and their children.

Often, people in poverty are not just facing poverty – their vulnerability relates to many different positions, including those positions created by ableism, patriarchy, racism, heterosexism, and other forms of stratification. For instance, it is important to consider how women, whose bodies are a major site of struggle for control due to their role in childbirth and sexuality, are situated in relationships that may restrict their freedom, in a culture that devalues them, and in a social welfare system that treats them with suspicion. Poverty is multidimensional, intersecting with a variety of strengths and vulnerabilities.

And it is these social relations that need to be addressed. For instance, the section in Chapter 6 on employment relations revealed that it is not just that the labor market is problematic – it is the relation people have to the labor market that is problematic. It is not just the employer or employee who is problematic; it is the relation between them such that the employee has no recourse. But I have argued that these difficulties people in poverty find themselves in are not issues restricted to the world of the poor. These difficulties are connected to the workplace and political economy that we all live by. Workplaces are draining, and demand much from employees. Workers who want to spend more time with family and caring for dependents may not be able to do so without risking poverty. People face discrimination in the workplace for characteristics such as race, ethnicity, disabilities, gender, accent, age, and sexual orientation. Thus, the problems of the poor are not disconnected from the issues the majority of Americans face; conditions of poverty are simply at the worse end of the continuum, compounding issues, and signaling problems with the society we all live in.

Changing Our Thinking about Poverty

Three tendencies need to change in general thinking about poverty: (1) the belief that the poor constitute a separate and homogeneous group of people; (2) the idea of poverty as an individual condition that is disconnected from the rest of us; and (3) the view that people in poverty are solely responsible for their situation. Although everyone who is in poverty at a given point in time may share similar challenges related to economic distress, there are few other problems or characteristics that are shared by a majority of the poor. In Chapter 2, I identified three different types of poverty status: deep and chronic poverty; insecurity, including those who may not be financially poor at a given point in time, but remain at risk; and temporary poverty, which relates to a time of transition for someone who may have assets, tangible or intangible, that will allow them to become financially secure in the future. Moreover, people enter and exit poverty frequently, such that the people who are actually in poverty change from year to year. We need an intersectional approach that takes into account how poverty varies for people in different social positions. People in poverty confront many of the same individual-level problems that exist throughout the country, including substance abuse, disability, and single motherhood. These problems are not responsible for their poverty. Rather, poverty is perpetuated by the relations through which people are denied rights, options, opportunities, or basic securities.

The American middle class are confronting the same sets of conditions that accompany poverty, including economic insecurity, constant stress, and relations of vulnerability. The very foundations for a middle-class existence are eroding. In fact, the pandemic-caused recession of 2020 may split America into diverging trajectories – of those who have maintained decent income and saved during the pandemic, and those who have had their savings emptied and their security undermined. Goldblum and Shaddox (2021:xvii) have noted that the pandemic not only seriously impaired those "with underlying vulnerabilities," but also increased the vulnerability of most Americans who were living paycheck to paycheck prior to the pandemic in a "strong" economy. According to results of the Current Population Survey for 2019, more than 1 in 3 Americans are under the 1.5 income-to-poverty ratio, meaning their income is 150% of the poverty threshold or below (US Census Bureau 2020c). About 1 in 3 Americans are in or near poverty. Combined with the "affordability" crisis, and recent inflation, Americans increasingly struggle – even if they do not technically count as poor – with attaining adequate healthcare, education or childcare for their children, safe housing, and other requirements for well-being as defined under the capability approach. Klein (2022) reports that, as the "trappings" of a middle-class lifestyle became more affordable over the past few decades, the important relational and capability-oriented resources grew pricier: housing, education, childcare, and healthcare. Cheap consumer goods and debt have "papered over the affordability crisis," but papering only lasts so long. In fact, the retrenchment in the cheapness of consumer goods has already begun with the inflation of the early 2020s. The ranks of people with relations of deep and persistent vulnerability will likely swell in the years to come.

Although the individual bears some responsibility for their behavior, the consequences of that behavior are not justly distributed; social relations of poverty punish the poor out of proportion to their mistakes, and unfairly in comparison to others making similar mistakes. Thus, the notion that the poor perpetuate their own poverty, for this and the many reasons given throughout this text, is simply false. The traditional understanding of a particular and inferior "culture of poverty" is certainly not sustained by the evidence. As Goldblum and Shaddox (2021:235) wrote: "People are poor because the money they have is insufficient to pay for the things they need."

Not things they want. Not because of their own actions. They simply do not have the ability to access the essentials without extensive efforts. Far from being wasteful or irresponsible, many people in poverty survive only because they cleverly, and sometimes desperately, balance demands. Rank (2004:49) has written: "In short, living in poverty is epitomized by the struggle to acquire, and at times, the need to forgo, the daily necessities and resources that most Americans take for granted." Sociology offers some different ways to think about the daily lives of people in poverty. This does not have to entail releasing individuals from responsibility for their actions or whitewashing the harsh effects of living in poverty. Rather, we need to recognize the complexity of human social behavior in terms of both the causes and effects of poverty. One way to look at the lives of the poor is to emphasize their behavior, another is to emphasize the larger circumstances. Both approaches by themselves fail to grasp how behavior of any group of people in society is going to be a matter of complex social processes and never a straightforward matter of responsibility and blame.

The Significance of a Relational Approach

I have noted that relationality is an approach or analytic, not a fully formed theory. Theories can be more or less relational. But, on its own, the relational approach is necessarily circular. People are poor due to relations, poverty is itself a relation, and this in turn impacts relations. But I am not making an argument about what causes poverty. Those would be specific relations, which vary from individual to individual and from group to group. Nor am I saying the individual does not matter. Rather, my approach has been to recognize the constant change and feedback processes of society, without privileging any one set of processes. It is about using the sociological imagination, as C. Wright Mills ([1959] 2000) termed it, on a specific issue – poverty, while being a bit more specific about what the sociological imagination entails.

I have used a relational approach in conjunction with social scientific research to identify some of the relations of importance for understanding poverty. This has largely involved interpreting actions and outcomes for people in poverty as matters of relational construction. Because relations are both broad and specific, such a task does require recognition of complex social processes at different levels and across different situations. Hence, the use of structure and culture to identify relevant sets of conditions helps us to generalize about important social processes without homogenizing people in poverty.

The troubles of the poor, as I describe and analyze them, come down to relational challenges, not merely individual problems such as mental health issues, addiction, low self-esteem, lack of motivation, lack of social skills, etc. It is how *we* relate to the poor and how they find themselves relating to other people that render these issues barriers to autonomous decision-making.

I wish to emphasize that, under a relational approach, individual responsibility is as important as ever. Individuals are implicated not only in their own actions, but for others as well. It is not that we should blame other people for our own behavior, but that we recognize our behavior is not inherent to us as an individual, and that the behavior is partly in response to conditions. This means responsibility and agency are admittedly more complex than how we typically moralize about them.

But the general lesson from taking a relational lens to poverty is not all that complex: connections are critical. Eliminating poverty requires the integration of the poor in society, not their further disenfranchisement. There are many ways in which people in poverty are disenfranchised, and these processes should be targeted for change by policy and programming.

Implications for Policy and Programs

True integration into society would have to include jobs with prospects, secure housing, a safety net in crisis, and the decriminalization of poverty. Charity is not going to help people escape poverty because charity entails a relationship between the giver and the recipient that is inherently disempowering to the recipient. The poor must insist on justice, not charity. For instance, Amartya Sen (1999) has emphasized the importance of political freedoms for poverty alleviation. Social arrangements and actions of the state determine the extension of individual freedoms. Programs to address poverty should stress dissemination of skills and leadership amongst the people themselves so that they can continue their own development (Sen 1999). Responsibility requires freedom and autonomy, including the opportunity to make one's own choices, and practice in doing so (Seale 2017). By exercising agency through institutions such as education, social services, the labor market, politics, and family, individuals are further empowered to address social problems (Khader 2011).

Perhaps the two most immediate concerns are education and housing, followed closely by healthcare and childcare. Education is an important piece of a comprehensive program to balance social relations. Education empowers people in relating to others by providing feelings of self-worth, skills, and options. Housing is another critical piece, given the enormous problem with affordable housing in the United States in the twenty-first century, and the far-reaching implications of having a safe place to live (Cunningham 2016; Desmond 2016). Housing is arguably the single most urgent problem to tackle in the short term, assisting the deep poor and the near poor in attaining a critical stability. Having stable housing affects one's relations to the criminal justice system, social services, and the labor market, to name a few institutions. Healthcare is a more complex problem to tackle, worth at least few hundred pages in its own right. Access to healthcare can be critical for people in poverty when we consider the high rates of mental health issues, indicators of despair, unplanned pregnancy, disability, work injury, and the effects of constant stress among people in poverty. The other high-priced item that parents need in order to be successful is quality childcare. Making quality childcare affordable is a requirement if we want to better enable parents' employment and improve children's well-being, as demonstrated by the welfare-to-work and child maltreatment literatures.

Policy changes can occur at two levels: change in how we distribute jobs, wealth, and resources; and change in terms of empowering people in poverty in their actual relations with others. The two levels are linked, but it is important to remember that poverty is not just about income – it is about the relations between people. Poverty is a profound imbalance in power. To address poverty, ultimately, we have to address that imbalance in power. Better education for all is one way to do this, but we can also consider political power in terms of voting and having a seat at the table of local government. In terms of programs to address poverty, it is essential to treat people in poverty as equal partners in the endeavor, as opposed to recipients of aid. We should not assume we know what people in poverty in a specific context need without consulting them. We should recognize their strengths as well as their vulnerabilities if we want to remedy those vulnerabilities.

In social work practice, community programs, and support centers, relationships are central mechanisms for success (Davidson et al. 2018). For programs and practitioners addressing populations in poverty, interactions with clients may be viewed as part of the "therapy" or treatment. Under a relational approach, the practitioner–client relationship is itself the therapy (Bondi 2008). This involves the building of trust, while recognizing that process as complex and ongoing (Smith and Romero 2010). Referencing their experience with a program addressing mental health in a poor urban community, Smith and Romero (2010) emphasize the importance of transparency in this process, arguing that transparency is a necessary part of transcending the detached, authoritarian method. A power-sharing approach is more difficult and laborious than the authoritarian approach, but can powerfully transform participants' orientations to the program and to themselves (Smith and Romero 2010). Anything that gives people in poverty greater sense of control over their lives has the potential to improve quality of life (Goodman et al. 2010). Additional benefits of a power-sharing participatory process include the development of pride and changing participants' orientation toward – and ultimately their relationship with – the community at large (Smith and Romero 2010).

Even more transient encounters can benefit from a relational approach to serving people in poverty. Intakes can be formulated to address relational issues, including questions about relationships and violence (Sharam and Hulse 2014) and relations with key authority figures such as landlords, employers, and police officers (Feldman 2019). Basic interactions and procedures can be developed to enhance clients' sense of control, choice, and connection (Goodman et al. 2010). As Goodman et al. (2010:9) emphasize, "new possibilities for practitioners and participants open when an understanding of poverty's dynamism – its tight grip on people's choice, control, and connections – is built into practice from the outset." Providing choice, control, and connections for people in poverty may not be as straightforward and bureaucratically measurable as providing food, shelter, and healthcare, but even small indications of respect and regard for people improve the sense that all is not lost – there is hope.

Implications for Research

It is important to reflect on the limitations of what we can know and understand. Recognition of such limits should engender an abiding respect for the unknowable, and subjectivity is never truly knowable in its entirety. Even the experience of poverty will elude us to some degree – even if *I* am impoverished, *I* cannot know what the experience is like for another. The limits to intersubjectivity must be acknowledged in respect of other people's suffering, their perseverance, their joys, and, ultimately, their inalienable worth as persons. As Gunzenhauser (2006:642) has written:

> Morally and epistemologically rich relations reflect the context in which they occur, and they are exceedingly difficult to reproduce. Of further significance is the need for establishment of multiple relations in the field, not just with the primary informant, but with a wide range of participants in the social setting. Needed is an ability to attempt an empathetic understanding of multiple actors in a social milieu. This may guard against demonizing certain participants and undertheorizing the complexity of power relations ... What Code (1995) calls enhanced subjectivity should be understood not as an alternative road to objectivity but rather always what it is – a partial intersubjectivity.

Yet the subjective is still worth scientific study (see Solli and Barbosa da Silva 2018). For one thing, subjective and objective reality are closely connected, as many theorists have tried to account for: "The acting individual needs to be grasped as entangled in symbolic knowledge structures of power that are part of the objective world" (Dreher and López 2015:218). For instance, we can appreciate an individual's attempts to create a subjective sense of dignity in relation to the social and cultural arrangements that demean them. This is essential to understanding the utility behind many choices that appear irrational. A poor person who spends $200 on a hairstyle is not mindlessly wasting money. That person may be creating dignity and self-worth in a society that says they are worthless.

Thus, a relational approach to poverty involves attention to subjective and objective dimensions in concert. I am defining subjectivity as pertaining to the perspective and experience of an individual. Objectivity refers to facts or objects that do not rely on one's perspective or experience, but that can be identified as existing outside of one's perspective on or experience of them. Subjective aims of methodology pertain to the perspective and portrayal of experiences of the researcher, the research participant, or the research audience. Objective aims of methodology pertain to the facts, objects, and situations of the social world that can be replicated and tested. I address many ways of achieving this objective subjectivity in a 2020 article (Seale 2020), including depth in data collection, making sense of conflicting information, and extending the time points of research. Two major research designs or orientations that help us achieve some of these goals are life course design and Participatory Action Research. These approaches to data collection and analysis can illuminate important social relations in addition to context. Critically, they allow us to consider variation across the life course or across situation, and to see the exercising of agency.

The life course design, for instance, makes sense given that people do cycle in and out of poverty, and some poverty may be specific to a life stage. The life course perspective also recognizes that socialization continues throughout the adult years, especially in terms of the demands that other members of society place on us (Clausen 1986). Another useful feature of the life course perspective is the focus on transitions between social roles (Donnelly et al. 2001; Carpenter 2010). Snow et al.'s (1994) critiques of research on the homeless can be partly addressed by utilizing these tools. We might indeed find that, rather than biological or feature dysfunctions of the person, "backgrounds of poverty, disrupted family arrangements, foster care, fragile social support networks, and even plain bad luck . . . may be far more important in understanding who is vulnerable to homelessness" (Snow et al. 1994:467). Life course research is greatly promising for demonstrating the agency of people in poverty, while also highlighting the challenges they face.

Participatory Action Research (PAR) is not a set of methods for data collection, but an orientation toward research that draws upon an epistemology of subjective knowledge construction (Minkler and Wallerstein 2008). One of the major criteria for PAR is that the researchers reflect on and discuss the outcomes of subjects' participation in the research (Shamrova and Cummings 2017). Research subjects are positioned to help frame research questions, collect data, and/or identify issues and solutions, since they have unique access to knowledge about their own lives (Quijada Cerecer et al. 2013). This is particularly relevant to research aimed at informing policy. Self-representation and the process of deliberation and advocacy can also directly change the cultural context of subjects' lives (Quijada Cerecer et al. 2013). For ethical reasons and research validity, Participatory Action Research is best done over a long period of time, allowing for the formation of reciprocal relationships and community investment (Belsky 1999). Unfortunately, such a long period of PAR is often not feasible for researchers – particularly for those working on master's or doctoral theses which typically only last one to three years – unless the researcher is already a long-term member of that community. Nonetheless, elements can be incorporated into research that is not fully fledged PAR by re-envisioning the researcher–subject relation as a collaboration in the production of knowledge. Not only are the ethical implications profound, but the data will be richer for it.

I believe that, while we might strive for objectivity in data collection, we should strive for a certain kind of subjectivity in representation. Erdmans and Black (2015) explain the difficulty in representing the experiences of those in poverty without stigmatizing them in their book *On Becoming a Teen Mom: Life before Pregnancy*. In their chapter on child sexual abuse, an unexpected topic that arose from their interviews with young mothers, they write:

> The politics of representation is a tricky issue because bearing witness to and exposing unnecessary pain and misery is a practice intended to inspire moral outrage and political action, and yet these representations folded into different interpretative frames can result in voyeuristic feasting and moralistic victim blaming . . . To address the problem of representation, we remind readers that child sexual abuse is a type of violence that occurs in all racial, ethnic, and social class communities; that it is a structural issue integral to the social organization of patriarchy and expressed as male entitlement to younger bodies for sexual pleasure and domination . . . The horrific abuse told by these mothers can steamroll our senses and prevent us from seeing the moments of redemption, forgiveness, and kindness embedded in their stories as well. Alisha told us that her mother had been clean from drugs for 14 years. Deidre will never forget what her similarly aged uncle did to her, but she saw him as an ally in neighborhood conflicts. Their childhood stories were laced with contradictory experiences and emotions that provide us with a complex profile of human experience. (Erdmans and Black 2015:86)

How do we address unsavory characters among the poor who take advantage of others, but who must be counted among the very people they exploit, abuse, or cheat? Unscrupulous individuals lurk everywhere, among all demographic groups. Yet, because people in poverty are more vulnerable, they can be victimized more easily and with less risk of repercussion. Some researchers also argue that, in some social worlds of deprivation, people learn to view personal relations as things to be exploited (Rainwater 1970; Sánchez-Jankowski 2008). Perhaps not all people can be or should be made into sympathetic characters, but here again comparison with the middle class becomes important. Indeed, middle-class subjects also learn to view personal relations as resources to be exploited, except this is portrayed positively in the literature and in many institutional spaces as "networking." In addition, we must keep in mind that living in poverty makes it more difficult to hide one's unscrupulousness behind a veil of legitimacy and respectability. But if we avoid being open about this reality, we make it easier for those who recognize or encounter these characters to reject our claims that the poor as a group are not blameworthy. Such acts of harm also form a part of the reality of poverty for individuals who are relatively less powerful than other people in their families and communities, including but not limited to children and battered women.

Although qualitative research is often designed to examine subjective experience in the context of relations, quantitative research can also be relational. Survey research can pair or triangulate people who are connected to one another. Another approach is to measure aspects of relationships and relations that people hold with authority figures and institutions. For instance, including questions about the level of autonomy one has at work or the number of different childcare providers one has relied upon may provide important information about social relations. Researchers can also conceptualize characteristics in more relational terms in measurement and interpretation. I advocate for less essentialist interpretations of characteristics such as sex, race, disability, substance abuse, such that the researcher interprets these characteristics not so much as directly causal in affecting outcomes, but as indicative of the social relations of which people are a part. Certain other research traditions do tend toward the relational, including social-ecological perspectives and social network research. Human ecologists often measure relational aspects, as in child maltreatment research by Belsky (1993) and Kotch et al. (1995) that examined the role of parents' social support in mitigating likelihood of child maltreatment. Social network research also entails a relational approach by the measurement of individuals' social networks and social capital (Klärner and Knabe 2019).

In addition, the extensive quantitative research on measurement of poverty should locate important subcategories of poverty to avoid homogenizing the poor. Green (2006:1112) writes that measuring poverty, including its distribution and depth, "assumes that poverty is a state universally accessible to these technologies of representation." In fact, however, poverty can manifest very differently across geographic areas. Research in the United States has focused on the urban poor to such an extent that the different circumstances of the rural poor have been ignored by policy reforms. The poor who live in the suburbs or in mixed-income metropolitan areas are even further off the policy radar. International differences are likely to be even greater and more critical. As a social relation, poverty will differ in manifestation, experience, and perpetuation across different contexts.

Toward a Global Reckoning

Just as social class groups in the United States are intertwined with each other, so are social class groups intertwined internationally. We may be able to identify groups of people in terms of their relations to power and resources on a global level, rather than relying only on nation-centric conceptualizations. Certain people in the world are far more vulnerable as a result of social relations spanning across and between nations. Meanwhile, the low- and middle-wealth sectors of the global population fight over who pays the price of postcolonial power imbalances. How we relate to people in other nations has been fundamental to national politics, especially with the recent rise in nativist and nationalist sentiment and populist uprisings.

Global capitalism and other forms of imperialism have altered people's ability to survive. Whether for the positive or negative is debated, but, regardless, the world we now live in can be improved by modifying and challenging global capitalism, whatever its merits may be.

For instance, global poverty rates have decreased over the past two centuries, though how rates of poverty might compare to a preindustrial world is another matter. At the same time, a small minority of people have become superrich. Such extreme wealth should be interrogated for what it means for the rest of us. On a global level, justice for the poor must be fought through those very issues that so profoundly affect power relations between nations and people. Debt forgiveness, tax reconstruction, land reform, and the end of the privatization of natural resources top the list.

Immigration and climate change affect vulnerabilities and other relations, as they are in turn created by imbalanced social relations and structural and cultural factors. Many scholars of poverty have argued that providing aid to poor nations is insufficient for addressing global poverty. For one thing, the majority of the poor do not currently live in the poorest nations, as one might expect, but in middle-income countries (Kanbur and Sumner 2012). Rather, addressing human rights accountability and expanding state capacity in middle- and low-income countries with democracies will be required (Haugen and Boutros 2014; Page and Pande 2018). As in the USA, changing the relations between people in poverty and the nation-state they live in, such that people can demand human rights and reforms, is critical to the problem of poverty. Though this discernment is not the focus of this book, a fundamental change in the foundations of contemporary social relations entails challenging the hegemony of capital. Structurally and culturally, capitalism directly contributes to the denigration of people in poverty. It does this through technological advances, the prioritization of profit over human need, and externalizing of costs. Finance capital, as theorized by Fraser and Jaeggi (2018:113), needs "subjects to exploit and expropriate." The best and most enduring solution to poverty-causing factors will not be found in so-called "free" markets, since capitalist markets are based on the exploitation of labor. Ultimately, whatever one's view on capitalism, if one wishes to end poverty, the central question is: who benefits from poverty?

Conclusion

Poverty occurs when a person is positioned relative to others such that they have less power to demand accountability for how they are treated and what resources are accorded them. Poverty means others – actors of the state, the criminal justice system, businesses, the financial industry, abusers, criminals, traffickers, grifters, loan sharks, tax dodgers, employers, managers, harassers, customers, polluters, political authorities, global elites, trade agreement enforcers, basically anyone in authority – can take advantage of certain people with little accountability. Poverty is due not only to a lack of economic means, but the vulnerability entailed by the lack of economic means combined with sociocultural disadvantages. Pay attention to the structural and cultural processes that contribute to these relations. Pay attention to how social relations reinforce people's vulnerability. All are implicated; all are affected.

References

Aalbers, Manuel B. 2018. "Financial Geography I: Geographies of Tax." *Progress in Human Geography* 42(6):916–27.

AAUW. 2021. "The Simple Truth about the Gender Pay Gap: 2021 Update." AAUW Reports. www.aauw.org.

Abrego, Leisy J. 2014. *Sacrificing Families: Navigating Laws, Labor, and Love across Borders.* Stanford University Press.

Acs, Gregory, and Austin Nichols. 2010. "Changes in the Economic Security of American Families." Washington, DC: Urban Institute.

Addams, Jane. 1910. *Twenty Years at Hull-House.* New York: Macmillan.

Addo, Fenaba R., and William A. Darity. 2021. "Disparate Recoveries: Wealth, Race, and the Working Class after the Great Recession." *The Annals of the American Academy of Political and Social Science* 695(1):173–92.

Addo, Fenaba R., William A. Darity, Jenifer Romich, Timothy M. Smeeding, and Michael R. Strain. 2021. "Disparate Recoveries: Wealth, Race, and the Working Class after the Great Recession." *The Annals of the American Academy of Political and Social Science* 695(1):173–92.

Agnitsch, Kerry, Jan Flora, and Vern Ryan. 2006. "Bonding and Bridging Social Capital: The Interactive Effects on Community Action." *Community Development* 37(1):36–51.

Aguayo-Romero, Rodrigo A. 2021. "(Re)centering Black Feminism into Intersectionality Research." *American Journal of Public Health* 111(1):101–3.

Ainsworth-Darnell, J. W., and D. B. Downey. 1998. "Assessing the Oppositional Culture Explanation for Racial/Ethnic Differences in School Performance." *American Sociological Review* 63(4):536–53.

Akee, Randall, William Copeland, E. Jane Costello, and Emilia Simeonova. 2018. "How Does Household Income Affect Child Personality Traits and Behaviors?" *American Economic Review* 108(3):775–827.

Albelda, Randy, and Michael Carr. 2014. "Double Trouble: U.S. Low-Wage and Low-Income Workers, 1979–2011." *Feminist Economics* 20(2):1–28.

Ali, Mehvash. 2021. "Educational Disparities due to the COVID-19 Pandemic." *Academic Advising Today* (NACADA). May 23. https://na cada.ksu.edu/Resources/Academic-Advising-Today/View-Articles/Edu cational-Disparities-Due-to-the-COVID-19-Pandemic.aspx.

Altman, Claire E., Colleen M. Heflin, Chaegyung Jun, and James D. Bachmeier. 2021. "Material Hardship among Immigrants in the United States: Variation by Citizenship, Legal Status, and Origin in the 1996–2008 SIPP." *Population Research and Policy Review* 40:363–99.

Álvarez, Rodrigo González, Luis Armando Parra, Mijntje ten Brummelaar, Lucy Avraamidou, and Mónica López López. 2022. "Resilience among LGBTQIA+ Youth in Out-of-home Care: A Scoping Review." *Child Abuse & Neglect* 129(105660).

Anakwenze, Ujunwa, and Daniyal Zuberi. 2013. "Mental Health and Poverty in the Inner City." *Health & Social Work* 38(3):147–57.

Appell, Annette R. 1998. "On Fixing 'Bad' Mothers and Saving Their Children." Pp. 356–80 in *"Bad" Mothers: The Politics of Blame in Twentieth-Century America*, ed. M. Ladd-Taylor and L. Umanski. New York University Press.

Archer, Margaret S. 1996. *Culture and Agency: The Place of Culture in Social Theory*. Cambridge University Press.

Archer, Margaret S. 2010. "Morphogenesis versus Structuration: On Combining Structure and Action." *The British Journal of Sociology* 61(1):225–52.

Assink, Mark, Anouk Spruit, Mendel Schuts, Ramón Lindauer, Claudia E. van der Put, and Geert-Jan J. M. Stams. 2018. "The Intergenerational Transmission of Child Maltreatment: A Three Level Meta-analysis." *Child Abuse & Neglect* 84:131–45.

Ayers, Susan, Rod Bond, Rebecca Webb, Pamela Miller, and Karen Bateson. 2019. "Perinatal Mental Health and Risk of Child Maltreatment: A Systematic Review and Meta-analysis." *Child Abuse & Neglect* 98(104172).

Bacon, David. 2008. *Illegal People: How Globalization Creates Migration and Criminalizes Immigrants*. Boston: Beacon Press.

Bailey, Beth A., and Ruth Ann Daugherty. 2007. "Intimate Partner Violence during Pregnancy: Incidence and Associated Health Behaviors in a Rural Population." *Maternal and Child Health Journal* 11(5):495–503.

Bailey, Nancy E. 2016. *Losing America's Schools: The Fight to Reclaim Public Education*. Lanham, MD: Rowman & Littlefield Publishers.

Bane, Mary Jo, and David T. Ellwood. 1994. *Welfare Realities: From Rhetoric to Reform*. Cambridge, MA: Harvard University Press.

Banfield, Edward C. 1970. *The Unheavenly City*. Boston, MA: Little, Brown, and Co.

Barnes, Sandra L. 2008. "A Case Study of the Working Poor Single Mother Experience: An Analysis of the Structure versus Agency Discourse." *Journal of Poverty* 12(2):175–200.

Barnett, Cynthia, and F. Carson Mencken. 2002. "Social Disorganization Theory and the Contextual Nature of Crime in Nonmetropolitan Counties." *Rural Sociology* 67(3):372–93.

Baron, Juan D., Deborah A. Cobb-Clark, and Nisvan Erkal. 2015. "Welfare Receipt and the Intergenerational Transmission of Work–Welfare Norms." *Southern Economic Journal* 82(1):208–34.

Baum, Sandy, Charles Kurose, and Michael S. McPherson. 2013. "An Overview of American Higher Education." *The Future of Children* 23(1):17–39.

Belsky, Jay. 1993. "Etiology of Child Maltreatment: A Developmental-Ecological Analysis." *Psychological Bulletin* 114(3):413–34.

Belsky, JiU M. 1999. "Misrepresenting Communities: The Politics of Community-Based Rural Ecotourism in Gales Point, Manatee, Belize." *Rural Sociology* 64(4):641–66.

Bennett, Fran. 2014. "The Living Wage, Low Pay and In Work Poverty: Rethinking the Relationships." *Critical Social Policy* 34(1):46–65.

Bernstein, Jared. 1999. "Demand Shifts and Low-Wage Workers." *Eastern Economic Journal* 25(2):191–208.

Bernstein, Sara. 2020. "The Metaphysics of Intersectionality." *Philosophical Studies* 177:321–35.

Bernstein, Shayna Fae, David Rehkopf, Shripad Tuljapurkar, Carol C. Horvitz, and Natalia L. Komarova. 2018. "Poverty Dynamics, Poverty Thresholds and Mortality: An Age-Stage Markovian Model." *PloS One* 13(5).

Bettie, Julie. 2003. *Women without Class: Girls, Race, and Identity*. Berkeley: University of California Press.

Bhandari, Shreya, Linda F. C. Bullock, Kim M. Anderson, Fran S. Danis, and Phyllis W. Sharps. 2011. "Pregnancy and Intimate Partner Violence: How Do Rural, Low-Income Women Cope?" *Health Care for Women International* 32(9):833–54.

Blank, Rebecca. 1997. *It Takes a Nation: A New Agenda for Fighting Poverty*. New York: Russell Sage Foundation.

Blau, Joel. 2006. "Welfare Reform in Historical Perspective." Pp. 49–120 in *The Promise of Welfare Reform: Political Rhetoric and the Reality of Poverty in the Twenty-First Century*, ed. K. M. Kilty and E. A. Segal. New York: The Haworth Press.

Blokland, Talja. 2012. "Blaming Neither the Undeserving Poor Nor the Revanchist Middle Classes: A Relational Approach to Marginalization." *Urban Geography* 33(4):488–507.

Bondi, Liz. 2008. "On the Relational Dynamics of Caring: A Psychotherapeutic Approach to Emotional and Power Dimensions of Women's Care Work." *Gender, Place and Culture* 15(3):249–65.

Bonds, Anne. 2009. "Discipline and Devolution: Constructions of Poverty, Race, and Criminality in the Politics of Rural Prison Development." *Antipode* 41(3):416–38.

Bourdieu, Pierre. 1977. *Outline of a Theory of Practice*. Cambridge University Press.

Bourdieu, Pierre. 1990. *The Logic of Practice*. Stanford University Press.

Bowen, Sarah, Joslyn Brenton, and Sinikka Elliott. 2019. *Pressure Cooker: Why Home Cooking Won't Solve Our Problems and What We Can Do about It*. New York: Oxford University Press.

Bradford, Scott. 2019. "Protection and Skills: Does Trade Policy Favor Low-Skill Workers?" *Review of International Economics* 27(3):981–1000.

Bradshaw, Daragh, Ann-Marie Creaven, and Orla T. Muldoon. 2021. "Parental Incarceration Affects Children's Emotional and Behavioral Outcomes: A Longitudinal Cohort Study of Children Aged 9 to 13 Years." *International Journal of Behavioral Development* 45(4):310–16.

Brady, David, and Rebekah Burroway. 2012. "Targeting, Universalism, and Single-Mother Poverty: A Multilevel Analysis across 18 Affluent Democracies." *Demography* 49:719–46.

Brandolini, Andrea, Silvia Magri, and Timothy M. Smeeding. 2010. "Asset-Based Measurement of Poverty." *Journal of Policy Analysis and Management* 29(2):267–84.

Brewer, Joe, Martin Kirk, Alnoor Ladha, and Think Africa Press. 2013. "It's Time to Shine a Light on the Poverty Creation Industry." *Truthout*. April 14. https://truthout.org/articles/its-time-to-shine-a-light-on-the -poverty-creation-industry.

Browne-Yung, Kathryn, Anna Ziersch, and Fran Baum. 2013. "'Faking til You Make It': Social Capital Accumulation of Individuals on Low Incomes Living in Contrasting Socio-economic Neighbourhoods and Its Implications for Health and Wellbeing." *Social Science & Medicine* 85:9–17.

Burkitt, Ian. 2016. "Relational Agency: Relational Sociology, Agency and Interaction." *European Journal of Social Theory* 19(3):322–39.

Burns, Kalee, Liana Fox, and Danielle Wilson. 2022. "Expansions to Child Tax Credit Contributed to 46% Decline in Child Poverty Since 2020." US Census Bureau. September 13. www.census.gov/library/stories/20 22/09/record-drop-in-child-poverty.html#:~:text=ARPA%20increased %20the%20value%20of,the%20taxpayer%27s%20income%20tax%20 liability.

Bursik, Robert J., Jr. 1988. "Social Disorganization and Theories of Crime and Delinquency: Problems and Prospects." *Criminology* 26(4):519–51.

Burton, Candace W., Kevin Nolasco, and Dave Holmes. 2021. "Queering Nursing Curricula: Understanding and Increasing Attention to LGBTQIA+ Health Needs." *Journal of Professional Nursing* 37(1):101–7.

Burton, Linda M. 2009. "Uncovering Hidden Facts that Matter in Interpreting Individuals' Behaviors: An Ethnographic Lens." Pp. 20–3 in *Families as They Really Are*, ed. B. J. Risman. New York: Norton Publishers.

Butz, Adam M. 2016. "Theorizing about Poverty and Paternalism in Suburban America: The Case of Welfare Sanctions." *Poverty & Public Policy* 8(2):129–40.

Cahill, Sean, and Sarah Tobias. 2007. *Policy Issues Affecting Lesbian, Gay, Bisexual, and Transgender Families*. Ann Arbor: University of Michigan Press.

Callan, Francesca Delaney, and Elizabeth M. Dolan. 2013. "Parenting Constraints and Supports of Young Low-income Mothers in Rural United States." *Journal of Comparative Family Studies* 44(2): 157–74.

Caner, Asena, and Edward Wolff. 2004. "Asset Poverty in the United States, 1984–1999." *Challenge* 47(1):5–52.

Carpenter, Laura M. 2010. "Gendered Sexuality over the Life Course: A Conceptual Framework." *Sociological Perspectives* 53(2):155–78.

Carter, Michael R., and Christopher B. Barrett. 2006. "The Economics of Poverty Traps and Persistent Poverty: An Asset-Based Approach." *The Journal of Development Studies* 42(2):178–99.

Carter, Prudence. 2005. *Keepin' It Real: School Success Beyond Black and White*. Transgressing Boundaries: Studies in Black Politics and Black Communities. New York: Oxford University Press.

Case Anne, and Angus Deaton. 2020. *Deaths of Despair and the Future of Capitalism*. Princeton University Press.

Cassino, Dan, and Yasemin Besen-Cassino. 2019. "Race, Threat and Workplace Sexual Harassment: The Dynamics of Harassment in the United States, 1997–2016." *Gender, Work, and Organization* 26(9):1221–40.

Catte, Elizabeth. 2018. *What You Are Getting Wrong about Appalachia*. Cleveland, OH: Belt Publishing.

Center for Women's Welfare. 2022. Home page. University of Washington School of Social Work, Seattle, WA. https://selfsufficiencystandard.org.

Chablani, Aneel. 2016. "Legal Aid's Once and Future Role for Impacting the Criminalization of Poverty and the War on the Poor." *Michigan Journal of Race & Law* 21(2):349–60.

Chen, Edith, Gene H. Brody, and Gregory E. Miller. 2022. "What Are the Health Consequences of Upward Mobility?" *Annual Review of Psychology* 73(1):599–628.

Cheng, Ping, Zhenguo Lin, and Yingchun Liu. 2014. "Racial Discrepancy in Mortgage Interest Rates." *The Journal of Real Estate Finance and Economics* 51(1):101–20.

Chetty, Raj, Nathaniel Hendren, Patrick Kline, Emmanuel Saez, and Nicholas Turner. 2014. "Is the United States Still a Land of Opportunity? Recent Trends in Intergenerational Mobility." *American Economic Review* 104(5):141–7.

Chetty, Raj, Matthew O. Jackson, Theresa Kuchler, et al. 2022. "Social Capital and Economic Mobility." Opportunity Insights, Harvard University. opportunityinsights.org.

Choi, Jeong-Kyun, Dan Wang, and Aurora P. Jackson. 2019. "Adverse Experiences in Early Childhood and Their Longitudinal Impact on Later Behavioral Problems of Children Living in Poverty." *Child Abuse & Neglect* 98(104181).

Christiansen, Isaac. 2017. "Commodification of Healthcare and Its Consequences." *World Review of Political Economy* 8(1):82–103.

Cicero, Theodore J., Matthew S. Ellis, Hilary L. Surratt, and Steven P. Kurtz. 2014. "The Changing Face of Heroin Use in the United States: A Retrospective Analysis of the Past 50 Years." *The Journal of the American Medical Association Psychiatry* 71(7):821–6.

Civic Enterprises & Everyone Graduates Center, Johns Hopkins University School of Education. 2016. *Building a Grad Nation: Data Brief: Overview of 2013–14 High School Graduation Rates.* Washington, DC: America's Promise Alliance.

Clark, David, and David Hulme. 2010. "Poverty, Time and Vagueness: Integrating the Core Poverty and Chronic Poverty Frameworks." *Cambridge Journal of Economics* 34:347–66.

Clausen, John A. 1986. *The Life Course: A Sociological Perspective.* Upper Saddle River, NJ: Prentice Hall.

Cleaveland, Carol L. 2013. "'I Stepped Over a Dead Body...': Latina Immigrant Narratives of Immigration and Poverty." *Journal of Human Behavior in the Social Environment* 23:1–13.

Clemens, Michael A., Ethan G. Lewis, and Hannah M. Postel. 2018. "Immigration Restrictions as Active Labor Market Policy: Evidence from the Mexican Bracero Exclusion." *The American Economic Review* 108(6):1468–87.

Code, L. (1995). *Rhetorical Spaces: Essays on Gendered Locations.* New York: Routledge.

Coleman, James S. 1966. *Equality of Educational Opportunity.* Washington, DC: US Government Printing Office.

Coleman-Jensen, Alisha, Matthew P. Rabbitt, Christian A. Gregory, and Anita Singh. 2022. "Household Food Security in the United States in 2021." Economic Research Service. Washington, DC: USDA.

Coleman-Jensen, Alisha, and Barry Steffen. 2017. "Food Insecurity and Housing Insecurity." Ch. 10 in *Rural Poverty in the United States,* ed. J. Sherman, A. Tickamyer, and J. Warlick. New York: Columbia University Press.

Collins, Patricia Hill. 2015. "Intersectionality's Definitional Dilemmas." *Annual Review of Sociology* 41:1–20.

Collins, Randall. 2010. "The Contentious Social Interactionism of Charles Tilly." *Social Psychology Quarterly* 73(1):5–10.

Congressional Research Service. 2018. "Supplemental Nutrition Assistance Program (SNAP): A Primer on Eligibility and Benefits." https://crsrepo rts.congress.gov.

Conley, Dalton. 1999. *Being Black, Living in the Red: Race, Wealth and Social Policy in America.* Berkeley: University of California Press.

Corra, Mamadi, Scott Carter, and Shannon Carter. 2011. "The Interactive Impact of Race and Gender on High School Advanced Course Enrollment." *Journal of Negro Education* 80(1):33–46.

Costello, E. Jane, William Copeland, and Adrian Angold. 2016. "The Great Smoky Mountains Study: Developmental Epidemiology in the Southeastern United States." *Social Psychiatry and Psychiatric Epidemiology* 51:639–46.

Council of Economic Advisers (CEA). 2018. "Expanding Work Requirements in Non-Cash Welfare Programs." Executive Office of the President (July 2018). www.whitehouse.gov/wp-content/uploads/2018/07/Expanding-Work-Requirements-in-Non-Cash-Welfare-Programs.pdf.

Crenshaw, Kimberle. 1989. "Demarginalizing the Intersection of Race and Sex: A Black Feminist Critique of Antidiscrimination Doctrine, Feminist Theory, and Antiracist Politics." *University of Chicago Legal Forum* 1989(1):139–67.

Crookston, Andrew, and Gregory Hooks. 2012. "Community Colleges, Budget Cuts, and Jobs: The Impact of Community Colleges on Employment Growth in Rural U.S. Counties, 1976–2004." *Sociology of Education* 85(4):350–72.

Crossley, Nick. 2015. "Relational Sociology and Culture: A Preliminary Framework." *International Review of Sociology* 25(1):65–85.

Cunningham, Mary K. 2016. "Reduce Poverty by Improving Housing Stability." June 26. Urban Institute. www.urban.org/urban-wire/reduce -poverty-improving-housing-stability.

Curran, Megan A. 2022. "Research Roundup of the Expanded Child Tax Credit: One Year On." November 15. Poverty and Social Policy Report 6(9). Center on Poverty & Social Policy, Columbia University.

Davidai, Shai, and T. Gilovich. 2018. "How Should We Think about Americans' Perceptions of Socioeconomic Mobility?" *Judgment and Decision Making* 13(3):297–304.

Davidson, Danielle, Greg Marston, Jennifer Mays, and Jeffery Johnson-Abdelmalik. 2018. "Role of Relational Case Management in Transitioning from Poverty." *Australian Social Work* 71(1):58–70.

Dépelteau, François. 2008. "Relational Thinking: A Critique of Co-Deterministic Theories of Structure and Agency." *Sociological Theory* 26(1):51–73.

Desmond, Matthew. 2016. *Evicted: Poverty and Profit in the American City.* New York: Crown Publishers.

Diamond, John B., and James P. Huguley. 2014. "Testing the Oppositional Culture Explanation in Desegregated Schools: The Impact of Racial

Differences in Academic Orientations on School Performance." *Social Forces* 93(2):747–77.

Dickeman, Mildred. 1971. "The Integrity of the Cherokee Student." Pp. 140–79 in *The Culture of Poverty: A Critique,* ed. E. B. Leacock. New York: Simon and Schuster.

Dickey, Madison S., Elizabeth A. Mosley, Elizabeth A. Clark, Sarah Cordes, Eva Lathrop, and Lisa B. Haddad. 2022. "'They're Forcing People to Have Children that They Can't Afford': A Qualitative Study of Social Support and Capital among Individuals Receiving an Abortion in Georgia." *Social Science & Medicine* 315(115547).

Dodson, Lisa. 2007. "Wage-Poor Mothers and Moral Economy." *Social Politics* 14(2):258–80.

Donnelly, Denise, Elisabeth Burgess, Sally Anderson, Regina Davis, and Joy Dillard. 2001. "Involuntary Celibacy: A Life Course Analysis." *Journal of Sex Research* 38(2):159–69.

Dreher, Jochen, and Daniela Griselda López. 2015. "Subjectivity and Power." *Human Studies* 38:197–222.

Drucker, Ernest. 1971. "Cognitive Styles and Class Stereotypes." Pp. 41–61 in *The Culture of Poverty: A Critique,* ed. E. B. Leacock. New York: Simon and Schuster.

Du Bois, W. E. B. [1899] 1967. *The Philadelphia Negro: A Social Study.* New York: Schocken Books.

Due, Pernille, Juan Merlo, Yossi Harel-Fisch, et al. 2009. "Socioeconomic Inequality in Exposure to Bullying during Adolescence: A Comparative, Cross-Sectional, Multilevel Study in 35 Countries." *American Journal of Public Health* 99(5):907–14.

Duncan, Cynthia M. 1999. *Worlds Apart: Why Poverty Persists in Rural America,* 2nd edition. New Haven, CT: Yale University Press.

Duncan, Greg J., and Katherine Magnusson. 2013. "The Long Reach of Early Childhood Poverty." Pp. 57–70 in *Economic Stress, Human Capital, and Families in Asia: Research and Policy Challenges,* ed. W. J. J. Yeung and M. T. Yap. Dordrecht : Springer Netherlands.

Eason, John M., L. Ash Smith, Jason Greenberg, Richard D. Abel, and Corey Sparks. 2017. "Crime, Punishment, and Spatial Inequality." In *Rural Poverty in the United States,* ed. J. Sherman, A. Tickamyer, and J. Warlick. New York: Columbia University Press.

Edelman, Peter. 2019. "The Criminalization of Poverty and the People Who Fight Back." *Georgetown Journal on Poverty Law & Policy* 26(2):213–28.

Edin, Kathryn, and Maria Kefalas. [2005]. 2011. *Promises I Can Keep: Why Poor Women Put Motherhood before Marriage,* reprint. Berkeley: University of California Press.

Edin, Kathryn, and Laura Lein. 1997. *Making Ends Meet: How Single Mothers Survive Welfare and Low-Wage Work.* New York: Russell Sage Foundation.

Edin, Kathryn, and Timothy Jon Nelson. 2013. *Doing the Best I Can: Fatherhood in the Inner City.* Berkeley: University of California Press.

Edin, Kathryn J., and H. Luke Shaefer. 2015. *$2.00 a Day: Living on Almost Nothing in America.* Boston: Mariner Books.

Eldeib, Duaa, Adriana Gallardo, Akilah Johnson, et al. 2020. "The First 100: COVID-19 Took Black Lives First. It Didn't Have To." May 9. ProPublica Illinois. https://features.propublica.org/chicago-first-deaths /covid-coronavirus-took-black-lives-first.

Elwood, Sarah, Victoria Lawson, and Eric Sheppard. 2017. "Geographical Relational Poverty Studies." *Progress in Human Geography* 41(6): 745–65.

Emirbayer, Mustafa, and Jeff Goodwin. 1994. "Network Analysis, Culture, and the Problem of Agency." *American Journal of Sociology* 99(6):1411–54.

Erdmans, Mary Patrice, and Timothy Black. 2015. *On Becoming a Teen Mom: Life before Pregnancy.* Oakland: University of California Press.

Erickson, W., C. Lee, and S. von Schrader. 2020. "2018 Disability Status Report." Ithaca, NY: Cornell University Yang-Tan Institute (YTI). www.disabilitystatistics.org.

Espinosa, Adriana, Lesia M. Ruglass, Naomi Dambreville, Alina Shevorykin, Ron Nicholson, and Kelly M. Sykes. 2017. "Correlates of Child Abuse Potential among African American and Latina Mothers: A Developmental-Ecological Perspective." *Child Abuse & Neglect* 70:222–30.

Evans, Sally, and Wanda Anderson. 2013. "Demetrio's Story: Socialization and Family Adjustments Based on Long-Term Immersion in a Culture of Poverty." *Children & Schools* 35(4):244–7.

Faber, Jacob William. 2019. "Segregation and the Cost of Money: Race, Poverty, and the Prevalence of Alternative Financial Institutions." *Social Forces* 98(2):817–46.

Fain, Paul. 2019. "Wealth's Influence on Enrollment and Completion." *Inside Higher Ed.* May 23.

Falk, William W., and Linda M. Lobao. 2003. "Who Benefits from Economic Restructuring? Lessons from the Past and Challenges for the Future." Pp. 152–65 in *Challenges for Rural America in the Twenty-First Century*, ed. D. L. Brown and L. E. Swanson. University Park: The Pennsylvania State University Press.

Farber, Naomi B. 1997. "Americans All: Black and Single Parent Families in the Inner City." *Ethnic and Racial Studies* 20(1):200–9.

Farmer, Paul. 2003. *Pathologies of Power: Health, Human Rights, and the New War on the Poor.* Berkeley: University of California Press.

Feijen-de Jong, Esther I., Danielle Jansen, Frank Baarveld, Cornelis van der Schans, Francois G. Schellevis, and Sijmen A. Reijneveld. 2012. "Determinants of Late and/or Inadequate Use of Prenatal Healthcare in High-Income Countries: A Systematic Review." *European Journal of Public Health* 22(6): 904–13.

Feldman, Deborah L., Antony T. Smith, and Barbara L. Waxman. 2017. *"Why We Drop Out": Understanding and Disrupting Student Pathways to Leaving School.* New York: Teachers College Press.

Feldman, Guy. 2019. "Towards a Relational Approach to Poverty in Social Work: Research and Practice Considerations." *British Journal of Social Work* 49:1705–22.

Figlio, D. N. 2005. "Boys Named Sue: Disruptive Children and Their Peers." National Bureau of Economic Research Working Paper No. W11277.

Fisher, Gordon M. 1992. "The Development and History of the Poverty Thresholds." *Social Security Bulletin* 55(4). www.ssa.gov/history/fisheronpoverty.html.

Fitchen, Janet M. 1981. *Poverty in Rural America: A Case Study.* Boulder, CO: Westview Press.

Fizaine, Florian, and Sondès Kahouli. 2019. "On the Power of Indicators: How the Choice of Fuel Poverty Indicator Affects the Identification of the Target Population." *Applied Economics* 51(11):1081–1110.

Fogle, Nikolaus. 2011. *The Spatial Logic of Social Struggle: A Bourdieuian Topology.* Lanham, MD: Lexington Books.

Foley, Michael W., John D. McCarthy, and Mark Chaves. 2001. "Social Capital, Religious Institutions, and Poor Communities." Pp. 215–45 in *The Community Development Reader*, ed. J. DeFilippis and S. Saegert. New York: Russell Sage Foundation.

Ford, Timothy G., Kyong-Ah Kwon, and Jessica D. Tsotsoros. 2021. "Early Childhood Distance Learning in the U.S. during the COVID Pandemic: Challenges and Opportunities." *Children and Youth Services Review* 131:106297.

Foster, James E. 1998. "Absolute versus Relative Poverty." *The American Economic Review* 88(2):335–41.

Fox, Liana E., and Kalee Burns. 2021. "The Supplemental Poverty Measure: 2020." Current Population Reports P60-273. US Census Bureau.

Fraser, Nancy, and Rahel Jaeggi (2018). *Capitalism: A Conversation in Critical Theory*, ed. B. Milstein. Cambridge: Polity.

Frazier, Franklin E. 1937. "The Impact of Urban Civilization upon Negro Family Life." *American Sociological Review* 2(5):609.

Frazier, Franklin E. 1950. "Problems and Needs of Negro Children and Youth Resulting from Family Disorganization." *The Journal of Negro Education* 19(3):269–77.

Friedrichs, Chad, dir.. 2011. *The Pruitt–Igoe Myth.* Columbia, MO: Unicorn Stencil Documentary Films.

Fryer, Jr., Roland G., and Lawrence F. Katz. 2013. "Achieving Escape Velocity: Neighborhood and School Interventions to Reduce Persistent Inequality." *American Economic Review* 103(3):232–7.

Fuchs, Victor. 1969. "Comment on Measuring the Size of the Low-Income Population." Pp. 198–202 in *Six Papers on the Size Distribution of Wealth and Income*, ed. L. Soltow. New York: National Bureau of Economic Research.

Fuhse, Jan A. 2013. "Social Relationships between Communication, Network Structure, and Culture." Pp. 181–206 in *Applying Relational Sociology: Relations, Networks, and Society*, ed. F. Dépelteau and C. Powell. New York: Palgrave Macmillan.

Fulkerson, Gregory M., and Alexander R. Thomas, 2014. *Studies in Urbanormativity: Rural Community in Urban Society*. Lanham, MD: Lexington Books.

Fulkerson, Gregory M., and Gretchen H. Thompson. 2008. "The Evolution of a Contested Concept: A Meta-Analysis of Social Capital Definitions and Trends (1988–2006)." *Sociological Inquiry* 78(4):536–57.

Furstenberg, Frank F. 2007. *Destinies of the Disadvantaged: The Politics of Teen Childbearing*. New York: Russell Sage Foundation.

Gans, Herbert J. 1967. "The Negro Family: Reflections on the Moynihan Report." Pp. 445–57 in *The Moynihan Report and the Politics of Controversy*, ed. L. Rainwater and W. L. Yancey. Cambridge, MA: MIT Press. Originally published in part in *Commonweal*, October 15, 1965.

Gans, Herbert J. 2010. "Concentrated Poverty: A Critical Analysis." *Challenge* 53(3):82–96.

Garcia, Angela. 2010. *The Pastoral Clinic: Addiction and Dispossession along the Rio Grande*. Berkeley: University of California Press.

Gautié, Jérôme and John Schmitt, eds. 2010. *Low-Wage Work in the Wealthy World*. New York: Russell Sage Foundation.

George, Janel. 2015. "Stereotype and School Pushout: Race, Gender, and Discipline Disparities." *Arkansas Law Review* 68(1):101–29.

Genter, Shaun, Gregory Hooks, and Clayton Mosher. 2013. "Prisons, Jobs and Privatization: The Impact of Prisons on Employment Growth in Rural US Counties, 1997–2004." *Social Science Research* 42(3):596–610.

Geraghty, Sarah. 2016. "Keynote Remarks: How the Criminalization of Poverty Has Become Normalized in American Culture and Why You Should Care." *Michigan Journal of Race & Law* 21(2):195–203.

Gerdts, Caitlin, Loren Dobkin, Diana Greene Foster, and Eleanor Bimla Schwarz. 2016. "Side Effects, Physical Health Consequences, and Mortality Associated with Abortion and Birth after an Unwanted Pregnancy." *Women's Health Issues* 26:55–9.

Gerlock, April A., Jackie Grimesey, and George Sayre. 2014. "Military-Related Posttraumatic Stress Disorder and Intimate Relationship Behaviors: A Developing Dyadic Relationship Model." *Journal of Marital and Family Therapy* 40(3):344–56.

Geronimus, Arline T., and Sanders Korenman. 1992. "The Socioeconomic Consequences of Teen Childbearing Reconsidered." *The Quarterly Journal of Economics* 107(4):1187–1214.

Giddens, Anthony. 1984. *The Constitution of Society: Outline of the Theory of Structuration*. Berkeley: University of California Press.

Giefer, Katherine G., and Tracy A. Loveless. 2021. "Benefits Received by Veterans and Their Survivors: 2017." Current Population Reports P70BR-175. US Census Bureau.

Gilder, George. 1981. *Wealth and Poverty*. New York: Basic Books.

Glenn, Evelyn Nakano. 2002. *Unequal Freedom: How Race and Gender Shaped American Citizenship and Labor*. Cambridge, MA: Harvard University Press.

Goffman, Erving. 1959. *The Presentation of Self in Everyday Life*. New York: Anchor Books.

Goldblum, Joanne Samuel, and Colleen Shaddox. 2021. *Broke in America: Seeing, Understanding, and Ending US Poverty*. Dallas, TX: BenBella Books.

Goldrick-Rab, Sara, Jed Richardson, and Anthony Hernandez. 2017. "Hungry and Homeless in College: Results from a National Study of Basic Needs Insecurity in Higher Education." Madison, MI: Wisconsin HOPE Lab. https://hope4college.com/wp-content/uploads/2018/09 /Hungry-and-Homeless-in-College-Report.pdf.

Goldsmith, William W., and Edward J. Blakely. 1992. *Separate Societies: Poverty and Inequality in U.S. Cities*. Philadelphia: Temple University Press.

Goodman, Lisa A., Katya Fels Smyth, and Victoria Banyard. 2010. "Beyond the 50-Minute Hour: Increasing Control, Choice, and Connections in the Lives of Low-Income Women." *American Journal of Orthopsychiatry* 80(1):3–11.

Gordon, David. 2017. "PSE-UK 2012 Survey: Producing an 'Objective' Poverty Line in Eight Easy Steps." Poverty and Social Exclusion: UK. www.poverty.ac.uk/pse-research/pse-uk-2012.

Gottschalk, Peter, and Sheldon Danziger. 2009. "Inequality of Wage Rates, Earnings and Family Income in the United States, 1975–2002." Pp. 216–38 in *Inequality and Society: Social Science Perspectives on Social Stratification*, ed. J. Manza and M. Sauder. New York: W.W. Norton & Co.

Granovetter, Mark. 1974. *Getting a Job: A Study of Contacts and Careers*. University of Chicago Press.

Green, Maia. 2006. "Representing Poverty and Attacking Representations: Perspectives on Poverty from Social Anthropology." *Journal of Development Studies* 42(7):1108–29.

Green, Maia, and David Hulme. 2005. "From Correlates and Characteristics to Causes: Thinking about Poverty from a Chronic Poverty Perspective." *World Development* 33(6):867–79.

Greenhouse, Steven. 2014. "Low-Wage Workers Are Finding Poverty Harder to Escape." *The New York Times*. March 16. www.nytimes.com /2014/03/17/business/economy/low-wage-workers-finding-its-easier-to -fall-into-poverty-and-harder-to-get-out.html?emc=edit_th_20140317 &nl=todaysheadlines&nlid=59821686&_r=0.

Grusky, David B., Peter A. Hall, and Hazel Rose Markus. 2019. "The Rise of Opportunity Markets: How Did It Happen & What Can We Do?" *Daedalus* 148(3):19–45.

Gunzenhauser, Michael G. 2006. "A Moral Epistemology of Knowing Subjects: Theorizing a Relational Turn for Qualitative Research." *Qualitative Inquiry* 12(3):621–47.

Guterman, Neil B., and Yookyong Lee. 2005. "The Role of Fathers in Risk for Physical Child Abuse and Neglect: Possible Pathways and Unanswered Questions." *Child Maltreatment* 10(2):136–49.

Guttmacher Institute. 2022a. "Sex and HIV Education." December 1. www .guttmacher.org/state-policy/explore/sex-and-hiv-education.

Guttmacher Institute. 2022b. "United States Abortion Demographics." www.guttmacher.org/united-states/abortion/demographics.

Ha, Yoonsook, Mary Elizabeth Collins, and David Martino. 2015. "Child Care Burden and the Risk of Child Maltreatment among Low-Income Working Families." *Children and Youth Services Review* 59:19–27.

Haberly, Daniel, and Dariusz Wójcik. 2015. "Tax Havens and the Production of Offshore FDI: An Empirical Analysis." *Journal of Economic Geography* 15(1):75–101.

Hacker, Jacob S. 2006. *The Great Risk Shift: The New Economic Insecurity and the Decline of the American Dream.* New York: Oxford University Press.

Hacker, Jacob S. 2019. *The Great Risk Shift: The New Economic Insecurity and the Decline of the American Dream,* 2nd edition. New York: Oxford University Press.

Hagler, Matthew, Sherry Hamby, John Grych, and Victoria Banyard. 2015. "Working for Well-Being: Uncovering the Protective Benefits of Work through Mixed Methods Analysis." *Journal of Happiness Studies* 17(4):1493–1510.

Hahamovitch, Cindy. 2011. *No Man's Land: Jamaican Guestworkers in America and the Global History of Deportable Labor.* Princeton University Press.

Hall, Abigail R., Jerod T. Hassell, and Chivon H. Fitch. 2021. "Militarized Extremism: The Radical Right and the War on Terror." *The Independent Review* 26(2):225–42.

Hall, Matthew, and George Farkas. 2008. "Does Human Capital Raise Earnings for Immigrants in the Low-Skill Labor Market?" *Demography* 45(3):619–39.

Halpern, Robert. 1995. *Rebuilding the Inner City: A History of Neighborhood Initiatives to Address Poverty in the United States.* New York: Columbia University Press.

Han, JooHee. 2018. "Who Goes to College, Military, Prison, or Long-Term Unemployment? Racialized School-to-Labor Market Transitions among American Men." *Population Research and Policy Review* 37(4):615–40.

Harding, David. 2010. *Living the Drama: Community, Conflict, and Culture among Inner-City Boys.* University of Chicago Press.

Harrell, Zaje A. T., Jason L. Huang, and Dawn M. Kepler. 2013. "Affluence and College Alcohol Problems: The Relevance of Parent- and Child-Reported Indicators of Socioeconomic Status." *Journal of Adolescence* 36:893–7.

Harrington, Michael. 1962. *The Other America: Poverty in the United States.* New York: The MacMillan Company.

Harris, Alexes. 2016. *A Pound of Flesh: Monetary Sanctions as Punishment for the Poor.* New York: Russell Sage Foundation.

Harris, Kathleen Mullan. 1993. "Work and Welfare among Single Mothers in Poverty." *American Journal of Sociology* 99(2):317–52.

Harvey, Mark H. 2017. "Racial Inequalities and Poverty in Rural America." Ch. 6 in *Rural Poverty in the United States*, ed. J. Sherman, A. Tickamyer, and J. Warlick. New York: Columbia University Press.

Haskins, Ron, and Isabel V. Sawhill. 2016. "The Decline of the American Family: Can Anything Be Done to Stop the Damage?" *The Annals of the American Academy of Political and Social Science* 667:8–34.

Haugen, Gary A., and Victor Boutros. (2014) *The Locust Effect: Why the End of Poverty Requires the End of Violence.* New York: Oxford University Press.

Hazen, Kirk. 2018. "Rural Voices in Appalachia: The Shifting Sociolinguistic Reality of Rural Life." Pp. 75–90 in *Rural Voices: Language, Identity, and Social Change across Place*, ed. E. Seale and C. Mallinson. Lanham, MD: Lexington Books.

Hegewisch, Ariane, and Heidi Hartmann. 2014. "Occupational Segregation and the Gender Wage Gap: A Job Half Done." Institute for Women's Policy Research. https://iwpr.org/iwpr-issues/esme/occupational-segre gation-and-the-gender-wage-gap-a-job-half-done.

Heimlich, Russell. 2007. "See Poor as Too Dependent on Government Aid." The Pew Research Center. www.pewresearch.org/fact-tank/2007 /07/21/see-poor-as-too-dependent-on-government-aid.

Henry, Meghan, Anna Mahathey, Tyler Morrill, et al. 2018. "The 2018 Annual Homeless Assessment Report (AHAR) to Congress." Office of Community Planning and Development, US Department of Housing and Urban Development. www.hudexchange.info/resource/5783/2018 -ahar-part-1-pit-estimates-of-homelessness-in-the-us.

Herring, Chris. 2019. "Complaint-Oriented Policing: Regulating Homelessness in Public Space." *American Sociological Review* 84(5): 769–800.

Herring, Chris, Dilara Yarbrough, and Lisa Marie Alatorre. 2020. "Pervasive Penality: How the Criminalization of Poverty Perpetuates Homelessness." *Social Problems* 67(1):131–49.

Ho, Vivian. 2020. "'A True Emergency': Covid-19 Pushes Homeless Crisis in San Francisco's Tenderloin to the Brink." *The Guardian.* May 19. www.theguardian.com/world/2020/may/19/a-true-emergency-covid-19 -pushes-homeless-crisis-in-san-franciscos-tenderloin-to-the-brink.

Hochschild, Arlie. 2012. *The Outsourced Self: Intimate Life in Market Times.* New York: Metropolitan Press.

Hochschild, Arlie. 2016. "Foreword: Invisible Labor, Inaudible Voice." Pp. xi–xiv in *Invisible Labor: Hidden Work in the Contemporary World*, ed. M. Crain, W. Poster, and M. Cherry. Berkeley: University of California Press.

Howell, David R., and Arne L. Kalleberg.2019. "Declining Job Quality in the United States: Explanations and Evidence." *RSF: The Russell Sage Foundation Journal of the Social Sciences* 5(4):1–53.

Huff, Charlotte. 2022. "A Crisis of Campus Sexual Assault." *Monitor on Psychology* (Washington, DC: American Psychological Association) 53(3).

Human Rights Campaign. 2021. "A Call to Action: LGBTQ Youth Need Inclusive Sex Education." HRC Foundation. www.hrc.org/resources /a-call-to-action-lgbtq-youth-need-inclusive-sex-education.

Hunt, Joshua. 2022. "How I Became a Pathological Liar." *The New York Times*, July 13. www.nytimes.com/2022/07/13/opinion/class-poverty-lying.html?searchResultPosition=1.

Iceland, John. 2013. *Poverty in America: A Handbook*, 3rd edition. Berkeley: University of California Press.

Institute for Children, Poverty, and Homelessness. 2022. "Understanding Homelessness in Rural America." www.icphusa.org/rural.

Isaacs, Julia B. 2008. "Economic Mobility of Families across Generations." In *Getting Ahead or Losing Ground: Economic Mobility in America*. Washington, DC: The Brookings Institute.

Isenberg, Nancy. 2016. *White Trash: The 400-Year Untold History of Class in America*. New York: Viking.

Israeli, O., and M. Weber. 2014. "Defining Chronic Poverty: Comparing Different Approaches." *Applied Economics* 46(31): 3874–81.

Jacobs, Anna W., and Irene Padavic. 2015. "Hours, Scheduling and Flexibility for Women in the US Low-Wage Labour Force." *Gender, Work & Organization* 22(1):67–86.

Jargowsky, Paul A. 1996. "Beyond the Street Corner: The Hidden Diversity of High Poverty Neighborhoods." *Urban Geography* 17(7):579–603.

Jargowsky, Paul A., and Mary Jo Bane. 1991. "Ghetto Poverty in the United States, 1970–1980." Pp. 235–73 in *The Urban Underclass*, ed. C. Jencks and P. E. Peterson. Washington, DC: The Brookings Institute.

Jeffrey, Wesley. 2020. "Crossing the Finish Line? A Review of College Completion Inequality in the United States by Race and Class." *Sociology Compass* 14(5).

Jencks, Christopher, and Susan E. Mayer. 1990. "The Social Consequences of Growing Up in a Poor Neighborhood." Pp. 111–86 in *Inner-City Poverty in the United States*, ed. L. E. Lynn, Jr., and M. G. H. McGeary. Washington, DC: National Academies Press.

Jencks, Christopher, and Paul E. Peterson, eds. 1991. *The Urban Underclass.* Washington, DC: The Brookings Institute.

Jenkins, Janis H. 2015. *Extraordinary Conditions: Culture and Experience in Mental Illness.* Berkeley: University of California Press.

Jensen, Leif, and Danielle Ely. 2017. "Measures of Poverty and Implications for Portraits of Rural Hardship." Ch. 3 in *Rural Poverty in the United States,* ed. J. Sherman, A. Tickamyer, and J. Warlick. New York: Columbia University Press.

Johnson, Anna D., Anne Martin, Anne Partika, Deborah A. Phillips, and Sherri Castle. 2022. "Chaos during the COVID-19 Outbreak: Predictors of Household Chaos among Low-Income Families during a Pandemic." *Family Relations* 71(1):18–28.

Kalleberg, Arne L. 2011. *Good Jobs, Bad Jobs: The Rise of Polarized and Precarious Employment Systems in the United States, 1970s to 2000s.* New York: Russell Sage Foundation.

Kalleberg, Arne L. 2018. *Precarious Lives: Job Insecurity and Well-Being in Rich Democracies.* Cambridge: Polity.

Kanbur, Ravi, and Andy Sumner. 2012. "Poor Countries or Poor People? Development Assistance and the New Geography of Global Poverty." *Journal of International Development* 24(6):686–95.

Katz, Sheila M. 2018. "Pride and Hope, Shame and Blame: How Welfare Mothers in Higher Education Juggle Competing Identities." Pp. 11–24 in *Marginalized Mothers, Mothering from the Margins,* ed. T. Taylor and K. Bloch. Bingley, UK: Emerald Publishing.

Kerber, Linda K. 1998. *No Constitutional Right to Be Ladies: Women and the Obligations of Citizenship.* New York: Hill and Wang.

Khader, Serene J. 2011. *Adaptive Preferences and Women's Empowerment.* New York: Oxford University Press.

Kim, Dong Ha, Sarah M. Bassett, Lois Takahashi, and Dexter R. Voisin. 2018. "What Does Self-Esteem Have to Do with Behavioral Health among Low-Income Youth in Chicago?" *Journal of Youth Studies* 21(8):999–1010.

Kim, Hyunil, Christopher Wildeman, Melissa Jonson-Reid, and Brett Drake. 2017. "Lifetime Prevalence of Investigating Child Maltreatment among US Children." *American Journal of Public Health* 107(2):274–80.

Klärner, Andreas, and André Knabe. 2019. "Social Networks and Coping with Poverty in Rural Areas." *Sociologia Ruralis* 59(3):447–73.

Klein, Ezra. 2022. "Why a Middle-Class Lifestyle Remains out of Reach for So Many." *New York Times,* July 17. www.nytimes.com/2022/07/17/opinion/inflation-prices-affordability.html?campaign_id=2&emc=edit_th_20220718&instance_id=66918&nl=todaysheadlines&regi_id=64924513&segment_id=98816&user_id=aa15fe8237e0e69db3d05350 5e9c7648.

Kneebone, Elizabeth, and Alan Berube. 2014. *Confronting Suburban Poverty in America.* Washington, DC: Brookings Institute Press.

Kotch, Jonathan B., Dorothy C. Browne, Christopher L. Ringwalt, et al. 1995. "Risk of Child Abuse or Neglect in a Cohort of Low-Income Children." *Child Abuse & Neglect* 19(9):1115–30.

Kristof, Nicholas. 2016. "3 TVs and No Food: Growing Up Poor in America." *New York Times*. October 28.

Krysan, Maria. 2011. "Race and Residence: From the Telescope to the Microscope." *Contexts* 10:38–42.

Ladson-Billings, Gloria. 2006. "It's Not the Culture of Poverty, It's the Poverty of Culture: The Problem with Teacher Education." *Anthropology & Education Quarterly* 37(2):104–9.

Lansberry, Kasey, Tiffany Taylor, and Elizabeth Seale. 2017. "Welfare and the Culture of Conservatism: A Contextual Analysis of Welfare-to-Work Participation in North Carolina." *Journal of Poverty* 21(1): 20–41.

Lareau, Annette. 2003. *Unequal Childhoods: Class, Race, and Family Life.* Berkeley: University of California Press.

Lather, Patricia A., and Christine S. Smithies. 1997. *Troubling the Angels: Women Living with HIV/AIDS*. New York: Westview Press.

Laughlin, Lynda, and Kelly Ann Holder (US Census Bureau). 2017. "Service over College: Does Military Service Act as a Bridge to Better Economic Opportunities for Post-9/11 Non-College-Degreed Female Veterans?" Population Association of America. Poster, April 27–29.

Lawson, Monica, Megan H. Piel, and Michaela Simon. 2020. "Child Maltreatment during the COVID-19 Pandemic: Consequences of Parental Job Loss on Psychological and Physical Abuse towards Children." *Child Abuse & Neglect* 110(104709).

Leacock, Eleanor Burke. 1971. "Introduction." Pp. 9–37 in *The Culture of Poverty: A Critique*, edited by E. B. Leacock. New York: Simon and Schuster.

Leaman, Jeremy, and Attiya Waris. 2013. *Tax Justice and the Political Economy of Global Capitalism, 1945 to the Present*. New York: Berghahn Books.

Lee, Matthew R., Michael O. Maume, and Graham C. Ousey. 2003. "Social Isolation and Lethal Violence across the Metro/Nonmetro Divide: The Effects of Socioeconomic Disadvantage and Poverty Concentration on Homicide." *Rural Sociology* 68(1):107–31.

Lee, Shawna J., Kaitlin P. Ward, Joyce Y. Lee, and Christina M. Rodriguez. 2022. "Parental Social Isolation and Child Maltreatment Risk during the COVID-19 Pandemic." *Journal of Family Violence* 37:813–24.

Leeds, Anthony. 1971. "The Concept of the 'Culture of Poverty': Conceptual, Logical, and Empirical Problems, with Perspectives from Brazil and Peru." Pp. 226--84 in *The Culture of Poverty: A Critique*, edited by E. B. Leacock. New York: Simon and Schuster.

Lemke, Sieglinde. 2016. *Inequality, Poverty, and Precarity in Contemporary American Culture*. New York: Palgrave Macmillan.

Lengermann, Patricia Madoo, and Jill Niebrugge-Brantley. 2002. "Back to the Future: Settlement Sociology, 1885–1930." *The American Sociologist* 33(3):5–20.

Levey, Elizabeth J., Bizu Gelaye, Paul Bain, et al. 2017. "A Systematic Review of Randomized Controlled Trials of Interventions Designed to Decrease Child Abuse in High-Risk Families." *Child Abuse & Neglect* 65:48–57.

Levey, Noam. 2022. "Sick and Struggling to Pay, 100 Million People in the U.S. Live with Medical Debt." June 16. National Public Radio and Kaiser Health News. www.npr.org/sections/health-shots/2022/06/16/11 04679219/medical-bills-debt-investigation.

Levine, Judith A. 2013. *Ain't No Trust: How Bosses, Boyfriends, and Bureaucrats Fail Low-Income Mothers*. Berkeley: University of California Press.

Lewis, Oscar. [1959] 1975. *Five Families: Mexican Case Studies in the Culture of Poverty*, reprint. New York: Basic Books.

Lewis, Oscar. 1965. *La Vida: A Puerto Rican Family in the Culture of Poverty – San Juan and New York*. New York: Random House.

Lichter, Daniel T., Gail M. Johnston, and Diane K. McLaughlin. 1994. "Changing Linkages between Work and Poverty in Rural America." *Rural Sociology* 59(3):395–415.

Lichter, Daniel T., Scott R. Sanders, and Kenneth M. Johnson. 2015. "Hispanics at the Starting Line: Poverty among Newborn Infants in Established Gateways and New Destinations." *Social Forces* 94(1):209–35.

Lichter, Daniel T., and James P. Ziliak. 2017. "The Rural–Urban Interface: New Patterns of Spatial Interdependence and Inequality in America." *Annals of the American Academy of Political and Social Science* 672:6–25.

Lindo, Jason M., Jessamyn Schaller, and Benjamin Hansen. 2018. "Caution! Men Not at Work: Gender-Specific Labor Market Conditions and Child Maltreatment." *Journal of Public Economics* 163:77–98.

Linnan, Laura, Gabriela Arandia, Lori A. Bateman, Amber Vaughn, Natalie Smith, and Dianne Ward. 2017. "The Health and Working Conditions of Women Employed in Child Care." *International Journal of Environmental Research and Public Health* 14:283.

Lloyd, Margaret H., and Nancy Jo Kepple. 2017. "Unpacking the Parallel Effects of Parental Alcohol Misuse and Low Income on Risk of Supervisory Neglect." *Child Abuse & Neglect* 69:72–84.

Lobao, Linda. 2004. "Continuity and Change in Place Stratification: Spatial Inequality and Middle-Range Territorial Units." *Rural Sociology* 69(1):1–30.

Lofstrom, Magnus, and Steven Raphael. 2016. "Crime, the Criminal Justice System, and Socioeconomic Inequality." *Journal of Economic Perspectives* 30(2):103–26.

Long, Cindy. 2006. "Understanding Poverty: An Innovative Workshop Helps Educators Close the Achievement Gap." *NEA Today* (April):16.

Ludwig, Jens, and Susan Mayer. 2006. "'Culture' and the Intergenerational Transmission of Poverty: The Prevention Paradox." *The Future of Children* 16(2):175–96.

Luker, Kristin. 1996. *Dubious Conceptions: The Politics of Teenage Pregnancy.* Cambridge, MA: Harvard University Press.

MacGillis, Alec, and ProPublica. 2016. "The Original Underclass." *The Atlantic* (September). www.theatlantic.com/magazine/archive/2016/09/the-original-underclass/492731.

Maclean, Johanna Catherine, Justine Mallatt, Christopher J. Ruhm, and Kosali Simon. 2021. "Economic Studies on the Opioid Crisis: A Review." Working Paper 28067. National Bureau of Economic Research. www.nber.org/papers/w28067.

Maloney, Tim, Nan Jiang, Emily Putnam-Hornstein, Erin Dalton, and Rhema Vaithianathan. 2017. "Black–White Differences in Child Maltreatment Reports and Foster Care Placements: A Statistical Decomposition Using Linked Administrative Data." *Maternal and Child Health Journal* 21(3):414–20.

Mammen, Sheila, Elizabeth Dolan, and Sharon B. Seiling. 2015. "Explaining the Poverty Dynamics of Rural Families Using an Economic Well-Being Continuum." *Journal of Family & Economic Issues* 36:434–50.

Mann, Charles C. 2006. *1491: New Revelations of America before Columbus.* New York: Knopf.

Martin, Joyce A., Brady E. Hamilton, Michelle J. K. Osterman, and Anne K. Driscoll. 2021. "Births: Final Data for 2019." *National Vital Statistics Reports* 70(2):1–51.

Marwell, Nicole P., and Shannon L. Morrissey. 2020. "Organizations and the Governance of Urban Poverty." *Annual Review of Sociology* 46:233–50.

Mason, Geoff, and Wiemer Salverda. 2010. "Low Pay, Working Conditions, and Living Standards." Pp. 35–90 in *Low-Wage Work in the Wealthy World*, ed. J. Gautie and J. Schmitt. New York: Russell Sage Foundation.

Massey, Douglas S., and Nancy A. Denton. 1993. *American Apartheid: Segregation and the Making of the Underclass.* Cambridge, MA: Harvard University Press.

Mather, Mark, and Beth Jarosz. 2014. "The Demography of Inequality in the United States." Population Bulletin 69(2). Washington, DC: Population Reference Bureau.

Mauldin, Teresa, and Yoko Mimura. 2001. "Exits from Poverty among Rural and Urban Black, Hispanic, and White Young Adults." *The Review of Black Political Economy* 29(1):9–23.

McCall, Leslie. 2005. "The Complexity of Intersectionality." *Signs* 30(3): 1771–1800.

McDermott, Monica. 2006. *Working-Class White: The Making and Unmaking of Race Relations.* Berkeley: University of California Press.

McGhee, Heather. 2021. *The Sum of Us: What Racism Costs Everyone and How We Can Prosper Together*. New York: One World.

McKernan, Signe-Mary, Caroline Ratcliffe, Eugene Steuerle, and Sisi Zhang. 2014. "Disparities in Wealth Accumulation and Loss from the Great Recession and Beyond." *The American Economic Review* 104(5):240–4.

McLaughlin, Katie A., Jennifer Greif Green, Margarita Alegría, et al. 2012: "Food Insecurity and Mental Disorders in a National Sample of U.S. Adolescents." *Journal of the American Academy of Child & Adolescent Psychiatry* 51(12):1293–1303.

McLeod, Jay. 1995. *Ain't No Makin' It: Aspirations and Attainment in a Low Income Neighborhood*. Boulder, CO: Westview Press.

McNay, Lois. 2008. "The Trouble with Recognition: Subjectivity, Suffering, and Agency." *Sociological Theory* 26(3):271–96.

McNichol, Liz, and John Springer. 2004. "State Policies to Assist Working Poor Families." Center on Budget and Policy Priorities. www.cbpp.org /12-10-04sfp.htm.

McPherson, Craig. 2019. "You Can't Kill Chairman Fred: Examining the Life and Legacy of a Revolutionary." *Journal of African American Studies* 23:276–98.

Meehan, Mary. 2019 "Unsheltered and Uncounted: Rural America's Hidden Homeless." National Public Radio, July 4. www.npr.org/sec tions/health-shots/2019/07/04/736240349/in-rural-areas-homeless-pe ople-are-harder-to-find-and-to-help.

Méhaut, Philippe, Peter Berg, Damian Grimshaw, and Karen Jaehrling, with Marc van der Meer and Jacob Esklidsen. 2010. "Cleaning and Nursing in Hospitals: Institutional Variety and the Reshaping of Low-Wage Jobs." Pp. 319–66 in *Low-Wage Work in the Wealthy World*, ed. J. Gautie and J. Schmitt. New York: Russell Sage Foundation.

Meyer, Bruce D., and James X. Sullivan. 2017. "Annual Report on U.S. Consumption Poverty: 2016." American Enterprise Institute Report. https://leo.nd.edu/assets/249750/meyer_sullivan_cpr_2016_1_.pdf.

Milanovic, Branko. 2016. *Global Inequality: A New Approach for the Age of Globalization*. Cambridge, MA: Belknap Press.

Mills, C. Wright. [1959]. 2000. *The Sociological Imagination*, reprint. Oxford University Press.

Mills, Charles W. 1999. *The Racial Contract*. Ithaca, NY: Cornell University Press.

Minkler, Meredith, and Nina Wallerstein. 2008. *Community-Based Participatory Research for Health from Process to Outcomes*. San Francisco: Jossey-Bass.

Mirza, M. Usman, Andries Richter, Egbert H. van Nes, and Marten Scheffer. 2019. "Technology Driven Inequality Leads to Poverty and Resource Depletion." *Ecological Economics* 160:215–26.

Mitra, Sophie, Aleksandra Posarac, and Brandon Vick. 2013. "Disability and Poverty in Developing Countries: A Multidimensional Study." *World Development* 41:1–18.

Moffitt. Robert A. 2015. "The Deserving Poor, the Family, and the U.S. Welfare System." *Demography* 52:729–49.

Monnat, Shannon M. 2010. "The Color of Welfare Sanctioning: Exploring the Individual and Contextual Roles of Race on TANF Case Closures and Benefit Reductions." *Sociological Quarterly* 51(4): 678–707.

Monnat, Shannon M., and Raeven Faye Chandler. 2017. "Immigration Trends and Immigrant Poverty in Rural America." In *Rural Poverty in the United States*, ed. J. Sherman, A. Tickamyer, and J. Warlick. New York: Columbia University Press.

Montopoli, Brian. 2010. "S.C. Lt. Gov. Andre Bauer Compares Helping Poor to Feeding Stray Animals." *CBS News*, January 25. www.cbsne ws.com/news/sc-lt-gov-andre-bauer-compares-helping-poor-to-feeding -stray-animals.

Morris, Aldon D. 2015. *The Scholar Denied: W. E. B. Du Bois and the Birth of Modern Sociology*. Oakland: University of California Press.

Morris, Edward W. 2012. *Learning the Hard Way: Masculinity, Place, and the Gender Gap in Education*. New Brunswick, NJ: Rutgers University Press.

Moynihan, Daniel. P. [1965] 1967. *The Negro Family: The Case for National Action*. United States Department of Labor, Office of Policy Planning and Research. Available in *The Moynihan Report and the Politics of Controversy*, ed. L. Rainwater and W. L. Yancey. Cambridge, MA: MIT Press.

Mullainathan, Sendhil, and Eldar Shafir. 2013. *Scarcity: The New Science of Having Less and How It Defines Our Lives*. New York: Picador.

Munck, Ronaldo. 2004. "Globalization, Labor and the 'Polanyi Problem.'" *Labor History* 45(3):251–69.

Murray, Charles. 1984. *Losing Ground: American Social Policy, 1950–1980*. New York: Basic Books.

Myrdal, Gunnar (with the assistance of Richard Sterner and Arnold Rose). 1944. *An American Dilemma: The Negro Problem and Modern Democracy*. New York: Harper.

Napolitano, Laura J., Shelley Pacholok, and Frank F. Furstenberg. 2014. "Educational Aspirations, Expectations, and Realities for Middle-Income Families." *Journal of Family Issues* 35(9):1200–26.

National Alliance to End Homelessness. 2022. "Unsheltered and Rural Homelessness Supplemental NOFO Resource Series." Washington, DC. https://endhomelessness.org/resource/2022-unsheltered-and-rural -homelessness-supplemental-nofo-resource-series.

National Coalition for the Homeless. 2009. "Rural Homelessness." Washington, DC. https://nationalhomeless.org/factsheets/rural.html.

National Research Council. 1993. *Understanding Child Abuse and Neglect*. Washington, DC: National Academy Press.

Nelson, Margaret K. 2006. "Ongoing Challenges in the Understanding of Rural Poverty." *Journal of Poverty* 10(4):89–108.

Newman, Katherine S. 1999. *No Shame in My Game: The Working Poor in the Inner City*. New York: Russell Sage Foundation.

Nickell, Doug, Jana Kliestikova, and Maria Kovacova. 2019. "The Increasing Casualization of the Gig Economy: Insecure Forms of Work, Precarious Employment Relationships, and the Algorithmic Management of Labor." *Psychosociological Issues in Human Resource Management* 7(1):60–5.

Nussbaum, Martha. 2000. *Women and Human Development: The Capabilities Approach*. Cambridge University Press.

Oberman, Michelle, Robert M. Sade, Lois Shepherd, and Robin Fretwell Wilson. 2018. "Motherhood, Abortion, and the Medicalization of Poverty." *Journal of Law, Medicine & Ethics* 46(3):665–71.

Obernesser, Laura, and Elizabeth Seale. n.d. "The Dark Side of Agency: A Life Course Exploration of Agency and Family among White, Rural, and Impoverished South-Central New Yorkers." Unpublished manuscript.

O'Connor, Alice. 2001. *Poverty Knowledge: Social Science, Social Policy, and the Poor in Twentieth-Century U.S. History*. Princeton University Press.

Ogbu, John Uzo. 1978. *Minority Education and Caste: The American System in Cross-Cultural Perspective*. San Diego, CA: Academic Press.

Orshansky, Mollie. 1965. "Counting the Poor: Another Look at the Poverty Profile." *Social Security Bulletin* 28(1):3–29.

Oyserman, Daphna. 2013. "Not Just Any Path: Implications of Identity-based Motivation for Disparities in School Outcomes." *Economics of Education Review* 33:179–90.

Padavic, Irene, and Barbara F. Reskin. 2002. *Women and Men at Work*. Thousand Oaks, CA: Sage Publications.

Page, Joshua, and Joe Soss. 2020. "Who's Looting Whom? Criminal Justice as Revenue Racket." *Footnotes* 48(4):11–12. American Sociological Association. www.asanet.org/news-events/footnotes/jul-aug-2020/featu res/whos-looting-whom-criminal-justice-revenue-racket.

Page, Lucy, and Rohini Pande. 2018. "Ending Global Poverty: Why Money Isn't Enough." *Journal of Economic Perspectives* 32(4):173–200.

Park, Robert, Ernest Burgess, and Roderick Mckenzie. 1925. *The City*. University of Chicago Press.

Partridge, Sarah, Jacques Balayla, Christina A. Holcroft, and Haim A. Abenhaim. 2012. "Inadequate Prenatal Care Utilization and Risks of Infant Mortality and Poor Birth Outcome: A Retrospective Analysis of 28,729,765 U.S. Deliveries over 8 Years." *American Journal of Perinatology* 29(10):787–94.

Patterson, James T. 1981. *America's Struggle against Poverty, 1900–1980*. Cambridge, MA: Harvard University Press.

Patton, Desmond U., and Benjamin J. Roth. 2016. "Good Kids with Ties to 'Deviant' Peers: Network Strategies Used by African American and

Latino Young Men in Violent Neighborhoods." *Children and Youth Services Review* 66:123–30.

Pavetti, LaDonna. 1992. *Learning from the Voices of Mothers: Single Mothers' Perceptions of the Trade-offs between Welfare & Work.* New York: Manpower Demonstration Research Corporation.

Payne, Ruby K. 1995. *A Framework for Understanding Poverty.* Highlands, TX: AHA! Process, Inc.

Pendo, Elizabeth. 2016. "Hidden from View: Disability, Segregation, and Work." Pp. 115–29 in *Invisible Labor: Hidden Work in the Contemporary World,* ed. M. Crain, W. Poster, and M. Cherry. Berkeley: University of California Press.

Perna, Laura W. 2005. "The Benefits of Higher Education: Sex, Racial/ Ethnic, and Socioeconomic Group Differences." *Review of Higher Education* 29(1):23–52.

Peterson, Janice. 2020. "Welfare Policy and Precarious Lives: 'Welfare Reform' Revisited." *Journal of Economic Issues* LIV(2):377–83.

Petterson, Steve, John M. Westfall, and Benjamin F. Miller. 2020. "Projected Deaths of Despair during the Coronavirus Recession." Well Being Trust. WellBeingTrust.org, https://wellbeingtrust.org/wp-con tent/uploads/2020/05/WBT_Deaths-of-Despair_COVID-19-FINAL -FINAL.pdf.

Pettinicchio, David, and Michelle Maroto. 2017. "Employment Outcomes among Men and Women with Disabilities: How the Intersection of Gender and Disability Status Shapes Labor Market Inequality." *Research in Social Science and Disability* 10:3–33.

Pew Charitable Trust, The. 2013. "Moving On Up: Why Do Some Americans Leave the Bottom of the Economic Ladder, but Not Others?" www.pew trusts.org/~/media/assets/2013/11/01/movingonuppdf.pdf.

Phillips, Joshua D. 2016. *Homeless: Narratives from the Streets.* Jefferson, NC: McFarland & Company.

Phillips, Susan D., and Patricia O'Brien. 2012. "Learning from the Ground Up: Responding to Children Affected by Parental Incarceration." *Social Work in Public Health* 27:29–44.

Pickering, Kathleen Ann, Mark H. Harvey, Gene F. Summers, and David Mushinski. 2006. *Welfare Reform in Persistent Rural Poverty: Dreams, Disenchantments, and Diversity.* University Park: The Pennsylvania State University Press.

Pilisuk, Marc, and Phyllis Pilisuk, eds. 1971. *Poor Americans: How the White Poor Live.* Chicago, IL: Aldine Publishing Company.

Pistor, Katharina. 2019. *The Code of Capital: How the Law Creates Inequality and Wealth.* Princeton University Press.

Polikoff, Nancy D. 2016. "Marriage as Blindspot: What Children with LGBT Parents Need Now." Pp. 127–56 in *After Marriage Equality: The Future of LGBT Rights,* ed. C. A. Ball. New York University Press.

Porpora, Douglas V. 2015. *Reconstructing Sociology: The Critical Realist Approach*. Cambridge University Press.

Porpora, Douglas V. 2016. "The Meaning of Culture and the Culture of Empiricism in American Sociology." *The American Sociologist* 47:430–41.

Preble, Edward, and John J. Casey. 1969. "Taking Care of Business: The Heroin Addict's Life on the Street." Pp. 190–204 in *The American Drug Scene: An Anthology*, ed. J. Inciardi and K. McElrath. New York: Oxford University Press.

President's National Advisory Committee on Rural Poverty. 1967. *The People Left Behind*. Washington, DC: US Government Printing Office. https://archive.org/details/ERIC_ED016543/page/n9/mode/2up.

Pugh, Allison J. 2015. *The Tumbleweed Society: Working and Caring in an Age of Insecurity*. New York: Oxford University Press.

Purnell, Derecka. 2020. "They Said I Could Break out of the Curse of Poverty: Coronavirus Proves Them Wrong." *Guardian*, April 29. www.theguardian.com/commentisfree/2020/apr/29/curse-poverty-coronavirus?CMP=GTUS_email.

Quadagno, Jill. 1995. *The Color of Welfare: How Racism Undermined the War on Poverty*. New York: Oxford University Press.

Quijada Cerecer, David Alberto, Caitlin Cahill, and Matt Bradley. 2013. "Toward a Critical Youth Policy Praxis: Critical Youth Studies and Participatory Action Research." *Theory into Practice* 52(3):216–23.

Quinn, Eithne. 2016. "Occupy Wall Street, Racial Neoliberalism, and New York's Hip-Hop Moguls." *American Quarterly* 68(1):75–99.

Radey, Melissa, and Lenore M. McWey. 2021. "Safety Nets, Maternal Mental Health, and Child Mental Health Outcomes among Mothers Living in Poverty." *Journal of Child and Family Studies* 30:687–98.

Rainwater, Lee. 1970. *Behind Ghetto Walls: Black Families in a Federal Slum*. Chicago, IL: Aldine Publishing Company.

Rank, Mark R. 1994. "A View from the Inside Out: Recipients' Perceptions of Welfare." *Journal of Sociology and Social Welfare* 21(2):27–47.

Rank, Mark R. 2004. *One Nation, Underprivileged: Why American Poverty Affects Us All*. Oxford University Press. Electronic version obtained through ProQuest Ebook Central.

Rank, Mark R. 2011. "Rethinking American Poverty." *Contexts* 10:16–21.

Rank, Mark R., Lawrence Eppard, and Heather Bullock. 2021. *Poorly Understood: What America Gets Wrong about Poverty*. New York: Oxford University Press.

Rank, Mark R., and Thomas A. Hirschl. 1999. "The Likelihood of Poverty across the American Adult Life Span." *Social Work* 44(3):201–16.

Rank, Mark R., Thomas A. Hirschl, and Lidia Adriana Braunstein. 2015. "The Likelihood of Experiencing Relative Poverty over the Life Course." *PloS One* 10(7).

Rao, Vijayendra, and Paromita Sanyal. 2010. "Dignity through Discourse: Poverty and the Culture of Deliberation in Indian Village

Democracies." *Annals of the American Academy of Political and Social Science* 629:146–72.

Ratcliffe, Caroline, and Emma Kalish. 2017. "Escaping Poverty: Predictors of Persistently Poor Children's Economic Success." Research Report. US Partnership on Mobility from Poverty. www.urban.org/mobilitypa rtnership.

Raz, Mical. 2013. *What's Wrong with the Poor? Psychiatry, Race, and the War on Poverty*. Chapel Hill: University of North Carolina Press.

Rein, Martin, and Lee Rainwater. 1978. "Patterns of Welfare Use." *The Social Service Review* 52(4):511–34.

Ribar, David C., and Karen Hamrick. 2003. "Dynamics of Poverty and Food Sufficiency." US Department of Agriculture. Food Assistance & Nutrition Research Program No. FANRR-36. www.ers.usda.gov/pub lications/pub-details/?pubid=46766.

Riffkin, Rebecca. 2014. "In U.S., 67% Dissatisfied with Income, Wealth Distribution." *Economy*, January 20. Gallup. www.gallup. com/poll/166904/dissatisfied-income-wealthdistribution.aspx.

Rist, Carl. 2022. "Wealth and Health: Exploring Asset Poverty as a Key Measure of Financial Security." *North Carolina Medical Journal* 83(1):11–16.

Robertson, Raymond, Drusilla Brown, Gaelle Pierre, and Maria Laura Sanchez-Puerta. 2009. *Globalization, Wages, and the Quality of Jobs: Five Country Studies*. The World Bank.

Robinson, Brandon Andrew. 2020. "The Lavender Scare in Homonormative Times: Policing, Hyper-incarceration, and LGBTQ Youth Homelessness." *Gender & Society* 34(2):210–32.

Rooks, Noliwe. 2017. *Cutting School: Privatization, Segregation, and the End of Public Education*. New York: New Press.

Roscigno, Vincent J., Donald Tomaskovic-Devey, and Martha L. Crowley. 2006. "Education and the Inequalities of Place." *Social Forces* 84(4):2121–45.

Rosenbaum, Dottie. 2013. "SNAP Is Effective and Efficient." Washington D.C.: Center of Budget and Policy Priorities. https:// www.cbpp.org/research/snap-is-effective-and-efficient#_ftn4.

Rosenwohl-Mack, Amy, Darin Smith, Meredith Greene, et al. 2022. "Building H.O.U.S.E (Healthy Outcomes Using a Supportive Environment): Exploring the Role of Affordable and Inclusive Housing for LGBTQIA+ Older Adults." *International Journal of Environmental Research and Public Health* 19(3).

Rugh, Jacob S., and Douglas S. Massey. 2010. "Racial Segregation and the American Foreclosure Crisis." *American Sociological Review* 75(5):629–51.

Salamon, Sonya, and Katherine MacTavish. 2017. *Singlewide: Chasing the American Dream in a Rural Trailer Park*. Ithaca, NY: Cornell University Press.

Salazar, Amy M. 2013. "The Value of a College Degree for Foster Care Alumni: Comparisons with General Population Samples." *Social Work* 58(2):139–50.

Sánchez-Jankowski, Martín. 2008. *Cracks in the Pavement: Social Change and Resilience in Poor Neighborhoods*. Berkeley: University of California Press.

Sanyal, Paromita, Vijayendra Rao, and Shruti Majumdar. 2015. "Recasting Culture to Undo Gender: A Sociological Analysis of Jeevika in Rural Bihar, India." World Bank Group: Development Research Group: Poverty and Inequality Team. WPS7411.

Sassen, Saskia. 1998. *Globalization and Its Discontents*. New York: New Press.

Sassen, Saskia. 2002. "Towards a Sociology of Information Technology." *Current Sociology* 50(3):365–88.

Sawyer, Wendy, and Peter Wagner. 2020. "Mass Incarceration: The Whole Pie: 2019." Northhampton, MA: Prison Policy Initiative. https://www.prisonpolicy.org/reports/pie2019.html.

Schaffer, Bradley J. 2014. "Female Military Veterans: Crime and Psychosocial Problems." *Journal of Human Behavior in the Social Environment* 24:996–1003.

Schifter, Laura A., Todd Grindal, Gabriel Schwartz, and Thomas Hehir. 2019. "Students from Low-Income Families and Special Education." Special Report by The Century Foundation. https://tcf.org/content/report/students-low-income-families-special-education.

Schnitzer, Patricia G., and Bernard G. Ewigmen. 2005. "Child Deaths Resulting from Inflicted Injuries: Household Risk Factors and Perpetrator Characteristics." *Pediatrics* 116 (5):e687–e693.

Schram, Sanford F., Joe Soss, Richard C. Fording, and Linda Houser. 2009. "Deciding to Discipline: Race, Choice, and Punishment at the Frontlines of Welfare Reform." *American Sociological Review* 74(3):398–422.

Scourfield, Jonathan. 2014. "Improving Work with Fathers to Prevent Child Maltreatment." *Child Abuse & Neglect* 38(6):974–81.

Seale, Elizabeth. 2013. "Coping Strategies of Rural and Urban Welfare Agencies and the Regulation of the Poor." *New Political Economy* 18(2):141–70.

Seale, Elizabeth. 2017. "The Relational Experience of Poverty: Challenges in Family Planning and Health Autonomy among the Rural Poor." *Poverty & Public Policy* 9(3):331–54.

Seale, Elizabeth. 2020. "Strategies for Post-Culture-of-Poverty Research on Poverty, Meaning, and Behavior." *The American Sociologist* 51(4):402-424.

Sears, Brad, Christy Mallory, Andrew R. Flores, and Kerith J. Conron. 2021. "LGBT People's Experiences of Workplace Discrimination and Harassment." Los Angeles, CA: UCLA School of Law Williams Institute.

Sen, Amartya. 1981."Public Action and the Quality of Life in Developing Countries." *Oxford Bulletin of Economics and Statistics* 43(4):287–319.

Sen, Amartya. 1999. *Development as Freedom*. New York: Anchor Books.

Shaefer, H. Luke, and Italo A. Gutierrez. 2013. "The Supplemental Nutrition Assistance Program and Material Hardships among Low-Income Households with Children." *Social Service Review* 87(4):753–79.

Shamrova, Daria P., and Cristy E. Cummings. 2017. "Participatory Action Research (PAR) with Children and Youth: An Integrative Review of Methodology and PAR Outcomes for Participants, Organizations, and Communities." *Children and Youth Services Review* 81:400–12.

Shapiro, Eliza. 2020. "These Families Feel Forgotten as N.Y.C. Pushes to Open Schools." *The New York Times*, September 14.

Sharam, Andrea, and Kath Hulse. 2014. "Understanding the Nexus between Poverty and Homelessness: Relational Poverty Analysis of Families Experiencing Homelessness in Australia." *Housing, Theory & Society* 31(3):294–309.

Sharkey, Patrick, and Jacob W. Faber. 2014. "Where, When, Why, and for Whom Do Residential Contexts Matter? Moving Away from the Dichotomous Understanding of Neighborhood Effects." *Annual Review of Sociology* 40:559–79.

Shaw, Clifford R., and Henry D. McKay. 1969. *Juvenile Delinquency and Urban Areas: A Study of Rates of Delinquency in Relation to Differential Characteristics of Local Communities in American Cities*. University of Chicago Press.

Sheely, Amanda. 2012. "Devolution and Welfare Reform: Re-evaluating 'Success.'" *Social Work* 57(4):32131.

Sherman, Jennifer. 2006. "Coping with Rural Poverty: Economic Survival and Moral Capital in Rural America." *Social Forces* 85(2):891–913.

Sherwin, Susan B. 1998. "A Relational Approach to Autonomy in Health Care." Pp. 19–47 in *The Politics of Women's Health: Exploring Agency and Autonomy*. Philadelphia: Temple University Press.

Shrider, Emily A., Melissa Kollar, Frances Chen, and Jessica Semega. 2021. "Income and Poverty in the U.S.: 2020." Current Population Reports P60-273. US Census Bureau.

Simi, Pete, Bryan F. Bubolz, and Ann Hardman. 2013. "Military Experience, Identity Discrepancies, and Far Right Terrorism: An Exploratory Analysis." *Studies in Conflict and Terrorism* 36(8):654–71.

Slack, Kristen Shook, Lawrence M. Berger, Kimberly DuMont, et al. 2011. "Risk and Protective Factors for Child Neglect during Early Childhood: A Cross-study Comparison." *Children & Youth Services Review* 33:1354–63.

Slack, Tim. 2010. "Working Poverty across the Metro–Nonmetro Divide: A Quarter Century in Perspective, 1979–2003." *Rural Sociology* 75(3):363–87.

Slack, Tim, Brian C. Thiede, and Leif Jensen. 2020. "Race, Residence, and Underemployment: Fifty Years in Comparative Perspective, 1968–2017." *Rural Sociology* 85(2):275–315.

Slotnik, Daniel E. 2020. "What Happened When Homeless Men Moved into a Liberal Neighborhood." *The New York Times*, Aug. 18. www.nyt

imes.com/2020/08/18/nyregion/uws-homeless-hotels-nyc.html?campa
ign_id=2&emc=edit_th_20200819&instance_id=21393&nl=todayshe
adlines&regi_id=64924513&segment_id=36478&user_id=aa15fe8237
e0e69db3d053505e9c7648.

Small, Mario Luis. 2002. "Culture, Cohorts, and Social Organization
Theory: Understanding Local Participation in a Latino Housing
Project." *American Journal of Sociology* 108(1):1–54.

Smith, R. Drew. 2001. "Churches and the Urban Poor: Interaction and
Social Distance." *Sociology of Religion* 62(3):301–13.

Smith, Brenda D., Emma Sophia Kay, and Tracy D. Pressley. 2018. "Child
Maltreatment in Rural Southern Counties: Another Perspective on
Race, Poverty and Child Welfare." *Child Abuse & Neglect* 80:52–61.

Smith, Brenda D., Qingyi Li, Kun Wang, and Angela M. Smith. 2021. "A
National Study of Child Maltreatment Reporting at the County Level:
Interactions among Race/Ethnicity, Rurality and Poverty." *Children and
Youth Services Review* 122(105925).

Smith, Laura, and LeLaina Romero. 2010. "Psychological Interventions
in the Context of Poverty: Participatory Action Research as Practice."
American Journal of Orthopsychiatry 80(1):12–25.

Snapp, Shannon D., Jennifer M. Hoenig, Amanda Fields, and Stephen T.
Russell. 2015. "Messy, Butch, and Queer: LGBTQ Youth and the
School-to-Prison Pipeline." *Journal of Adolescent Research* 30(1):57–82.

Snow, David A., Leon Anderson, and Paul Koegel. 1994. "Distorting
Tendencies in Research on the Homeless." *The American Behavioral
Scientist* 37(4):461–75.

Solli, Hans Magnus, and António Barbosa da Silva. 2018. "Objectivity
Applied to Embodied Subjects in Health Care and Social Security
Medicine: Definition of a Comprehensive Concept of Cognitive
Objectivity and Criteria for Its Application." *BMC Medical Ethics* 19(1).

Soss, Joe, Sanford F. Schram, Thomas P. Vartanian, and Erin O'Brien.
2001. "Setting the Terms of Relief: Explaining State Policy Choices
in the Devolution Revolution." *American Journal of Political Science*
45(2):378–95.

Stacciarini, Jeanne-Marie R., Rebekah Smith, Cynthia Wilson Garvan,
Brenda Wiens, and Linda B. Cottler. 2015. "Rural Latinos' Mental
Wellbeing: A Mixed-Methods Pilot Study of Family, Environment and
Social Isolation Factors." *Community Mental Health Journal* 51:404–15.

Stack, Carol. 1974. *All Our Kin: Strategies for Survival in a Black Community.*
New York: Harper & Row.

Stiffman, Michael N., Patricia G. Schnitzer, Patricia Adam, Robin L. Kruse,
and Bernard G. Ewigmen. 2002. "Household Composition and Risk of
Fatal Child Maltreatment." *Pediatrics* 109(4):615–21.

Stith, Sandra M., Ting Liu, L. Christopher Davies, et al. 2009. "Risk Factors
in Child Maltreatment: A Meta-Analytic Review of the Literature."
Aggression and Violent Behavior 14:13–29.

Stoll, Steven. 2017. *Ramp Hollow: The Ordeal of Appalachia*. New York: Hill and Wang.

Stullich, Stephanie, Ivy Morgan, and Oliver Schak. 2016. "State and Local Expenditures on Corrections and Education." A brief from the US Department of Education, Policy and Program Studies Service, July.

Sullivan, Teresa A., Elizabeth Warren, and Jay Lawrence Westbrook. 2000. *The Fragile Middle Class: Americans in Debt*. New Haven, CT: Yale University Press.

Surratt, Hilary L., James A. Inciardi, Steven P. Kurtz, and Marion C. Kiley. 2004. "Sex Work and Drug Use in a Subculture of Violence." *Crime and Delinquency* 50(1):43–59.

Swartz, David. 1997. *Culture & Power: The Sociology of Pierre Bourdieu*. University of Chicago Press.

Sweeney, Kathryn A. 2012. "The Culture of Poverty and Adoption: Adoptive Parent Views of Birth Families." *Michigan Family Review* 16(1):22–37.

Sykes, Bryan L., and Becky Pettit. 2014. "Mass Incarceration, Family Complexity and the Reproduction of Childhood Disadvantage." *Annals of the American Academy of Political and Social Science* 654:127–49.

Syrek, Steven. 2012. "'Why Am I Talking?' Reflecting on Language and Privilege at Occupy Wall Street." *The Critical Quarterly* 54(2):72–5.

Taylor, Tiffany, and Katrina Bloch, eds. 2018. *Marginalized Mothers, Mothering from the Margins*. Bingley, UK: Emerald Publishing.

Taylor, Tiffany, and Elizabeth Seale. 2013. "Implementing Welfare-to-Work: Program Managers' Identities and Service Delivery in North Carolina." *Sociological Focus* 46:295–313.

Theodore, Nik. 2010. "Urban Underclass: The Wayward Travels of a Chaotic Concept." *Urban Geography* 31(2):169–74.

Thiede, Brian C., and Matthew M. Brooks. 2018. "Child Poverty across Immigrant Generations in the United States, 1993–2016: Evidence using the Official and Supplemental Poverty Measures." *Demographic Research* 39:1065–80.

Thiede, Brian C., Daniel T. Lichter, and Tim Slack. 2018. "Working, but Poor: The Good Life in Rural America?" *Journal of Rural Studies* 59:183–93.

Thompson, Alexandra, and Susannah N. Tapp. 2022. *Criminal Victimization, 2021*. US Department of Justice, Office of Justice Programs, Bureau of Justice Statistics. NCJ 305101.

Thompson, E. P. 1966. *The Making of the English Working Class*. New York: Vintage Books.

Tickamyer, Ann R., and Cynthia M. Duncan. 1990. "Poverty and Opportunity Structure in Rural America." *Annual Review of Sociology* 16:67–86.

Tienda, Marta, and Haya Stier. 1991. "Joblessness and Shiftlessness: Labor Force Activity in Chicago's Inner City." Pp. 135–54 in *The Urban*

Underclass, ed. C. Jencks and P. E. Peterson. Washington, DC: The Brookings Institute.

Tomaskovic-Devey, Donald, and Dustin Avent-Holt. 2019. *Relational Inequalities: An Organizational Approach*. New York: Oxford University Press.

Townsend, Peter. 1962. "The Meaning of Poverty." *British Journal of Sociology* 13(3).

Townsend, Peter. 1979. *Poverty in the United Kingdom: A Survey of Household Resources and Standards of Living*. Berkeley: University of California Press.

Trachtenberg, Alan. 1982. *The Incorporation of America: Culture and Society in the Gilded Age*. New York: Hill and Wang.

United Nations. 1995. "Eradication of Poverty." Ch. 2 in *Programme of Action of the World Summit for Social Development*. World Summit for Social Development, Copenhagen. www.un.org/esa/socdev/wssd/text -version/agreements/poach2.htm.

United Nations. 2019. "Disability and Development Report: Realizing the Sustainable Development Goals by, for and with Persons with Disabilities, 2018." New York: United Nations Department of Economic Affairs. www.un.org/development/desa/disabilities/wp-conte nt/uploads/sites/15/2019/07/disability-report-chapter2.pdf.

United Nations. 2022. "Global Multidimensional Poverty Index (MPI)." United Nations Development Programme. https://hdr.undp.org/con tent/2022-global-multidimensional-poverty-index-mpi#/indicies/MPI.

US Bureau of Labor Statistics. 2009. "Women and Men in Management, Professional, and Related Occupations, 2008." *The Economic Daily*, August 7. www.bls.gov/opub/ted/2009/ted_20090807.htm.

US Census Bureau. 2020a. "Armed Forces Day: May 21, 2020." Release Number CB22SFS.71. www.census.gov/newsroom/stories/armed-for ces-day.html.

US Census Bureau. 2020b. "Wealth, Asset Ownership, & Debt of Households Detailed Tables: 2019." Survey of Income and Program Participation, Survey Year 2020. Public Use Data. www.census.gov/da ta/tables/2019/demo/wealth/wealth-asset-ownership.html.

US Census Bureau. 2020c. "People with Income below Specified Ratios of Their Poverty Thresholds by Selected Characteristics: 2019." Current Population Survey, 2020 Annual Social and Economic Supplement (CPS ASEC). Public Use Data. www.census.gov.

US Census Bureau. 2020d. Table B-1: "People in Poverty by Selected Characteristics: 2018 and 2019." Current Population Survey, 2019 and 2020 Annual Social and Economic Supplements.

US Census Bureau. 2022. "SIPP Introduction and History." www.census .gov/programs-surveys/sipp/about/sipp-introduction-history.html.

US Department of Agriculture. 2022a. "USDA Food Plans: Cost of Food Reports (Monthly Reports)." Washington, DC: USDA Food and

Nutrition Service. www.fns.usda.gov/cnpp/usda-food-plans-cost-food
-reports-monthly-reports.

US Department of Agriculture. 2022b. "SNAP Data Tables." Washington,
DC: USDA Food and Nutrition Service. www.fns.usda.gov/pd/suppl
emental-nutrition-assistance-program-snap.

US Department of Agriculture. 2022c. "Rural Poverty & Well-Being."
Washington, DC: USDA Economic Research Service. www.ers.usda
.gov/topics/rural-economy-population/rural-poverty-well-being.

US Department of Housing and Urban Development (HUD). 2022. "The
2021 Annual Homeless Assessment Report (AHAR) to Congress."
www.huduser.gov/portal/datasets/ahar/2021-ahar-part-1-pit-estimates
-of-homelessness-in-the-us.html.

US Department of Labor. 2022. "Facts over Time: Women in the Labor
Force." Washington, DC: Women's Bureau, US Department of Labor.
www.dol.gov/agencies/wb/data/facts-over-time#earningsratio.

Vaisey, Stephen. 2010. "What People Want: Rethinking Poverty, Culture,
and Educational Attainment." *ANNALS of the American Academy of
Political and Social Science* 629:75–101.

Valentine, Charles A. 1968. *Culture and Poverty: Critique and Counter-
Proposals.* University of Chicago Press.

Vallanti, Giovanna. 2018. "International Capital Mobility and Unemployment Dynamics: Empirical Evidence from OECD Countries." *World
Economy* 41(11):3130–71.

Vance, J. D. 2016. *Hillbilly Elegy: A Memoir of a Family and Culture in Crisis.*
New York: Harper.

Vu, Catherine M., and Michael J. Austin. 2007. "The Explosive Nature of
the Culture of Poverty: A Teaching Case Based on an Agency-Based
Training Program." *Journal of Human Behavior in the Social Environment*
16(1/2):167–82.

Wacquant, Loic J. D. 1997. "Three Pernicious Premises in the Study of the
American Ghetto." *Journal of Urban and Regional Research* 21(2):341–55.

Wacquant, Loïc J. D. 2008. *Urban Outcasts: A Comparative Sociology of
Advanced Marginality.* Cambridge: Polity.

Wald, Michael S. 2014. "Beyond Maltreatment: Developing Support for
Children in Multiproblem Families." Pp. 251–80 in *Handbook of Child
Maltreatment,* ed. J. E. Korbin and R. D. Krugman. New York: Springer.

Waller, Maureen R. 2010. "Viewing Low-Income Fathers' Ties to Families
through a Cultural Lens: Insights for Research and Policy." *ANNALS
of the American Academy of Political and Social Science* 629(1):102–24.

Walsh, Bridget A., Tricia A. Woodliff, Julie Lucero, et al. 2021. "Historically
Underrepresented Graduate Students' Experiences during the COVID-
19 Pandemic." *Family Relations* 70(4):955–72.

Wax, Murray L. 1971. "Poverty and Interdependency." Pp. 338–44 in *The
Culture of Poverty: A Critique,* ed. E. B. Leacock. New York: Simon and
Schuster.

Weber, Bruce, Leif Jensen, Kathleen Miller, Jane Mosley, and Monica Fisher. 2005. "A Critical Review of Rural Poverty Literature: Is There Truly a Rural Effect?" Rural Poverty Research Center Discussion Paper no. 1309-05, University of Iowa.

Weisbrod, Burton A., and Lee W. Hansen. 1968. "An Income – Net Worth Approach to Measuring Economic Welfare." *American Economic Review* 58(5):1315–29.

Wesling, Meg. 2008. "Why Queer Diaspora?" *Feminist Review* 90(1):30–47.

White, Deborah Gray. 1999. *Too Heavy a Load: Black Women in Defense of Themselves, 1896–1994*. New York: W.W. Norton & Co.

White, Roger, ed. 2017. *Measuring Multidimensional Poverty and Deprivation: Global Perspectives on Wealth and Distribution*. Cham: Palgrave Macmillan. https://doi-org.oneonta.idm.oclc.org/10.1007/978-3-319 -58368-6_8.

Whiteside, Jasmine L. 2021. "Becoming Academically Eligible: University Enrollment among First-Generation, Rural College Goers." *Rural Sociology* 86(2):204–28.

Whyte, William Foote. 1943. *Street Corner Society: The Social Structure of an Italian Slum*. Chicago University Press.

Wilkinson, Richard G., and Kate E. Pickett. 2009. "Income Inequality and Social Dysfunction." *Annual Review of Sociology* 35(1):493–511.

Williams, Natasha D., and Elaine A. Anderson. 2020. "A Critique of Repealing the Affordable Care Act: Implications for Queer People of Color." *Analyses of Social Issues and Public Policy* 20(1):195–210.

Williams, Terry, and William Kornblum. 1994. *The Uptown Kids: Hope and Struggle in the Projects*. New York: G. P. Putnam's Sons.

Williamson, Elizabeth. 2022. "Who Will Help Care for Texas' Post-Roe Babies?" *New York Times*, July 1. www.nytimes.com/2022/07/01/us/poli tics/texas-abortion-roe-wade.html?searchResultPosition=1.

Willis, Paul. [1977] 1981. *Learning to Labor: How Working Class Kids Get Working Class Jobs*. New York: Columbia University Press.

Wilson, William Julius. 1987. *The Truly Disadvantaged: The Inner City, the Underclass, and Urban Poverty*. University of Chicago Press.

Wilson, William Julius. 1996. *When Work Disappears*. New York: Random House, Inc.

Wirth, Louis. 1928. *The Ghetto*. University of Chicago Press.

Wolff, Jonathan, and Avner De-Shalit. 2007. *Disadvantage*. New York: Oxford University Press.

World Bank. 2022. "Poverty Headcount Ratio at $1.90 a day (2011 PPP) (% of population)." https://data.worldbank.org/indicator/SI.POV.DDAY.

World Population Review. 2022. "Poverty Rate by Country 2022." https:// worldpopulationreview.com/country-rankings/poverty-rate-by-country.

Zerr, Argero A., Rae R. Newton, Alan J. Litrownik, Kristen M. McCabe, and May Yeh. 2019. "Household Composition and Maltreatment

Allegations in the US: Deconstructing the At-Risk Single Mother Family." *Child Abuse & Neglect* 97:104–23.

Zimmer, Ron W., and Eugenia F. Toma. 2000. "Peer Effects in Private and Public Schools across Counties." *Journal of Policy Analysis and Management* 19(1):75–92.

Zuberi, Dan. 2006. *Differences that Matter: Social Policy and the Working Poor in the United States and Canada.* Ithaca, NY: Cornell University Press.

Zylan, Yvonne, and Sarah A. Soule. 2000. "Ending Welfare as We Know It (Again): Welfare State Retrenchment, 1989–1995." *Social Forces* 79(2):623–52.

Index

ableism 8, 39
abortion 75, 76, 77, 88–9
Abrego, L. J. 160, 176
absolute poverty
  defining and measuring 22, 23
  see also deep poverty
ACE (adverse childhood
  experiences) 171
Addams, J. 96, 97
addiction 5, 14, 171
Addo, F. R. 41
AFDC (Aid to Families with
  Dependent Children) 64–5,
  105–6, 107, 108, 136
African Americans *see* Black
  Americans
AFS (Alternative Financial
  Services) 130
age
  and capability poverty 30
  and risk of poverty 4
  and social relations 16
ageism 8
agency 3, 14, 15, 19, 169, 172, 180
  and the culture of poverty 121–3
  improving agency of the poor
    119–20
  and structure 143–4
Albelda, R. 69
Amazon 134, 135

American Rescue Plan legislation
  34
Appalachia 49, 113, 116, 121–3,
  124
Appell, A. R. 78
Archer, M. S. 143, 144, 145
art, US 120
asset poverty 58
  defining and measuring 25–6,
    33, 35
autonomy 168–72, 180
Avent-Holt, D. 11

Bacon's Rebellion (1676, Virginia)
  43
Bailey, B. A. 147
Bane, M. J. 36, 106–7
Banfield, E. C. 40
Bauer, Andre 120
behavioral change
  and the culture of poverty thesis
    119–20
Belsky, J. 186
Bernstein, S. 39
Berube, A. 51
Bettie, J. 153
Bhandari, S. 83, 147
Biden, Joe 34
birth control 74–5, 77, 88, 91
Black, T. 72, 91, 185

Black Americans 40–2, 43
  Black women and the War on
    Poverty 106
  and capability poverty 30
  and child maltreatment 81
  and chronic poverty 53
  and the culture of poverty thesis
    95, 97–9, 101, 102, 109,
    113, 117, 118
  education 47
  families and parenting 85
  housing 142
  middle-class 41, 50, 116, 117
  and military service 167
  and mobility 37, 38
  and oppositional culture theory
    154
  and religion 116
  risk of poverty 4–5
  in rural areas 48, 50
  single mother households 41, 62,
    64–5, 68
  teen motherhood 72, 73
  and the War on Poverty 104
  and work ethics 162
  see also race and ethnicity; racism
Black Panther Party 43
Blame Fallacy 164
Blank, R. 38
Blau, J. 136
Bloch, K. 140
bonding social capital 115–16
Booth, C. 96
Bourdieu, Pierre 10, 11, 114–15,
  117
Boutros, V. 20, 84, 165
bridging social capital 115–16
Browne-Yung, K., et al. 115–16
Burgess, E. 96
Burkitt, Ian 145
Burns, K. 32
Burton, L. M. 12

capability poverty
  defining and measuring 28–9, 30

capitalism 130, 187–8
Carr, M. 69
Catte, E. 123
CEA (Council of Economic
  Advisers) 106
Chandler, R. F. 47, 50
Chen, E. 166
Chetty, R. 149
Chicago School 96, 98, 99
child development
  and cultural deprivation theory
    100
child maltreatment 60, 77–85, 89,
  171, 181, 186
  abuse 18, 64, 78, 81
  cultural factors and violence
    84–5
  neglect 77, 79, 81
  relations of support 78, 81–3
child poverty 1, 4, 54–5
  poverty alleviation programs 32
  in rural places 48
child sexual abuse 185
child tax credits 34
childbirth
  health risks of early childbirth
    73–4
childcare 12, 29, 82, 102, 128,
  136, 157, 161, 181
children
  foster care 64, 78, 89
  and limited mobility 37
  long-term effects of poverty on
    170–1
  non-citizen 160
  in single mother households
    64–5
Choi, J.-K. 171
chronic poverty 18, 58, 177
  conditions of 53–5
  and the culture of poverty 111
  defining and measuring 22, 33, 35
  geographical variations in 5
  intergenerational 33
  see also deep poverty

citizenship 5, 16, 47, 159–61
Civil Rights movement 103
Clark, D. 22, 29
class
    and college attendance 153,
        154–5
    and cultural deprivation theory
        100, 101
    and the culture of poverty thesis
        108, 113, 117–18
    international social class groups
        187
    and intersectionality 39
    neighborhood inequality 132
    and single motherhood 61
    and social relations 13, 14
    and structural features of poverty
        127
    working-class Whites 42–3
    see also middle class
Cleaveland, C. L. 159
Clemens, Michael A. 130
climate change 187
Code, L. 183
cohabitation 62, 63
Coleman-Jensen, A. 54
college attendance 151–6, 173,
        176
colonialism 131
community action programs
        104–5, 181
concentrated poverty 101–2, 111,
        112
consumption-based poverty
    defining and measuring 26,
        32–3, 34, 35
contraception 74–5, 77, 88, 91
corporate scandals 134
COVID-19 pandemic 4, 14, 25,
        32, 34, 57, 132, 166
    and child maltreatment 82–3
    and chronic poverty 54
    and the culture of poverty 121
    and education 156
    and race inequality 44

    and social relations 145
    and support services 137
criminal justice system 14
cultural deprivation theory 100–1
cultural identity 5
cultural understandings of poverty
        2, 9, 14–15, 18–19
    contemporary research on
        114–20
    structure and culture 117, 118,
        125, 143, 145–50, 179–80
culture of poverty thesis 7–8, 19,
        92–125, 178
    conceptual issues 111–13
    defining 92
    dependency or blame 120–4
    four characteristics of (Lewis)
        93–4
    historical context of 96–103
    and parental choices 102
    problems with the arguments
        107–13
    and social disorganization 94,
        96–100, 102, 109
    and teen motherhood 72–3, 109,
        110
    and US public policy 103–7

Darity, W. A. 41
Daugherty, R. A. 147
De-Shalit, A. 147, 148–9
deaths
    alcohol, drugs, or suicide 57
debtors
    punishment of 141–2
deep poverty 18, 19, 58, 131, 164,
        177, 181
    defining and measuring 22–3,
        35, 36
    and social services 139
    and welfare reforms 106
    see also chronic poverty
democracies 29
Denmark 53
Denton, N. A. 50

dependency culture 120–4
"deserving" and "undeserving"
    poor 3, 113, 139
Desmond, M. 17
deviance
    and the culture of poverty 96,
        99–100
Dickey, M. S. 76
dignity, relations of 8, 17–18, 19,
    58, 172–3, 175–88
disability 5, 8, 50, 58, 141
    and chronic poverty 53–4
    and definitions of poverty 21
    and the Individual Blame Fallacy
        164
    social relations of 8, 12, 16
    and social services 138, 141
    VA (Veterans' Affairs) disability
        compensation 167
distrust
    and mothers in poverty 169–70
diversity 36, 38–52
    gender and sexuality 44–6
    immigration 46–7
    place 47–52
divorce 66
Dodson, L. 124
domestic violence 16, 165
Drucker, E. 100
drug convictions 141
drug use 49, 141, 142
DSS (Department of Social
    Services) 139–40
Du Bois, W. E. B. 96, 97–8, 102
Duncan, C. 114, 116–17

Earned Income Tax Credit 70
economic recession
    and poverty rates 34
Edin, K. 16, 18, 19, 34, 35, 63–4,
    65–6, 67–8, 71, 74–5, 86–7,
    89–90, 108, 157–9, 162,
    164, 165, 170, 172
education 1, 40
    college attendance 151–6, 173

and the culture of poverty thesis
    111, 117–18
effects of chronic poverty 54–5
families and parenting 61, 90, 91
and habitus 115
immigrants to the US 46–7
importance of relationships for
    success 153–4
and institutional racism 130
and labor market structure
    134–5
macro view of 151–2
and the middle class 55
policy and programs 180, 181
school disengagement 154–6
and social mobility 37–8
structural changes in 53
EITC (Earned Income Tax Credit)
    138, 139
Ellwood, D. T. 106–7
Ely, D. 22, 25
emotional labor 45
empirical issues
    and the culture of poverty thesis
        108–11
employers
    families and parenting 90, 91
    relations with employees 149–50
employment see labor market; work
EOA (Economic Opportunity Act)
    104
Erdmans, M. P. 14, 72, 91, 185
ethnicity see race and ethnicity
evictions 17, 54
extreme poverty see deep poverty

Faber, J. W. 130
family and parenting 5, 18, 60–91
    child maltreatment 60, 77–85,
        89, 171
    childbearing decisions 61
    family separation 89
    family size 3
    military service and familial
        relations 167

Faber, J. W. (*cont.*)
   mothers in poverty and parent–
      child relations 170–1
   obligations and expectations
      85–7
   players and power 87–91
   relations with the state 60
   reproductive rights 74–5, 88–9
   single mother households 18, 60,
      61–71, 85–7
   support systems 60–1
   vulnerability and dignity 176
   young motherhood 60, 71–7, 85,
      86, 87, 91
   see also fathers; mothers
famines 29
Farkas, G. 46–7
fathers 60, 86
   and child maltreatment 83–4
   and single mother households
      60, 65, 66–8, 70–1, 87
Feldman, D. L. 155
feminism 10
finance capital 188
financial services 130, 134
Fisher, G. M. 23, 24
Fizane, F. 26–7
Foley, M. W. 116
food costs
   and the Official Poverty Measure
      (US) 24
food insecurity 54, 137–8
   defining and measuring 27,
      32
food stamps *see* SNAP
      (Supplemental Nutritional
      Assistance Program)
Foster, J. E. 28
Fox, L. E. 32
Fraser, N. 188
Frazier, E. F. 98–9, 103
FREGs (Far-Right Extremist
      Groups) 167–8
Friedrichs, C. 112
Fuchs, V. 28

fuel poverty
   defining 26–7
   measuring 32
Fuhse, J. A. 149
Furstenberg, F. F. 73

Gans, H. J. 101–2, 112
Garcia, A. 14
gender 5, 19, 39
   changing gender norms 119–20
   and disability 53–4
   and the Individual Blame Fallacy
      164
   pay gap 69–70
   and sexuality 44–6
   social relations of 8, 12, 16
   see also men; women
genocide 40
geographical variations (US) 5
Giddens, A. 143–4
Gilder, G. 95
Glenn, Evelyn Nakano 148
global capitalism 187–8
global poverty 187–8
global shadow economy 134
globalization 130
Goffman, Erving 10–11
Goldblum, J. S. 69, 142, 178
Goodman, L. A. 182
Granovetter, M. 38
Great Recession (from 2007) 41, 56
Green, M. 22, 25, 28, 36, 186
guest workers 159–60
Gunzenhauser, M.G. 58, 183
Gutierrez, I. A. 54

Ha, Y. 81–2
habitus 115, 117
Hacker, J. S. 34, 56
Hall, A. R. 167
Hall, M. 46–7
Halpern, R. 100
Hampton, Fred 43
Han, J. 167
Hansen, L. W. 25

Harding, D. 84
harm, acts of 185–6
Harrington, M. 103
Haugen, G. A. 20, 84, 165
HeadStart 104, 105
health outcomes of poverty 1, 53,
    54, 161
    the rural poor 104
healthcare 90, 181
heterosexism 8
Hillbilly Elegy 121–4
Hispanics and Latinos 40, 46–7,
    142, 160
    young mothers 71–2
HIV/AIDS
    women living with 58
home ownership 26, 54
    African Americans 41–2
    mobile homes 33
homelessness 46, 51–2
    child and education 152
    and child maltreatment 80–1
    criminalization of 140–1
    and the culture of poverty 110,
    121
household composition
    and single motherhood 61
household incomes
    and the COVID-19 pandemic 34
housing 17, 112, 117, 165
    criminalizing poverty 142
    evictions 17, 54
    policy and programs 181
    race discrimination in 41, 132
    and social relations 146
    social services 138, 139
HUD (Department of Housing and
    Urban Development) 138
Hulme, D. 22, 25, 28, 29, 36
human agency *see* agency
human rights 187

IDA (Individual Development
    Account) Demonstration Act
    (1998) 25

immigration 46–7, 72, 187
    and the labor market 130, 135,
    159–61
    see also migration
impression management 11
incarceration 46, 49, 141
    parental incarceration and single
    motherhood 62–3
income
    and capability poverty 30
    and deep poverty 22–3
    inequalities 163–4
    low-income work 127–8, 129,
    134–5, 159, 161–2
    measuring poverty by 3–4, 33,
    35–6
    and social capital 115–16
India 119
Individual Blame Fallacy 164
individualism
    and autonomy 169
individuals
    and social relations 2, 16–17, 19,
    145–50
inequality
    and measures of poverty 28
    relations of 8–9
    and social mobility 37
    structural 105, 114–15, 127–31,
    132, 160
    of wealth and income 131,
    163–4
infant mortality 53, 104
informal economy
    in rural areas 49
insecure status 35, 56, 57, 58,
    177
institutional racism 129–30
intergenerational mobility 37,
    164
intergenerational poverty 22, 26,
    33, 131
    and the culture of poverty 108
    in rural areas 50
international trade 131

intersectional approach to poverty
8, 14, 16, 38–52, 58,
177–8
see also class; gender; race and
ethnicity
intimate partners
single mothers and relations with
63–8, 70, 86
violence by 78, 83, 147–8
and vulnerability 172
Isenberg, N. 43

Jacobs, A. W. 161
Jaeggi, R. 188
Jargowsky, P. A. 36
Jarosz, B. 58
Jencks, C. 109
Jenkins, J. 175
Jensen, L. 22, 25
Job Corps 104, 105
Johnson, Lyndon B. 103–4

Kahouli, S. 26–7
Kalleberg, A. 56
Katz, S. M. 140
Kefalas, M. 65–6, 74–5, 172
Kim, H. 85
kin networks
single mother households 63,
64–5
Klein, E. 178
Kneebone, E. 51
Kornblum, W. 116
Kotch, J. B. 82, 186
Kristof, Nicholas 33

labor market 149–50, 177
and education 151
families and parenting 61
and low-income fathers 60, 70–1
and the middle class 56–7
and military veterans 167, 168
rural economies 48–9
and single mother households
68–70

structure 53, 127–31, 134–5,
142, 143
and women 44–5
see also wages
Ladson-Billings, G. 95
Lareau, A. 108, 110–11, 114,
117–18
Lather, P. A. 58
Latinos *see* Hispanics and Latinos
Leacock, E. B. 94–5
Lein, L. 63–4, 71, 86–7, 89–90,
108, 157–9, 165
Lengermann, P. M. 97
Levine, J. A. 67, 86, 118–19, 169
Lewis, O.
and the culture of poverty 92,
93–4, 102, 103, 110, 111
LFOs (Legal Financial Obligations)
141, 142
LGBTQIA+ identities 45–6
life course design 183–5
low-income but not poor 5
low-income countries 187
low-income families
and education 152
low-income work 127–8, 129,
134–5, 159, 161–2
Luker, K. 72

McDermott, M. 42
McGhee, H. 43–4
McKay, H. D. 97, 99
McKenzie, R. 96
McKernan, S.-M. 25, 33
MacTavish, K. 33
McWey, L. M. 170
marriage
expectations of 86
and single motherhood 63, 66–7
Marwell, N. P. 132–3
Marxism 10
Massey, D. S. 50
maternal deprivation 101
Mather, M. 58
Mayer, S. E. 109

Mead, George Herbert 10
Medicaid 32, 69, 88, 104, 138,
    139, 157, 162
Medicare 104
men
    intimate partner relations and
        single mothers 63–8
    and social policy 139
    wealth and the labor market 45
    young men/boys and oppositional
        culture theory 154–5
    see also fathers
mental health 79, 100, 165, 171,
    173, 181
    and military veterans 168
mental illness 175
Meyer, B. D. 26, 32–3
middle class 58, 178
    Black Americans 41, 50, 116,
        117
    and the culture of poverty 7, 96,
        107, 109, 117, 118, 122
    overlap and similarities with the
        poor 53, 55–7
    and personal relations 185
    in rural places 49
    single motherhood 61
    women and childbearing choices
        76–7
Middle Eastern immigrants 46
middle-income countries 187
migration
    and citizenship 159–61
    immigration to the US 46–7
    rural–urban 48
    south-to-north 104, 116
    undocumented migrants 160
military service 157, 166–8, 176
Mills, C. Wright 179
Mills, Charles 129
mindset, poverty characterized as
    7–8
mobility 36–8
Moffitt, R. A. 139
Monnat, S. M. 47, 50

Morrissey, S. L. 132–3
mothers
    young motherhood 60, 71–7, 85,
        87, 91, 109, 110, 185
    see also single mother households
Moynihan, D. P. 40, 104
Mullainathan, S. 79
Murray, C. 73, 95
Muslims 46
Myrdal, G. 98, 99, 103

National Low Income Housing
    Coalition 138
nationalism 8
Native Americans 43, 44, 48, 50,
    113
neighborhood inequality 132–3
Nelson, M. K. 49, 50
Nelson, T. J. 67–8
network theory 38
Newman, K. S. 162, 163
Niebrugge-Brantley, J. 97
nonprofit agencies 139
North Carolina case study 6
Nussbaum, M. 29

Oberman, Michelle 89
Obernesser, L. 169
Occupy Wall Street movement 43
O'Connor, A. 102, 104–5
offshore jurisdictions 134
opioid crisis 57
OPM (Official Poverty Measure)
    23–4, 29, 30–1, 32, 35, 38
opportunity and personal autonomy
    151–72
    finding (better) employment
        156–68
    general autonomy 168–72
    going to college 151–6
    military service 157, 166–8
oppositional culture theory 154–5
Orshansky, M. 24
The Other America (Harrington)
    103

Padavic, I. 161
PAR (Participatory Action
    Research) 183–4
parent–child relations 170–1
Park, R. 96
Participatory Action Research
    (PAR) 183–4
Patterson, J. T. 95, 104, 105–6
Payne, R. 93
people of color *see* Black Americans
The People Left Behind (National
    Advisory Commission on
    Rural Poverty) 104
persistence of poverty 19
Peterson, J. 107
Phillips, Joshua 80–1
Pickering, K. A. 140
Pickett, K. E. 37
political economy
    and the creation of poverty
        127–31
Porpora, D. V. 143, 144
poverty, defining and measuring
    3–4, 20–36
    absolute definitions of 21, 23–7
    relative definitions of 21, 27–8
    US official measures of 20, 30–2
power relations 8, 12–13, 16–17,
    39, 181
    and global justice 187
precarity
    and child maltreatment 79–80
    and relations of vulnerability
        161
pregnancy
    and child maltreatment 83
    rural women and intimate partner
        violence 147–8
    single mothers 65–6
    teen mothers 71–7
prisons *see* incarceration
PTSD (post-traumatic stress
    disorder) 84
Pugh, A. J. 56
Purnell, D. 166

qualitative research 110–11, 114,
    186
quantitative research 186

race and ethnicity 19, 40–4
    and AFS (Alternative Financial
        Services) 130
    child maltreatment 81
    and the culture of poverty 98,
        100, 101, 108
    household incomes 34
    and the Individual Blame Fallacy
        164
    and intersectionality 39
    and limited mobility 37–8
    and military service 167
    neighborhood inequality 132
    racial minorities in rural places
        48, 50
    and risk of poverty 4–5
    and single motherhood 61, 65
    social relations of 8, 12, 16
    and the War on Poverty 104,
        105
    wealth gaps 40–2
    wealth and the labor market 45
    see also Black Americans;
        Hispanics and Latinos;
        Native Americans; White
        Americans
racism 8, 16, 39, 43–4
    and the culture of poverty 99,
        118
    institutional racism 129–30
Radey, M. 170–1
The Rainbow Coalition 43
Rank, M. R. 4, 112–13, 176, 179
Rao, V. 112, 119–20
Raz, M. 100, 101
Reagan, Ronald 95, 106
relational approach to poverty
    8–17, 19, 35, 59, 175–7
    contribution of 13–17
    culture, structure, and individuals
        145–50

and definitions of poverty 20
global perspective 187–8
implications for policy and
     programs 180–2
implications for research 182–6
obligations and expectations
     11–12, 146
opportunity and personal
     autonomy 151–72
significance of 179–88
subjective and objective
     dimensions to 183
relative poverty
defining and measuring 22, 23,
     27–9, 30, 35
religion
and social capital 116
reproductive rights 74–5, 88–9
research experience 5–7
residential segregation 144
risk of experiencing poverty 4, 35,
     53, 58
Risman, Dr. Barbara 5
Robertson, R. 130
Rodriguez, Antonia 75
Romero, L. 182
Roscigno, V. J. 152
rural areas 5, 47, 48–52
and the culture of poverty
     116–17, 124–5
identifying 25
and migration 47
National Advisory Commission
     report on 104
public schools 152
research on rural poverty 186
single mothers 69, 70, 157
spatial factors in 131
women and intimate partner
     violence 147–8

safety nets 2
Salamon, S. 33
Sánchez-Jankowski, M. 109, 154
Sanyal, P. 112, 119–20

savings 163
scarcity
and child maltreatment 79–81
Schifter, L.A. 55
Seale, E. 169
self-efficacy 171, 172
Sen, A. 28–9, 30, 180
settlement movement 97
sex education
and teen pregnancies 76
sexism 8
sexuality
and gender 44–6
Shaddox, C. 69, 142, 178
shadow economy 162
Shaefer, H. L. 16, 18, 19, 34, 35,
     54, 162, 164, 170
Shafir, E. 79
Shaw, C. R. 97, 99
single mother households 18, 60,
     61–73, 82
and the culture of poverty 102,
     107, 108, 109–10, 118–19
intimate partner relations 63–8,
     70, 86
and the labor market 68–70
and larger social trends 61–3
parenting strategies 89–90
players and power 87–8
relation to the state and the
     reliance on work 157–9
and social services 140
spending habits 163
SIPP (Survey of Income and
     Program Participation) 25,
     31
slavery 40
Slotnik, D. E. 121
Small, M. L. 117
Smith, L. 182
Smith, R. D. 116
Smithies, C. S. 58
SNAP (Supplemental Nutritional
     Assistance Program) 24, 31,
     32, 69, 136, 137–8, 139, 141

Snow, D. A. 110, 184
social capital 115–16, 149
social disorganization
    and the culture of poverty 94,
        96–100, 102, 109
social exclusion
    and the culture of poverty 94
    defining and measuring 21, 28,
        30, 33, 35
social inequality 8–9
social mobility 37, 166
    and chronic poverty 22
    and college attendance 153
    intergenerational 37, 164
    and the middle class 56
    and social capital 116
social network research 186
social relations *see* relational
        approach to poverty
Social Security 138
    poverty alleviation program 32
social services 135–40, 159
social support
    and child maltreatment 78, 81–3
    and single motherhood 61
sociological imagination 179
spatial factors
    in the structural understanding of
        poverty 131–5
spending habits, flexibility in 163
SPM (Supplemental Poverty
        Measure) 24–5, 31–2, 34,
        35
SSS (Self-Sufficiency Standard)
        29, 33
Stack, C. 64, 118, 166, 175
Steffen, B. 54
Stier, H. 162
Stith, S. M. 79
Stoll, S. 49, 113, 122–3
stress
    and child maltreatment 78, 79,
        85
structuralism and poverty 2, 9,
        14–15, 18–19, 126–50

criminalizing poverty 140–2
culture and structure 117, 118,
        125, 127, 144–50, 179–80
four characteristics of structure
        126–7
how structure creates poverty
        127–35
limits of 142–5
social policy 135–45
spatial and global factors 131–5
structural inequality 105,
        114–15, 127–31
subcultures 92, 99–100
substance abuse 5, 57, 58, 168
    and child maltreatment 79
    in rural areas 49
suburban areas 5, 47, 49, 51
Sullivan, J. X. 26, 32–3
support services 136
Swartz, D. 112
symbolic interactionism 10

TANF (Temporary Aid to Needy
        Families) 69, 107, 136,
        138–41, 157
tax credits 138
tax havens 134
Taylor, T. 140
technological change
    and the labor market 129
teen pregnancy/motherhood 18,
        60, 71–7, 85, 87, 91, 109,
        110, 185
temporary poverty 35, 58, 177
TFA (Teach for America) 170
Thatcher, Margaret 87
Thiede, B. C. 49
Thompson, E. P.
    *The Making of the English Working
        Class* 13, 14
Tienda, M. 162
Toma, E. F. 152
Tomaskovic-Devey, D. 11
tourism 131
Townsend, P. 21, 28, 33

trade unions 129
transgender women 39
Trump, Donald 106, 123

underclass thesis 50–1, 101–2,
    105–6, 112
unemployment 34, 102, 138, 162
    and rural poverty 104
    and single motherhood 62
United Nations
    and capability poverty 29
    Human Development Index 29
    Human Development Reports 29
    Human Poverty Index (HPI)
        29
urban poverty 48, 50–1
    identifying 25
US government
    and the culture of poverty thesis
        7, 120–1, 123
    measures of poverty 3–4
    social services 135–40
    and the War on Poverty 33–4,
        95, 103–5

VA (Veterans' Affairs) disability
    compensation 167
vagrancy laws 140–1
Vance, J. D. 121–4
violence 1
    child maltreatment 84
    and chronic poverty 53
    and definitions of poverty 36
    domestic violence 16, 165
    effect on opportunities 165
    and gender identity 45–6
    intimate partner 78, 83, 147–8
VISTA 104
vulnerability, relations of 8, 17–18,
    19, 52, 55, 161–2, 172–3,
    175–88
    defining and measuring poverty
        28, 33, 35, 36
    families and parenting 60
    immigrants 47, 160

LGBTQIA+ persons 46
    and military service 167–8
    and structure 148–9

Wacquant, L. 109
wages 161–2
    gender pay gap 45
    immigrants 47
    and the labor market 128, 129
    low 127–8, 129, 134–5, 159,
        161–2
    in rural places 49
    service sector 162
    single mothers and low wages
        69–70
Wal-mart 135
War on Poverty 33–4, 95, 103–5
wealth
    extreme wealth 187
    gender gap 45
    inequalities 131, 163–4
Weisbrod, B. A. 25
welfare
    and the culture of poverty 106–7,
        108, 125
    moving between welfare and
        work 157–9, 165
    reform legislation 157, 159
White Americans
    and the culture of poverty 98
    household income 34
    and military service 167
    poor Whites 40, 41–4
    risk of poverty 4–5
    in rural places 48
Whiteside, J. L. 153
Whyte, W. F.
    Street Corner Society 109
Wickenden, E. 95
Wilkinson, R. G. 37
Williams, T. 116
Willis, P. 154, 155
Wilson, W. J. 50, 51, 62, 90, 101,
    102
Wolff, J. 147, 148–9

women
    Black women 30, 42, 106
    and capability poverty 30
    early pregnancy 14
    female-headed households 40,
        44, 50, 53, 61–71
    improving agency of the poor
        119–20
    labor-market disadvantages
        44–5
    living with HIV/AIDS 58
    and military service 167
    single motherhood 44, 58
    and social relations 12, 14
    transgender 39
    vulnerability and dignity 176
    see also family and parenting;
        single mother households
work
    and the culture of poverty
        108
    finding (better) employment
        156–68

gender identity and workplace
    discrimination 45–6
low-income work 108, 127–8,
    129, 134–5, 159, 161
moving between welfare and
    work 157–9, 165
and personal autonomy 173
relation to the state and reliance
    on work 157–61
and self-efficacy 171
training 129, 157, 158, 165
work ethic 156–7, 162–3
work–family balance 61
workplace discrimination 177
workfare 136, 140, 157
World Bank 4, 30

The Young Patriots 43
young people
    college attendance 151–6
    and work ethics 162

Zimmer, R. W. 152